# Women and Sisters

# Women
# &Sisters

## JEAN FAGAN YELLIN

## The Antislavery Feminists
## in American Culture

Yale University Press
New Haven and London

Published with assistance from the Louis Stern Memorial Fund.

Designed by Jo Aerne

and set in Bodoni and Cheltenham type.

Printed in the United States of America.

**Library of Congress Cataloging-in-Publication Data**

Yellin, Jean Fagan.

  Women and sisters : the antislavery feminists in American culture / Jean Fagan Yellin.

      p.     cm.

  Bibliography: p.

  Includes index.

  ISBN 0–300–04515–8 (cloth)

      0–300–05236–7 (pbk.)

  1. Feminism—United States—History—19th century. 2. Slavery —United States—Anti-slavery movements. I. Title.

HQ1423.Y45   1989

305.42′0973—dc20                        89–16540

                                                  CIP

The paper in this book meets the guidelines for permanence and durability of the Committee on Production Guidelines for Book Longevity of the Council on Library Resources

10  9  8  7  6  5  4  3  2

*In memory of Sarah and Sarah, my mothers, and Ruth, my sister
and for my sisters Mary, Ann, and Esther
my daughters Lisa, Amelia, and Lisa
and my granddaughter Sarah*

# Contents

# List of Illustrations

# Preface

*Where have all the flowers gone,*
*Long time passing?*
*Where have all the flowers gone,*
*Long time ago?*
*Where have all the flowers gone?*
*Young girls picked them, every one.*

*When will they ever learn?*
*When will they ever learn?*
— Pete Seeger, "Where Have All the Flowers
Gone?"[1]

A generation after the 1960s, I won-
der what will remain of the culture that ended the Vietnam War. Will future
historians understand, after a century, that "Where Have All the Flowers
Gone" sang of politics? I come honestly by my interest in the culture of
social protest. The daughter of American radicals, I was born into the union
organizing of the Great Depression. Schooled by the resistance to McCarthy-
ism, then by the freedom struggles of the 1960s and the women's movement
of the 1970s, I was fully grown when I first saw the emblem of the kneeling
female slave that the antislavery feminists had popularized in the 1830s
and 1840s.

What struck me—it continues to strike me—is this image of a woman
exposed and enchained. Nineteenth-century American culture mandated
women's public invisibility; yet slave women were routinely displayed for
sale. When free women protested this, they were condemned for becoming

visible.[2] Reacting to this criticism, a small group of black and white abolitionist women demanded fuller participation in American life: more visibil-
ity, not less.

The antebellum period produced multiple and conflicting definitions of
"true womanhood." The dominant patriarchal culture endorsed the pattern
of purity, piety, domesticity, and obedience that Barbara Welter has identified.
Isolated within domestic spaces, this model was translated into a superior
spiritual being, the Angel in the House.[3] But against this confined nonhu-
man figure, black and white antislavery feminists projected an alternative:
the Woman and Sister. Their version of true womanhood, emphasizing humanity instead of superhumanity and community instead of isolation, was encoded
as icon in the emblem of the kneeling female slave.

This book examines the Woman and Sister emblem of the kneeling female
slave that the American antislavery feminists adopted. It traces its encoding, its recoding, and the reversal of this recoding in broadly diverse texts
produced from the 1830s to the 1850s. While explicitly addressing the
history of the discourse of American feminism, however, *Women and Sisters*
is more generally intended as a contribution to current efforts to use the
analysis of contradictions of race, caste, condition, ethnicity, and gender as
a way of opening up and redefining American literature and culture.[4]

Proposing a framework for the reconstruction of "so-called popular culture," Fredric Jameson has characterized class discourse as "essentially
dialogical in its structure." Its normal form, he continues, "is an *antagonistic*
one . . . in which two opposing discourses fight it out within the general
unity of a shared code." Seen from this perspective, "the individual utter-
ance or text is grasped as a symbolic move in an essentially polemic and
strategic ideological confrontation." Because the surviving cultural monuments of the past tend to perpetuate only the voice of the hegemonic group,
however, these monuments can be located within the dialogic system only by
restoring or reconstructing the voice that initially opposed them. This opposing voice, Jameson asserts, has been "for the most part stifled and reduced
to silence, marginalized, its own utterances scattered to the wind, or reappropriated in their turn by the hegemonic culture."[5]

Certainly, the discourse of the antislavery feminists has been lost. We
read neither their speeches nor their private and public writings. Although
historians have discussed some aspects of these women and their work, we
have not explored the culture that they created. Their cultural constructs
have not been examined in relation to the tensions between abolitionist and
feminist ideologies, nor has their complex discourse been identified as

structuring our own.[6] As to the women themselves as cultural texts, when we think of them at all, we have been taught to envision them as unwomanly —the blacks because of their color, the whites because of their public activity. (Or perhaps, if familiar with twentieth-century critiques of patriarchy, we define them as nineteenth-century true women who were pilloried by an aggressive violent patriarchal society—as victimized civic cousins of the Angel in the House.) My effort is to see these black and white women freshly and to hear their silenced discourse.

Rewriting their marginalized presence and their marginalized voices as essentially polemical, we can restore them to their appropriate place in the dialogic system. And we can do more. By restoring their confrontations with cultural monuments, with the literary and artistic canon, we can read that canon freshly. In Jameson's words, we can "reread or rewrite the hegemonic forms themselves . . . as a process of reappropriation and neutralization, the cooptation . . . the cultural universalization, of forms which originally expressed the situation of 'popular,' subordinate, or dominated groups." Such rereading and rewriting, Jameson points out, today "is of a piece with the reaffirmation of the existence of marginalized or oppositional cultures . . . and the reaudition of the oppositional voices of black or . . . women's . . . literature."[7]

This is the thrust of *Women and Sisters*. I want to locate, to rediscover, to resurrect, to legitimate, to *hear* the powerful discourse of the antislavery feminists; and I want to explore the political subtext of some of our nineteenth-century "classics."

The cultural productions and the public presence of the antislavery feminists that constitute my subject are open and broadly heterogeneous. I have not confined myself to texts that we understand as literature, but have traced both the motif and the motto of the supplicant slave emblem across the culture in visual icons as well as in written language.[8] Although tracking not a whale but an enchained female supplicant, like Melville's sub-sub Librarian, I too have found examples of my motif replicated on hugely divergent levels of artistic production and in wildly diverse media: in drawings, emblems, and political cartoons; in diaries, speeches, and polemics; in poems, tales, romances, and novels; in ceramic and in stone. All of these offer examples of the ways in which the discursive codes of the antislavery feminists were articulated in American nineteenth-century culture. And, as Jane Tompkins remarks about forms of verbal nonfictional discourse, these diverse texts "can be seen to construct the real world in the image of a set of ideals and beliefs in exactly the same ways that novels and stories do."[9]

The resulting dialogue of conflicting voices and forms embodies and expresses a dialectic that invites multiple readings when situated within its historical contexts. Parodying an aphorism, Roland Barthes wrote "that a little formalism turns one away from History, but that a lot brings one back to it."[10] My methodology is to identify the codes the antislavery feminists used, to examine the texts they produced both in terms of their internal dialectics and in terms of their relationships with the dominant codes, and then to examine the cultural "masterworks" that adopted their motifs and mottoes but emptied them of their antislavery feminist content and filled them instead with a contradictory content. In other words, it is to identify and analyze the tensions within a text, then to embed that text in relevant contexts in order to read it out of these, to historicize it. Implicit here are the notions, asserted by current critical theory, that it is possible and fruitful to use semiotic modes of analysis to discuss visual icons as well as literary texts, to use literary techniques to study the dynamics of culture, and to use historical analysis to open up literary interpretations as well as to explore the tensions within an individual text.

Part 1, "The Speechless Agony of the Fettered Slave," presents the emblem of the Woman and Sister, treating it both as icon (that is, as a culturally coded but not entirely arbitrary sign) and as symbol (or what Umberto Eco calls a "super-sign" conveying a complex discourse).[11] This section traces the history of the emblem as a gender-specific variant of the race-specific emblem of the enchained male slave, and it explores the significations of the emblem in relation to notions of true womanhood. Part 2, "Breaking Chains," discusses the varied significations that the antislavery feminists assigned to the emblem and the varied discourses that were structured by it. This section presents Angelina Grimké as representative of the free women who became platform speakers; L. Maria Child as representative of the free women writers; and Sojourner Truth and Harriet Jacobs as representative of the black women speakers and writers who had been held in slavery. Part 3, "Woman and Emblem in Stone and Story," traces the appropriation of the women's codes and the reversal of their significations in works canonized as "high art": Hiram Powers's sculpture *The Greek Slave*, and Nathaniel Hawthorne's *The Scarlet Letter*. The Coda, "Women Silenced," discusses the appropriation of the antislavery feminists themselves as text and the reversal of their signification, a generation later, in Henry James's satirical novel *The Bostonians*.

I am not happy about the results of my study of the flowering of antislavery feminist culture. Certainly the powerful iconography and the texts that the black and white women created are worth discovering and decoding. But even as these women spoke and wrote, their discourse was emptied of its content and recoded to oppose their efforts. When later they themselves were used as a literary subject to buttress things as they are, this process became complete.

To my mind, the reappropriation by the dominant culture of the antislavery feminists' oppositional discourse is a paradigm of the historic interaction between the culture of social protest and the dominant culture in America. Nevertheless, as Raymond Williams writes, "it would be wrong to overlook the importance of works and ideas which, while clearly affected by hegemonic limits and pressures, are at least in part significant breaks beyond them, which may again in part be neutralized, reduced, or incorporated, but which in their most active elements nevertheless come through as independent and original."[12] Certainly the antislavery feminists created an independent and original culture. So did the civil rights and antiwar activists of the 1960s and the feminists of the 1970s. Some flowers reseed.

# Acknowledgments

This book took almost too long, and it is good finally to be able to thank the many people who helped. I am, as always, grateful to my teacher Sherman Paul. And I am indebted to Nina Baym, Hazel V. Carby, Nancy Hewitt, Roger Stein, and Alan Wallach, who generously read sections of the manuscript. I am enormously beholden to Frederick C. Stern and Joseph T. Skerrett, who read through it all.

*Women and Sisters* was conceived during the tenure of my fellowship at the National Humanities Institute at Yale. It owes much to the fellows' discussions about American culture, and especially to Harry Burger, Clyde C. Griffen, John Herington, Marilyn Stokstad, and Patricia Meyer Spacks, as well as to the late Charles T. Davis. I explored nineteenth-century American art during the course of a fellowship at the National Museum of American Art of the Smithsonian Institution, where I learned from Lois Fink, Edith Mayo, Keith Melder, Lillian Miller, William Truettner, and the late Joshua Taylor, as well as from my colleagues Wanda Corn, Charles C. Eldredge, and Celia Betsky McGee. Later, a summer grant from the National Endowment for the Humanities enabled me to concentrate on Hawthorne, and still later, the American Association of University Women Founders Fellowship gave me time to think and to shape my thoughts into a book. I am most grateful for all this help. I am also indebted to the colleagues with whom I tested my ideas at meetings of the American Studies Association, the Modern Language Association, and at colleges and universities in the United States and abroad.

It seems that, over the years, I enlisted the aid of almost everyone I met. Among those who warmly responded were Ann U. Abrams, the late Marilyn Baily, Ruth Bogin, Rita Bradshaw-Beyers, Lee Chambers-Schiller,

Jules Chametsky, Bell Chevigny, Robert Corrigan, Margo Culley, Lauretta Demmick, Huston Diehl, Lee Edwards, Richard Fabrizio, Frances S. Foster, Philip Fulvi, William H. Gerdts, Lola B. Gellman, A. Bartlett Giamatti, Rita Gollin, Anne Coffin Hanson, Laura Hapke, Sharon Harley, Patricia G. Holland, Hugh Honour, Emma and Sid Kaplan, Carolyn Karcher, Ann Kliman, Phil Lapsansky, Margaret Neussendorfer, George Rehin, Claire Richter Sherman, Carroll Smith-Rosenberg, Judy Sokolov, Dorothy Sterling, Milton R. Stern, Howard Temperley, Alan Trachtenberg, Dorothy Porter Wesley, and Marilyn T. Williams. The others know who they are.

I also received indispensable assistance from archivists and librarians, in England at the Local Studies Department of the Public Libraries of Birmingham and the Department of Printed Books and the Department of Manuscripts at the British Library; and, in America, at the American Antiquarian Society; the Archives of American Art; the Division of Rare Books and Manuscripts, Boston Public Library; the Department of Rare Books and Manuscripts, Columbia University Library; the Rare Book Division and the Popular Print Division of the Library of Congress; the Duke University Library; the Essex Institute; the Haviland Records Room, New York Yearly Meeting of the Religious Society of Friends; the Clements Library of the University of Michigan; the Library Company of Philadelphia; the Moorland-Spingarn Research Center at Howard University; the New-York Historical Society; the Henry W. and Albert A. Berg Collection, the New York Public Library, Astor, Lenox and Tilden Foundations; the Schomburg Center for Research in Black Culture of the New York Public Library; the North Carolina State Archives; the Rush Rhees Library, University of Rochester; Sarah Lawrence College; the Arthur and Elizabeth Schlessinger Library of Radcliffe College; the Sophia Smith Collection, Smith College; the Stowe-Day Foundation; and the Yale University libraries.

At Pace University, the late Bruce Bergman, Director of the New York library, was patient and sometimes inspired, and his entire staff was consistently helpful. I have come to rely on the cooperation and encouragement of my chairman, Sherman Raskin, Dean Joseph E. Houle, Provost Joseph M. Pastore, President William Sharwell, and Chancellor Edward J. Mortola. At Yale University Press, I am deeply indebted to Ellen Graham and to Carl Rosen.

Although I became enmeshed for six years in chapter 4, researching Harriet Jacobs, *Women and Sisters* finally is finished. Today I feel relief that it is done, gratitude to those who helped, and joy. Ed thought I could live through it, and he was right.

Jean Fagan Yellin
New Rochelle, New York
April 1989

# PART ONE
## "The Speechless Agony
## of the Fettered Slave"

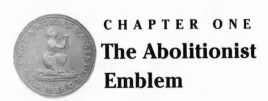

# CHAPTER ONE
# The Abolitionist Emblem

*Until the pictures of the slave's sufferings were drawn and held up to public gaze, no Northerner had any idea of the cruelty of the system . . . and those who had lived at the South . . . wept in secret places over the sins of oppression. . . . Prints . . . are powerful appeals.*
—*Angelina E. Grimké*[1]

Black, half nude, chained, kneeling in supplication—even now she retains her power (fig. 1). A century and a half ago, the emblem of the female slave popularized by black and white "antislavery females" triggered the outrage of American women and moved them to unprecedented action: direct involvement in the slavery controversy. Examining this emblem, briefly tracing its history and exploring the contradictions it embodies, will enable us to understand issues central to the culture of the antislavery women.

The Garrisonian abolitionists were routinely outrageous. In the early 1830s, when gender roles were in flux, their inclusion of women in the public debate over slavery challenged patriarchal codes restricting "true women" to the domestic sphere. When fifteen hundred women signed a petition "praying" the abolition of slavery in the District of Columbia, future president John Tyler expressed fears for the fate of the Republic:

> Woman is to be made the instrument of destroying our political paradise, the Union of these states; she is to be made the presiding genius over the councils of insurrection and discord, she is to be converted into a fiend, to rejoice over the conflagration of our dwellings and the murder of our people.[2]

3

Fig. 1. Hard Times Token. *Am I Not a Woman and a Sister?* (1838).

Equally unprecedented was the abolitionists' widespread use of printed propaganda in their efforts to win the hearts and minds of the American people. They published not only words, but pictures — "inflammatory appeals addressed to the passions of the slaves, in prints," President Andrew Jackson warned, that would incite the illiterate slaves to insurrection. In response, the abolitionists explained that the illustrated periodicals they "scattered unsparingly through the land" were intended for a northern audience. Charging that their prints were "the *occasion*, not the cause" of violence against travelers in the South who were found to have — or accused of having — antislavery papers in their possession, abolitionists launched a counter-attack against the criticisms of their graphics: "But the pictures! the pictures! these seem to have been specially offensive. And why, unless it is because they give specially distinct impressions of the horrors of slavery?"[3]

The antislavery women were quick to endorse this use of graphics. Angelina Grimké—a renegade Charleston aristocrat—dramatically argued their value in her historic "Appeal to the Christian Women of the South," and in 1837 the First Anti-Slavery Convention of American Women passed a formal resolution endorsing the use of visual images in the abolitionist cause:

> we regard anti-slavery prints as powerful auxiliaries in the cause of emancipation, and recommend that these "pictorial representations" be multiplied an hundred fold, so that the speechless agony of the fettered slave may unceasingly appeal to the heart of the patriot, the philanthropist, and the christian.[4]

Twentieth-century theorists who argue the cognitive signification of pictorial images explain that images make "understanding more rapid, more instinctive" than language "because the process is sensory rather than intellectual."[5] The resolution passed by the Anti-Slavery Convention of American Women, however, did not concern itself with how images function but with the relationship between signifier and signified. The abolitionists repeatedly asserted that their pictures were valid because they were accurate representations of actual events or individuals. This "journalistic vision," common in the nineteenth century, characterizes a large group of antislavery prints issued during the 1830s and 1840s. Hundreds of images dramatizing the violence related to the institution of slavery—the separation of families, the seizing, branding, selling, and torturing of men, women, and children—appeared in broadsides, newspapers, and books. During these same years American abolitionists also produced and distributed slave emblems. The emblems functioned both as icons and as symbols; in the language of the women's convention, they made an unceasing "appeal to the heart" by expressing figuratively "the speechless agony of the fettered slave."[6]

Like many other designs in nineteenth-century America, the male supplicant was an English import. There is some evidence that slavery had earlier been emblemized by the picture of an almost nude white male, whose head was shaved and whose hands and feet were loaded with chains, bowing under the burden of a heavy yoke weighted with a large stone. But in 1787 the Committee to Abolish the Slave Trade invented a new emblem to further their cause. Retaining the gender, nudity, and chains of the earlier figure, they posed the slave as a supplicant; blackening his skin, they made him race specific; and they added a motto. Abolitionist leader and historian Thomas Clarkson described the antislavery emblem they devised, first exe-

Fig. 2. Wedgwood medallion. *Am I Not a Man and a Brother?* (1787).

cuted by an anonymous craftsman, as showing "An African . . . in chains in a supplicating posture, kneeling with one knee upon the ground, and with both his hands lifted up to Heaven, and round the seal . . . the following motto, as if he was uttering the words himself—'Am I not a Man and a Brother?'"[7] The definitive form of this emblem was created later in 1787 when Josiah Wedgwood, an active member of the committee, employed his chief modeler, William Hackwood, to design a cameo (fig. 2). This cameo represents a fortuitous synthesis of advanced technological skills and radical political ideas. After lengthy experiments, Wedgwood had finally developed a clay body that could be colored effectively. Describing its use for the slavery emblem, Clarkson commented on the appropriateness of the sharp black-and-white contrast Wedgwood had achieved. "The ground was a most delicate white, but the Negro, who was seen imploring compassion in the middle of it, was his own native colour."[8]

Wedgwood distributed this image widely in England and in 1788 sent several to Benjamin Franklin, president of the Pennsylvania Abolition Society. Franklin responded with warmth. "I am persuaded," he wrote, "it may have an Effect equal to that of the best written pamphlet, in procuring favour to those oppressed People."[9] Coming from a man who knew the power of pamphlets, this was high praise. And Franklin was right. Wedgwood's work inspired a series of supplicants on cameos, coins, and medals, and on commercially produced and marketed crockery in England, France, and America. The kneeling slave also decorated needle-work made by women who organized themselves into antislavery sewing circles and sold the products of their labor at fairs to raise money for the cause. In 1836, Grimké noted the existence of sixty American female antislavery societies,

> telling the story of the colored man's wrongs, praying for his deliverance, and presenting his kneeling image constantly before the public eye on bags and needle-work, card-racks and pen-wipers, pin-cushions &c. Even the children of the North are inscribing on their handiwork, "May the points of our needles prick the slaveholders' conscience."[10]

The image of the supplicant slave appeared and reappeared in print — most notably, in America, over William Lloyd Garrison's column in Benjamin Lundy's early antislavery newspaper, *The Genius of Universal Emancipation*, and, later, on a broadside above John Greenleaf Whittier's poem "Our Countrymen in Chains"; for generations it decorated the title pages of books.[11]

All of the versions of this emblem function on both a social level and a religious level. From a religious perspective, this kneeling figure, with hands "lifted up to Heaven," addresses traditional ideas of the levels of Creation. The contradiction between the supplicant's prayerful gesture and the chains that degrade him like an animal signifies the sin the abolitionists held to be at the heart of slavery: the immoral subversion of the appropriate relationships between Creator and moral creature. In the words of abolitionist-feminist Sarah Grimké, "The essential sin of slavery consisted in reducing man to a brute."[12] Simultaneously, the emblem addresses the issue of race. While the nudity and the rendering of the figure emphasize its muscle

structure, they also emphasize its coloring. This image thus anatomizes the
humanity of its subject while dramatizing his black skin, as Clarkson points
out. In addition, the treatment of the hair and of the facial features insists
that this athletic young male figure, beautifully rendered in neoclassical
style and shown in what appears to be a religious pose, is not Greek, but
African.

The motto, Am I Not a Man and a Brother? functions as a prod. As
Clarkson notes, it is presented as if the slave "was uttering the words
himself." Its form — neither a declarative affirmation (I am) nor an affirmative
question (am I?) — at first appears doubly negative. But a question requires
an answer. Posed by the kneeling figure to himself, the halting double
inquiry suggests, albeit hesitantly, the issue of self-awareness, of the self-
affirmation of the figure as a morally responsible creature, and the issue of
his appropriate relationships with God's other creatures. If the double question is read as being posed by the figure to the unseen tyrant before whom he
kneels, it is an appeal for freedom. If directed to the observer, it is a plea for
help. His audience must either deny the carefully delineated humanity of
his form or, while acknowledging his insistent blackness, affirm it and act to
break his chains, so that like other men he can assume an upright position.

It was not this portrayal of the man and brother, however, that spoke most
deeply to the women who called themselves antislavery females but the
variant image of the Woman and Sister (fig. 1).

To those familiar with the design of the kneeling male African, this
female supplicant might appear to address social and religious issues identical to those raised by the Wedgwood figure. If women (like men) are God's
reasoning moral creatures, and if (like men) they are related to God's other
reasoning moral creatures, the situation of the female slave would seem to
be identical to that of the male. In this case, her image perhaps seems
interesting only because it presents a visual variation, and the inquiries
posed in her motto, Am I Not a Woman and a Sister? appear only verbal
variants.

But to my eyes, the female emblem is significantly different from that of
the male. Though posed as a supplicant, he is shown as powerful and
athletic; it is not impossible to imagine him bursting his fetters and asserting his freedom. Indeed, his right toes are curved underneath like those of a
runner ready to rise. (The sculptor Thomas Ball, who later modeled a figure
on Wedgwood's design, described his subject as "just rising from the earth"
and exerting his own strength to free himself.)[13] In contrast, the female
supplicant appears too weak to break her chains, especially since, unlike

those of the male, they fetter her to the ground. Thus despite her racial specificity the figure shown on the female slave emblem recalls the traditional emblem of Poverty, shown as a woman with one winged hand and the other hand weighed down by a chain attached to a stone.[14] The female slave cannot conceivably rise and free herself. All she can do is plead.

The draping and the gesture of the two figures, although like their physique reflecting neoclassical conventions, suggest contrasting gender patterns. The woman's drapery results in partial nudity that, like the male's, emphasizes her blackness. But conventions of nudity are gendered. Where the bared body of the male slave suggests strength, the exposure of the female suggests helplessness; in America today, the image of an enchained partially nude female signifies sexual bondage. By mimicking the gesture with which the male slave lifts his hands "up to heaven," the female slave both pleads against her violation and shields her body from our gaze—and perhaps partially hides it from the gaze of whomever she kneels to. Clearly this tyrant, who has social power over her and visual access to her, is not another woman. Whether the slave's gesture is read as an attempt to protect her body from the eye of her master or from our eyes, whether it is seen as sexual innocence threatened or sexual vulnerability revealed, it underscores the sexuality of the female emblem.[15]

The shift in the language of the motto also signifies a difference that is more than formal. Like "Man and Brother," the phrase "Woman and Sister" embodies tensions that are both spiritual and social—the tensions involved in coupling an individual's relationship to her Creator (woman/God) with her relationships to her fellow creatures (sister/sister, sister/brother): that is, neither a woman nor a man should be chained like a beast; both alike should pray to God; neither should do obeisance to a tyrant. Similarly, like a man, a woman should of course assume the posture common to her human community; she should not be placed on a level different from others of her kind but should participate in a common human brotherhood and sisterhood.

On the social level, however, a sexual shift is never insignificant. In a patriarchal society, while masculine terms are routinely used to signify women as well as men, feminine terms are gender specific. It is necessary, then, to examine the female slave emblem within the context of cultural codes of gender. Historians have pointed out that in nineteenth-century America, women were not generally acknowledged to be responsible moral agents in the same sense as men; conventionally and legally, they were accountable not only to their Creator, but to fathers and husbands as well. Women were not granted a role in public discussions of issues involving the national morality—issues such as slavery. Similarly, membership in a community of brothers was not equivalent to membership in a community of sisters. To be a brother was to join a common brotherhood, to be involved with one's peers in public debate and in undertaking civic action. But any woman attempting to participate in these ways found herself isolated from her sisters.[16] The dilemma that the nineteenth-century antislavery feminist faced was that if she affirmed herself on a spiritual level as a woman—as God's female reasoning creature—on a social level she relinquished her sisterhood, her community. Yet if she affirmed that community, it was at the price of abdicating her spiritual womanhood.

The earliest portrayal of a female supplicant that I have seen appears in a frontispiece published in France in 1789. Introducing Frossard's antislavery *La cause des esclaves Negres*, Soyez Libres et Citoyens shows a personification of France, a standing white female crowned and garbed in robes decorated with Bourbon lilies, clasping the hands of a kneeling black male slave whose shackles have been broken. Among the Africans kneeling behind him is a woman whose face is raised expectantly as she eyes the liberator; her hands are prayerfully clasped, although the chains shackling her wrists to her ankles remain intact (fig. 3).[17]

The female version of the supplicant slave emblem, however, was not imported to America from France. Like the Wedgwood figure, it came from England. Unlike the Wedgwood figure, however, which had been designed by an all-male committee and sent by male abolitionist leaders in England to their male counterparts in America, the female image was perhaps devised by British women. Certainly it was exported by them. Members of the Ladies Negro's Friend Society of Birmingham, England, chose this emblem to decorate the cover of their *First Report*, published in 1826. They discussed it in their *Second Report*, where, curiously, instead of signifying emblematic truth, it was used to illustrate the narrative of a Diaman woman who had asked—when told that some whites disapproved of those who had attacked her village, killed her baby, and enslaved her—"Why then do they not prevent it?"[18]

The Birmingham society made consistent use of graphics. In addition to publishing illustrated albums and reports, members sewed "ornamental work-bags," cloth purses decorated with "telling illustrations" picturing the evils of slavery. They stuffed these purses with antislavery pamphlets, then sold them or had them "sent among aristocratic circles"; Princess Victoria had one.[19]

SOYEZ LIBRES ET CITOYENS

Fig. 3. Frontispiece for B. Frossard, *La cause des esclaves Negres* (1789).

Evidently their propaganda, and that of other abolitionist women, was effective. In October 1828, *The Westminster Review* ran lead articles urging British women to redouble their abolitionist efforts and detailing the violence inflicted on female slaves in Jamaica and the Bahamas. Countering the *Review*'s antislavery politics, the cartoonist William McLean published a broadside lampooning the emblem of the supplicant female slave. His "Offended Dignity" presents a pastoral scene, perhaps in the West Indies, where an overdressed black couple wearing "Ball Dresses" appear in front of a group of barefooted black men in work clothes who are carrying agricultural implements. The dandified man in the foreground, garbed in striped trousers, jacket, vest, shirt, and tie, with shoes on his feet and a hat cocked on his head, is showing the woman *The Westminster Review*. Its cover pictures a supplicant female slave kneeling before a white man who brandishes a whip over her head. The dandy taunts his companion—a curvaceous black woman in a low-cut print dress who, bedecked with necklace and earrings, wears a feathered hat atop her bandana and carries a large umbrella—by commenting on the disparity between her resplendent appearance and the illustration of the pathetic female slave. Addressing her formally in broken English, he teases, "dem Buckra say darra you—Miss Leah Tomkin." She saucily responds, "Dem Buckra tell big lie, Massa Richard Tanton—an you an Buckra be one great fool" (fig. 4).[20]

The female slave image also appeared in American print in 1830. It was reproduced by editor Benjamin Lundy in the May issue of *The Genius of Universal Emancipation*, facing "The Ladies' Repository," a new feature designed to attract female readers. Lundy consistently used *The Genius* to report on women's participation in the struggle against slavery; he had discussed the work of the Birmingham society as early as 1827. In September 1829, as he republished the society's *Second Report* and described their *Album*, Lundy announced additions to his staff. The young William Lloyd Garrison would become his associate editor, and "an amiable and highly talented female writer" would "have the principal direction of a Ladies' Department." She was the young Philadelphia poet Elizabeth Margaret Chandler, who was to edit "The Ladies' Repository" until her early death in 1834.[21]

Chandler devoted her columns to "philanthropy and literature," featuring a wide variety of materials on women and slavery. She excerpted reports of female antislavery societies in America and in England, presented writings by black and white American women, and published her own abolitionist essays and poetry. Immediately after her appointment to *The Genius*, Chand-

Fig. 4. William McLean, "Offended Dignity" (1830).

ler issued "An Appeal to the Ladies of the United States"; she followed this, over the next few months, with "Letters on Slavery to the Ladies of Baltimore" and "Letters to Isabel." Writing these essays as a woman addressing other women, Chandler pressed her readers to take an antislavery stand. In an article called "Mental Metempsychosis" (the word signifies the soul's passage at death into another body) she urged them to try to identify with the enslaved. Insisting that her audience respond not only intellectually but also sensuously, she wrote that free women should strive to experience the brutalities inflicted on slave women. Imaginatively, they should "let the fetter be with its wearing weight upon their wrists, as they are driven off like cattle to the market, and the successive strokes of the keen thong fall upon their shoulders till the flesh rises to long welts beneath it, and the spouting blood follows every blow."[22]

Chandler was apparently the first in this country to make the image of the female supplicant a poetic subject. Immediately after Lundy printed the engraving, she published her "Kneeling Slave" in *The Genius*. In the same issue, she noted that among the items received from the Englishwomen was a "seal, bearing the device of a female kneeling slave, and the very appropriate motto Am I Not a Woman and a Sister?[23]

Chandler centers her poem on this motto. Moving toward gender identification, toward the assertion that an identical womanhood and sisterhood is shared by its genteel white female audience ("lady") and its enslaved black female subject ("negro"), the poem's opening line articulates the gulf between subject and audience, demanding that the reader bridge that distance.

Pity the negro, lady!

An explanation follows:

. . . her's is not,
Like thine, a blessed and most happy lot!

Most of this tightly structured neoclassical poem contrasts the lady's pleasant life with the slave's miserable existence. Its final lines, however, address the reader—now not as "lady" but as "woman." Following this rejection of class distinctions, the distinction of race is denied. The poem pivots on its assertion of the sisterhood of all women, reader and subject alike.

She is thy sister, woman! shall her cry,
Uncared for, and unheeded, pass thee by?
Wilt thou not weep to see her sink so low,
And seek to raise her from her place of woe?
Or has thy heart grown selfish in its bliss
That thou shouldst view unmoved a fate like this?

Making these inquiries, the poet does not question the humanity of her subject, nor does she inquire what the response of her audience should be. What is problematic here is her reader's humanity. She conjectures whether the lady has become dehumanized by her easy life: Will she pass on unmoved by the sight of the kneeling slave? Or will she hear the slave's cries, weep in pity, and try to raise her up? Assumed, asserted, never questioned is the legitimacy of the slave's appeal. At issue is not the womanhood and sisterhood of the poet's black female slave subject, but the womanhood and sisterhood of her genteel white female audience.

In 1832 when Garrison ran a wood engraving of the female supplicant and her motto as a stock heading above the "Ladies' Department" in his newly established newspaper, *The Liberator*, his female readers responded by answering the supplicant's double inquiries: "Yes! We acknowledge that thou art a woman and a sister . . . the thought is too revolting, that there is so much indifference manifested by our sex, on this subject, although one million of them are now groaning beneath the same oppressive yoke with thyself."[24]

In time, individually and informally, as well as collectively and officially, American antislavery women adopted the emblem of the female supplicant as their own. Some replicated it privately on paper, like black abolitionist Sarah Mapps Douglass, who sent her sketch of the image with a letter of appreciation to Chandler; and like black abolitionist Sarah Forten, who copied out one of Chandler's poems and filled a page in Elizabeth Smith's album with her drawing of the figure. Members of American antislavery sewing societies followed the British women's lead and transformed the female device into a decorative motif, using it, like the figure of the male supplicant slave, as a design for needlework. Some female antislavery societies printed up writing paper headed with the image of the female supplicant and sold it at fairs.[25]

While anonymous antislavery females were transforming the image into folk art by using it as a motif for traditional feminine crafts, prominent female abolitionist authors and editors were using it to illustrate books. L. Maria Child replicated the design repeatedly, patterning the frontispiece of her historic 1833 *Appeal in Favor of that Class of Americans Called Africans* on an engraving that the Chelmsford women had published in England and including a smaller, more spirited adaptation in her 1834 anthology *The Oasis*.[26]

The motif was domesticated in 1836 when it was reprinted in *The Slave's Friend* over the title "The Afflicted Mother" and explicated for a juvenile audience. This description is striking because it identifies the single figure in terms of a familial context that is absent. In doing so, however, it echoes the earliest British reading of this image by assigning to the supplicant the female role the nineteenth century prized most: motherhood. "See the afflicted mother! She is almost broken-hearted. Her husband and children have been torn from her; and her wrists and ancles are fastened with a chain. She has no one to go to now, to tell her sorrows, but God. Ah, she has thought of that."[27]

Such prints were effective. One abolitionist later wrote that a picture he had seen in childhood showing a slave woman being whipped "made a deep and lasting impression on my memory, which the lapse of more than half a century has not sufficed to erase." Another, recalling an illustration in *The Slave's Friend* that signified women's common sisterhood by picturing a black and a white girl playing together, remembered that this image had moved her to try to befriend a black child.[28]

The most important version of the female supplicant slave served as the frontispiece of Child's *The Fountain* (fig. 5). Omitting the double questions

Fig. 5. Patrick Reason, *Kneeling Slave* (1835).

of the motto and instead substituting the words "Engraved by P. Reason, a Colored Young Man of the City of New York, 1835," this variant embodies a new antislavery challenge. By accompanying the visual image of the female supplicant with this verbal assertion of the creativity and skill of a black artist, it counters the ideology of racism that buttressed slavery. The female antislavery societies evidently recognized the power of this version. Reason's design was reproduced and advertised for sale, then used as a decorative device on stationery. The strength of the response that this image evoked is demonstrated in a letter abolitionist Theodore Weld wrote to Angelina and Sarah Grimké. His handwriting almost out of control, he omits a formal salutation to begin with a passionate comment on Reason's image:

> Ah! Still kneeling, manacled, looking upward, pleading for help! As I caught a sheet at random from a large quantity on the desk at the office to write you a line my dear sisters, I had almost dashed my pen upon it before I saw *the kneeling slave!* The sudden sight drove home a deeper lesson than my heart has learned these many days!! The prayer of the slave! Perdition foretokened to the oppressor and deliverance to the oppressed! Blessed be God, "He taketh up the needy out of the dust."[29]

Abolitionist feminist Amy Post dramatized how grass-roots women used stationery decorated with antislavery emblems to express their commitment to the cause. In a letter to abolitionist lecturer Abby Kelley, Post explained that she had deliberately chosen this stationery to provoke Quaker authorities who, after cautioning her for neglecting her family while campaigning for abolition, had apparently dropped her "case." Writing on paper decorated with abolitionist emblems, Post asserted: "I expect they will have a fresh charge against me soon, as I yesterday transcribed Epistles for the Preparative meetings on such paper as this, and have but little doubt but that imploring image, [of the supplicant slave] will disturb their quiet, at least I hope it will."[30]

When, after Chandler's death, Lundy brought out an edition of her writings, he placed her portrait facing the title page of the *Poetical Works*, and he chose the female slave as the frontispiece of the *Essays*.[31] By 1836, the female supplicant had become the unofficial emblem of the antislavery women.

The major variant of this emblem shows the enchained woman faced by a female chain-breaking liberator (fig. 6). This represents an antislavery version of a very old design; classical art abounds with representations of the vanquished, fettered and kneeling or prone, with their victors standing above them, often planting a triumphant foot on the conquered. As the historian André Grabar explains, "The official language of the Empire saw these representations of victory as images of the 'liberation' of the vanquished, who were thought to have been torn from the tyranny of their leaders by the Roman emperors." This pattern was transformed and spiritualized with the adoption of Christianity. Using its old formula to depict the

Fig. 6. Cover vignette for Lydia Maria Child, *Authentic Anecdotes of American Slavery* (1838).

Harrowing of Hell, artists showed Christ, victorious over the tyrant Death, taking it unto himself and liberating Adam and Eve.[32]

During the eighteenth century, when the ideal of Liberty was secularized and related to national images, the neoclassical goddess Columbia appeared in American art as an active self-liberated young woman. Successfully breaking her fetters and triumphantly planting her foot on chains and crowns symbolic of Tyranny, this American Liberty was defined both positively by her pole and cap and negatively by the broken symbols of her erstwhile oppressor. Revolutionary France adopted a similar self-liberating chain-breaker, but the English abolitionists portrayed a figure that is significantly different. Although shown with cap and pole, instead of breaking her own chains, *Britannia Libertas* appears as the Genius of Emancipation to break the chains of enslaved Africans.[33]

This image, like the others, was exported to America by the women of the Birmingham society. In their *Album* and on their work-bags, it decorates William Cowper's antislavery poem "The Morning Dream" (fig. 7).[34] This illustration includes all of the characters in the drama of emancipation. As the chain-breaking Britannia appears, the slaveholding tyrant drops the bloody scourge he has used to brutalize the pair of enslaved African suppliants, still in fetters. Both are powerless, but in accord with patriarchal conventions the female is more debased. She assumes a prone position before the tyrant while the male appeals to him by raising his hands prayerfully. This design presents a corrected version of the sinful image of social and spiritual usurpation figured by the emblem of the supplicant slave who, chained like a beast, kneels before an unseen tyrant. Here the liberator's appearance between the tyrant and his victims ends their degradation. Momentarily the slaves' chains will be struck and their postures, which, when assumed before another human, signify oppression, will express appropriate reverence when they turn to worship the spirit of British liberty, whose interposition corrects the sin of the slaveholders' usurpation.

The implications of this action are significant both in religious and in political terms. With the inclusion of an empowered white chain-breaking liberator, the enchained black supplicants are seen as powerless. The appearance of the chain-breaker between slave and slaveholder makes it unnecessary for the slaves to rise and break their own chains, as perhaps Wedgwood's muscular male slave seemed capable of doing. Similarly, it makes impossible a reversal of roles in which the slaves might free themselves only to rivet their chains on the limbs of their former masters; that is, the chain-breaker's presence negates the possibility of a servile insurrection that would replace black slavery with black mastery—a threat that hung across the antebellum South. It was a threat that the abolitionists, accused of circulating pictures to foment insurrection among the illiterate slaves, said they abhorred as much as any.

As early as 1836, members of the Boston Female Anti-Slavery Society reproduced and disseminated the emblematic double image to celebrate their legal rescue of a young girl from slavery. To commemorate "little Med's case," they designed, made, and sold work-bags that pictured a slave kneeling before the figure of Justice.[35] Two years later, L. Maria Child illustrated *Authentic Anecdotes of American Slavery* with a cut repeating the double figures that had appeared on an English medal struck to celebrate the end of slavery in Britain (fig. 6).[36] Here a kneeling chained woman shares her abstract space with a chain-breaking liberator who is identified as Justice

*But soon as approaching the land,*

*That Goddess-like Woman he view'd;*

*The scourge he let fall from his hand,*

*With the blood of his subjects imbrued.*

Fig. 7. Illustration of William Cowper, *The Morning Dream* [1828].

by the scales and branch of palm leaves in her left hand. The liberator represents the principle on which legal systems are—or should be— founded. Evidently already having struck her balance, she is moving to redress the injustice to the slave, actively stepping forward as if to break the supplicant's chains and uplift her. Having condemned the institution of slavery as unjust, despite its historic legality, Justice is shown about to destroy it.

Although the surmounting words, Am I Not a Woman and a Sister? are identical to those on the emblem of the female supplicant, they gain an added complexity when displayed with these double figures. Interpreted one way, the supplicant now addresses her inquiries to Justice, whose affirmative response we are watching. Read another way, she questions us, the audience, and within this context urges us to emulate Justice, to answer positively, and to break her chains. A third reading presumes a female audience asking themselves the questions, responding appropriately in terms of their womanhood and sisterhood, consciously patterning themselves on Justice, and moving to free the slaves.

This device shows Justice about to enforce her decision, about to act, although she does not hold the sword traditionally symbolizing enforcement but instead carries Christ's sheaf of palm leaves. Bearing the motto, "Let us break their bonds asunder and cast away their chains. Psalm II:3," the English medal graphically and verbally commemorated the fact that the British had abolished slavery peacefully.[37]

American antislavery females were, like all Garrisonians, pacifists committed to nonviolence. A reading of the abolitionist press suggests, however, that it was not self-evident to antislavery activists in 1838 that the unarmed principle of Justice could transform the laws of the United States by peaceful means. If so, the millennium was approaching—as many believed. But what if it could not? What if, in a world still ruled by iron chains, ideal Justice lacked strength to enforce her decrees and to bring American laws into conformity with transcendent law?

Perhaps as a response to these concerns, when this image crossed the Atlantic and was reproduced as a wood engraving for Child's title page, its motto changed. Discarding the English command from the Old Testament to act as chain-breaker, the American version substitutes a more private imperative from the New Testament: "Remember them that are in bonds as bound with them. Heb. 13:3." Clearly this new injunction is not directed at the supplicant, already bound, or at the figure of Justice, shown demonstrating that she has indeed remembered. Read as if directed at us, the audience, it can be interpreted as a warning. The balance has already been struck and the emblem figures the test. If we respond as women and sisters, if we understand that while the supplicant remains bound we, too, wear chains, if we then become engaged, emulating transcendent Justice and breaking those chains by acting in the public sphere as a Woman and a Sister, it is we who will be lifted and exalted on Judgment Day. If not, we will justly be condemned. But another reading signifies something quite different. If to "remember" makes imperative interiorized feeling but not exteriorized action, if it simply involves our individual private sympathy, then the demand that we remember is consonant with patriarchal definitions of true womanhood, and we need take no public action.

The significance of this message is underscored by the fact that despite her neoclassical appearance, the chain-breaker holds scales that, like the chains of the supplicant, traditionally recall not only Greece and Rome but also the Last Judgment. For Christians the ultimate chain-breaker, the ultimate liberator, the ultimate judge is of course Jesus Christ. Artists traditionally pictured the Last Judgment with the Son of God enthroned, the vanquished serpent beneath his heel, the redeemed at his right hand freed into everlasting life, and at his left the condemned being led in chains by devils to their just slavery and damnation. Nineteenth-century American abolitionists were graphically reminded of this every week by the vignette on the masthead of Garrison's *Liberator* (fig. 8). Here Christ, who has made possible salvation and freedom from the slavery of sin, stands radiant at the center. Repeating standard Christian iconography, this political cut shows a former slave with chains struck, worshipping at his right hand and at his left, a former slaveholding tyrant turning aside and falling away. Surmounting all are the words, "I come to break the bonds of the oppressors."[38]

Like the Wedgwood slave and the emblem of the female supplicant, the double image of supplicant slave and liberator was widely replicated in the abolitionist press; like Reason's version of the kneeling female supplicant, it was used as a decorative device on stationery. The antislavery women produced a number of liberating chain-breakers who appeared in American print in conjunction with enchained supplicants. White women dressed in white neoclassical robes, posed either standing or elevated above the supplicant, their identity is variously defined by their surroundings and their attributes. Holding a torch, they represent Truth; placed in a printshop, they signify Freedom of the Press; usually, however, they carry the scales that identify them as Justice.[39]

In 1838, the image of the supplicant female slave was struck on a Hard

Fig. 8. Masthead of *The Liberator* (18 July 1862).

Times Token—a metal token issued as depression currency (fig. 1). By 1845, there was sufficient demand from printers to warrant the production of a commercial cut of the female supplicant. That year, the Boston Type Foundry, which used the stereotyping process to produce designs for printers, included among other products listed for sale in its *Specimen Book*, a version of the female slave design priced at seventy-five cents (fig. 9).[40] Thereafter, this device appeared and reappeared throughout the nation in newspapers and periodicals, as well as on printed artifacts. After the antislavery women had reproduced it for fifteen years, the female slave entered commercial discourse and became both figuratively and literally a stereotype.

The antislavery emblems focus, within a very limited range and with unusual clarity, the fundamental issues that the antislavery women faced. This book explores multiple and contradictory readings of the visual and verbal elements of the emblems, first as they were interpreted in the discourse of the black and white antislavery women, and then as this discourse was reinterpreted by white male practitioners of elite culture.

Both of Chandler's readings, by addressing the tensions between woman's elevated nature as God's reasoning moral creature and her debased condition in society, challenge patriarchal definitions of true womanhood that relegate God's female rational creature to the private sphere. The differences between these readings, however, are significant. Chandler implied the identity of her free white female audience and her enslaved black female

No. 844.    75 cts.

Fig. 9. *Specimen of Modern Printing Types, Cast at the Letter Foundry of the Boston Type and Stereotype Company* (Boston: White and Potter, 1845).

subject when she urged her audience to feel the chains' "wearing weight upon their wrists." Taken seriously, this assertion of gender identity challenges racist ideologies and the privileging of a white skin. Further, by asserting the identity between free women who conformed to patriarchal sexual codes of virginity before marriage and monogamy afterward and slave women not free to conform to these codes, it challenged the privileging of female "purity" central to patriarchal ideology. But precisely by asserting gender identity, this reading makes it possible to ignore the crucial differences between the situation of white free women and black slave women, to conflate the condition of free women and slaves.

Alternatively, when Chandler read the emblem as demanding that her readers rescue victimized slaves, she implied radical distinctions between her free white female audience and her enslaved black female subject. These distinctions, which suggest the superiority of the liberator and the inferiority of the slave, reinforce patriarchal ideas about the moral superiority of women who adhere to gender patterns mandated by the patriarchy; and they reinforce racist ideas about the moral superiority of whites — notions pictured clearly in the double emblem.

The antislavery emblems encoded a series of contradictions. The notion articulated by the women's convention that the emblem expresses "the speechless agony of the fettered slave," for example, on one level addresses the oppressiveness of American slavery, which denied slaves not only a voice in the government and the courts but even forbade their literacy (and of course denied their access to publishing). Yet on another level, this comment addresses the controversy concerning the humanity of the Africans: if they could not produce literature, the argument went, they were not truly human. Did the freeborn white abolitionist feminists see their task as speaking for the "voiceless" slave? Did they see it as enabling the slave to sound her own voice on the platform and in print?[41]

Or again: Did the emblemized critique of slavery present a female excluded from patriarchal definitions of true womanhood solely on grounds of race and condition? If so, it shows a woman who, although obedient and pious, has been denied sexual purity and a domestic life: it shows patriarchy's true woman degraded and brutalized. Or did the emblem signify a critique of patriarchy rooted in the notion that, in relegating women to the domestic sphere, patriarchal definitions functionally enslaved even women who were legally free by denying them the possibility of acting out their spiritual womanhood and their social sisterhood in the public sphere?[42]

The antislavery women who followed Chandler read the emblems variously and created multiple strategies, alternately addressing and avoiding issues of race, sexual conformity, and patriarchal definitions of true womanhood. At times, contradictorily, the antislavery women asserted their own right to be Women and Sisters, to define themselves and to act in the public sphere, while they condemned slavery because it excluded slave women from patriarchal definitions of true womanhood and from the domestic sphere. When taking this position, white antislavery feminists were identifying with female slaves in terms of gender but articulating a feminist consciousness that was race-specific. At other times, they asserted the womanhood and sisterhood of all women and claimed every woman's right to self-definition.

Enacting these complex patterns of address and avoidance, they recoded and re-recoded the emblem of the female supplicant, picturing themselves as chain-breaking liberators and as enchained slaves pleading for their own liberty, then asserting it and freeing themselves.

In all of their attempts to participate in the public struggle to end slavery in America, however, the activist abolitionist women inevitably embodied and projected versions of true womanhood that challenged patriarchal versions because the models of the Woman and Sister they advanced asserted female humanity and community not only in private but also in public life. All of these versions of the Woman and Sister contrast sharply with the patriarchal image of female superhumanity confined within the domestic sphere, the model of true womanhood that would find its avatar in the Angel in the House.

# PART TWO
# Breaking Chains

# CHAPTER TWO
# Angelina Grimké

*One sign that . . . [Grimké's] influence is felt is that the "sound part of the community" (as they consider themselves) seek to give vent to their vexation by calling her Devil-ina instead of Angel-ina. . . . Another sign is that we have succeeded in obtaining the Odeon . . . for her to speak in; and it is the first time such a place has been obtained for anti-slavery in this city.*
—*L. Maria Child*[1]

Angelina Grimké's speeches and writings transcribe into verbal arguments the ideas that the antislavery emblems present visually. Their ambiguous and contradictory articulation of the connections between the condition of women and slaves addressed the ambiguities and contradictions that the abolitionist women faced. Grimké appropriated the terms of these emblems and then reinscribed them to signify woman's struggle for self-liberation from patriarchal oppression, voicing her developing thoughts and attitudes concerning race and gender as she transformed herself first into an enchained victim and then, empowered, into a self-liberated woman. Simultaneously, supporters in her audiences appropriated and reinscribed the terms of the emblems to characterize Grimké's efforts as a lecturer-reformer.[2]

Grimké identified with the slave emblem early. Even before Chandler urged free women to practice "mental metempsychosis" and imagine themselves in chains, Grimké had seen herself as a shackled slave. Back home in Charleston after a visit to the North, this pampered daughter of a slaveholding family charted her transformation in her diary, where she was recording her spiritual autobiography, often in biblical language. In a series of ardently prayerful entries, Grimké, an Episcopalian-turned-Presbyterianturned-Quaker, articulated her belief in purification through suffering and her sense of mission. The most dramatic passage is dated April 1829.

> Whilst returning from meeting this morning, I saw before me a colored woman who in much distress was vindicating herself to two white boys. . . . The dreadful apprehension that they were leading her to the workhouse crossed my mind, and I would have avoided her if I could. As I approached, the younger said to her, "I will have you tied up." My knees smote together, and my heart sank within me. As I passed them, she exclaimed, "Missis!" But I felt all I had to do was to suffer the pain of seeing her. My lips were sealed, and my soul earnestly craved a willingness to bear the exercise which was laid on me. How long, O Lord, how long wilt thou suffer the foot of the oppressor to stand on the neck of the slave! None but those who know from experience what it is to live in a land of bondage can form any idea of what is endured by those whose eyes are open enough to feel for these miserable creatures. For two or three months after my return here it seemed to me that all the cruelty and unkindness which I had from my infancy seen practiced toward them came back to my mind as though it was only yesterday. And as to the house of correction, it seemed as though its doors were unbarred to me, and the wretched, lacerated inmates of its cold, dark cells were presented to my view. Night and day they were unbarred to me, and yet my hands were bound as with chains of iron. I could do nothing but weep over the scenes of horror which passed in review before my mind. Sometimes I felt as though I was willing to fly from Carolina, be the consequences what they might. At others, it seemed as though the very exercises I was suffering under were preparing me for future usefulness to them.[3]

Throughout this passage, Grimké focuses on herself, describing her own transformation into a powerless slave. The passivity, the apprehension — the shaking knees, the sinking heart, the prayer for strength — all are her own. The suffering painfully recounted is Grimké's own torture. As she writes, the black woman recedes, merging with countless other figures whose brutalization she has witnessed all her life. Assaulted by unbearable recollections, her normal modes of ordering perceptions fail. Present collapses into past; time, space, and matter become fluid. Grimké imaginatively penetrates the barred doors of the Charleston prison where, forced night and day to endure the sight of its victims, her identity is transformed. Her lips are sealed; her hands are bound. Powerless, she weeps. Perhaps, she thinks, she may escape; perhaps, she thinks, this torture may prepare her for some glorious future.

Grimké's diary entry sounds the authentic tones of classic American Gothicism. The inevitability of the experience, the fascinated horror, the obsessive reminiscence, the heightened sensibilities, the inability to act, the prospect of endless torment, the transport of torture—all point today's reader to Charles Brockden Brown and Edgar Allan Poe.

But in addition to the inevitable differences between diary entries and published fiction, there are other crucial differences. The origins of Grimké's responses are not private and obscure, like those of Poe's protagonists. Nor is her experience located outside common spatial and temporal contexts. On the contrary, Grimké describes her reactions to an actual encounter, a specific event that resulted from a routine incident attendant to an established social institution. Unlike American "classic" nineteenth-century writers, Grimké connects the American Gothic sensibility to its historic national subject: the debased relationships among the races.[4]

In making this connection, Grimké anticipates the responses of a number of other abolitionist women writers and speakers.[5] The diabolism of slavery, the urgency of the need to end it, the apparent impossibility of engaging in meaningful action to do so; the painful sensibility, the frantic powerlessness, the frustration of its victims (variously seen as slave, slaveholder, and observer), the inevitability of cataclysmic destruction—all occur and recur in the writings and speeches of these antislavery women in a peculiar mix of idealism, realism, social consciousness, religion, sentimentality, and sensationalism. Unlike writings by white men such as Poe, which circle around the peculiarly displaced sensations experienced by a unique asocial male narrator, the writings and speeches of the female abolitionists center on the figure of a social victim: a woman in chains.

In nineteenth-century America, the ways to feminism were many and varied. Male abolitionists routinely used the viewpoint, energy, and language of Christian evangelism in relation to the slavery question. Grimké herself recorded that when antislavery activist Theodore Weld (whom she would marry) described a male slave, he "proceeded to show that Slavery with an iron grip seized this Godlike being, wrested the sceptre of dominion from his hand, tore the crown from his head, and substituted for these the collar and the chain. Here was the sin of slavery."[6] Grimké's contribution was that, following Chandler's lead, she blazed a trail from abolitionism to feminism along which other women could proceed. She used the terms of the female antislavery emblem to explore slavery imaginatively from a woman's perspective.

At the heart of Grimké's remarkable impact as an abolitionist and femi-

nist was her success in making the imaginative and emotional leap that
Chandler had proposed. In a society with distinctive racial and gender
patterns, she developed a version of abolitionism in which both observer
and subject were female, and she transformed herself imaginatively from a
suffering white observer into a suffering black slave. Then Grimké went
further. She not only saw herself as a victimized slave, she extended this
identification to characterize the condition of all women. Fleshing out a
series of variations of the figures shown on the antislavery emblems, Grimké
reinterpreted these kneeling slaves in chains and erect chain-breaking liberators. In her speeches and writings, they came to represent what she
concluded was her own oppression as a woman, the oppression of all women,
and woman's struggle for liberation.

Grimké's first shift away from her identification as an enchained victim
appears in her 1835 letter to William Lloyd Garrison. She was shocked by
reports that *The Liberator*'s editor, as well as members of the Boston Female
Anti-Slavery Society, had been the targets of a mob. Sounding a note that
Garrison shrewdly identified as the ecstasy of martyrdom, she allied herself
with radical abolitionism: "It is my deep, solemn, deliberate conviction that
this is a cause worth dying for. . . . YES! LET IT COME—let us suffer, rather
than insurrections should arise."[7] As Grimké identifies herself with the
besieged abolitionists, she shifts the verbs from indicative to imperative and
the personal pronouns from singular to plural, transforming her private
despair into a shared hope for the future of the nation. By bearing the fury of
the proslavery mobs, by interposing themselves between master and slave,
she and the abolitionists will end slavery—and thus make unnecessary the
insurrection that many fear would otherwise surely transform black slaves
into masters and white masters into slaves.

In this letter, as in her diary, Grimké's female figure still kneels at the
center, but it has been transformed from passive to active, from despairing
to purposefully self-sacrificing. Although the notion of a private martyrdom,
with its implications of spiritual superiority and the value of suffering,
suggests a role consistent with patriarchal definitions of womanhood, a
martyrdom resulting from participation in a violent political event like the
Boston mobbing of 1835 suggests something quite different. Grimké's focus
here is not eternal but temporal. She believes that her torment will be of
value in this world, that it will redeem America. Transformed into a political
martyr whose suffering will save slave, slavemaster, and the entire nation,
she prays for strength: "LET IT COME—let us suffer." This letter changed her

life. When Garrison published it (without her permission or even her knowledge), she was urged to repudiate her words. Instead, in the tradition of Christian martyrdom, she asserted that God had inspired her testimony against slavery.

Grimké next characterized herself deliberately in a public testimony. The audience she targeted in her *Appeal to the Christian Women of the South* was one she knew well.[8] For years, in her diary she had recorded private efforts to convince friends and relatives, especially her mother, that slavery was a sin. Now, in 1836, she prefaced a public *Appeal* to these women with Queen Esther's words, "If I perish, I perish," the biblical statement of a woman's acceptance of the risk involved in presenting an illegal petition.

This problem of risk taking, of the risk involved in petitioning, is central to Grimké's *Appeal*. As her epigraph demonstrates, she had identified a scriptural model for the self-sacrificial female figure envisioned in her letter to Garrison; instead of being martyred, however, Esther had saved God's chosen nation. When Grimké now asks what women can do to end slavery, she answers that they can make a series of appeals: to God to enable them to bear witness against the system; to the men in their families to act to end it; and to their slaves to remain quiescent while enduring it. Urging her readers who hold slaves to take a greater risk, she proposes that they break the laws that prohibit emancipating slaves, paying them for their work and teaching them to read and write. Considering whether women are capable of enduring the punishments they will certainly incur for committing these crimes, Grimké confidently, even triumphantly, invokes the figure of Esther, who broke the law and saved her people:

> Yes, weak and trembling woman was the instrument appointed by God, to reverse the bloody mandate of the eastern monarch, and save the whole visible church from destruction. . . . Is there no Esther among you who will plead for the poor devoted slave? . . . Yes! if there were but one Esther at the South, she might save her country from ruin.[9]

Inscribing the biblical heroine she invokes, Grimké presents herself as a model for her readers. In making this *Appeal* she, like the Old Testament queen, knowingly violates established patterns of female behavior to plead for an oppressed people and an unpopular cause. Like Esther, she deliberately gambles.

Although her biblical model had won, Grimké lost badly—at least in the short term. Her pamphlet caused her to be estranged from her family, banished from her native city of Charleston, disowned by her conservative

Orthodox Quaker community in Philadelphia, and ostracized by most of her friends.

Despite this, within months she was drafting a second public document projecting an even more assertive and active image of woman. Its title, *An Appeal to the Women of the Nominally Free States*, signals its connections to her earlier pamphlet. [10] This time, however, Grimké did not write to express her own opinions but to make a collective statement for the 1837 Convention of American Women Against Slavery. Organized by the female antislavery societies, this convention brought more than seventy black and white women delegates together for four days to consider the issues of slavery and racism. Its members included prominent reformers Lucretia Mott, L. Maria Child, Sarah Mapps Douglass, and Anne Warren Weston. Angelina Grimké and her sister, Sarah, however, offered the resolutions on the public role of women. In discussions on the convention floor, Angelina Grimké again spoke of Queen Esther. Now, however, instead of referring to Esther as a model of principled self-sacrifice, Grimké used her to exemplify the tenacity that the delegates would need in order to undertake the unheard-of task of circulating political petitions. "It is the duty of every woman . . . annually to petition Congress with the faith of an Esther . . . for the immediate abolition of slavery."[11]

In addition to intense involvement in the daily work of the convention, Angelina and Sarah Grimké assumed primary responsibility for publications connected with it. Because of her concern about white racism, a problem she was currently discussing in her private correspondence and which she addressed in a resolution before the convention, Angelina Grimké assumed responsibility for a pamphlet designed for an audience of northern women. [12]

As its title suggests, *An Appeal to the Women of the Nominally Free States* again presents its female authors-narrators as supplicants. But here Angelina Grimké transforms that role. Where she had written her first *Appeal* in biblical phrases, her rhetoric now echoes the Constitution. As her reference to the "nominally free states" suggests, her focus is secular. Carefully listing as precedent the historic political involvement of women—from the Bible, Miriam and Deborah; from classical Rome, Venturia, Volumnia, and the Sabine women; from modern France, Joan of Arc; and from America Lydia Darrah, who had warned Washington of Howe's plans—she proposes that her northern female readers collect signatures on petitions being circulated by antislavery societies and sent to state and federal legislators. That is, she urges that they join an appeal that is not only public, but political.

In a passage crucial to the development of nineteenth-century American feminism, this *Appeal* by Grimké gives classic form to the connections she saw between the condition of women and the condition of slaves. Defining freedom as engagement in significant action and characterizing significant action as public speech, she develops the arguments implicit in the resolutions she had offered to the convention:

> All moral beings have essentially the same rights and duties, whether they be male or female. . . . The denial of our duty to act, is a bold denial of our right to act; and if we have no right to act, then may we well be termed "the white slaves of the North"—for, like our brethren in bonds, we must seal our lips in silence and despair.[13]

The unspoken corollary is, of course, that to be free is to act, to open one's lips in noise and in hope; that free women speak out in public.

The series of public actions Grimké proposes to northern women contrasts with the largely private actions she had suggested to southern women a few months earlier: she urges the northerners to organize antislavery societies, to inform themselves and others about slavery, and to sign and circulate abolitionist petitions. Grimké then addresses the crucial issue of racism. She asserts that her white readers must "break the cord of caste in the Free States" before they can appeal to southern white women "to break the yoke of bondage" and urges her black audience to continue "to mingle with us whilst we have the prejudice, because it is only by associating with you that we shall ever be able to overcome it." This pamphlet, which was presented to the interracial convention of women by an interracial committee, represents an important instance of the historic effort of black and white American women to address an audience of black and white American women on the subject of white racism.

An image new to abolitionist iconography concludes this extraordinary *Appeal*. In dramatic contrast to the kneeling form of the supplicant slave that Grimké had evoked in her letter to Garrison and in her first *Appeal*, she now describes an erect female figure actively engaged in liberating herself and in reforming the world. Neither the enchained supplicant nor the chain-breaking rescuer of the double antislavery emblem, this self-liberated figure is reminiscent of a popular revolutionary national image. Edward Savage's 1796 painting, *Liberty, in the Form of the Goddess of Youth Giving Support to the Bald Eagle*, shows a young woman in a cloudy setting that includes an American flag and a pole topped by a Liberty Cap; a wild storm rages in the distance (fig. 10).[14] Dressed in flowing garments, with blossoms in her hair, she is partially encircled by a chain of flowers that she holds in her left hand. Raising the goblet in her right hand, she offers nourishment to an eagle in flight as she strides forward, trampling monarchial decorations and symbols under her bare foot. Savage's engraving of his painting became immensely popular. His design was copied by Samuel L. Waldo and reworked by women into embroideries and paintings on glass.

This active goddess-like woman, whose natural beauty disdains artifice and who spurns trinkets with her foot, is suggested by the female figure Grimké describes. But the objects associated with Grimké's triumphant woman signify issues of gender, not of nationhood:

> Woman is now rising in her womanhood, to throw from her, with one hand, the paltry privileges with which *man* has invested her, of conquering by fashionable charms and winning by personal attractions, whilst, with the other, she grasps the right of woman, to unite in holy copartnership with man, in the renovation of a fallen world. She tramples these glittering baubles in the dust, and takes from the hand of her *Creator*, the Magna Charta of her high prerogatives as a *moral*, an *intellectual*, an accountable being, a *woman*, who, though placed in subjection to the monarch of the world, is still the crown and "the glory of man."[15]

I have been unable to find any illustrations of Grimké's new woman. Perhaps because her vital form so closely mirrored national images, no new pictures were designed for publications of the female antislavery societies.

During the summer of 1837, Angelina Grimké and her sister became public figures as they lectured throughout New England. Before June was done, the Grimké sisters faced large "promiscuous" audiences (audiences of both men and women). By mid-July, they were formally debating male proponents of slavery. In some places the sisters were warmly welcomed: in Salem, Massachusetts, by crowds at the Friends' Meeting House, the Howard Street Church, and the Colored Sabbath School; in Concord (where John Greenleaf Whittier and Samuel May had earlier been stoned), by Lydian Emerson and other members of the local "aristocracy."[16]

The extraordinary appearance of female speakers also triggered opposition. At a time when the names of respectable women did not appear in print, the Grimké sisters were clearly identified—but not named—as targets of a Pastoral Letter in which the Congregational Ministers of Massachusetts condemned the participation of women in public reforms as unbiblical

LIBERTY.

*In the form of the Goddess of Youth giving Support to the Bald Eagle.*

Fig. 10. Edward Savage, *Liberty as Goddess of Youth* (1796).

and urged that churches close their doors to antislavery speakers. And they were scurrilously abused by name in the public press. When Angelina Grimké was attacked by name in Catharine E. Beecher's *An Essay on Slavery and Abolitionism with Reference to the Duty of American Females Addressed to Miss A. E. Grimké*, she countered with a pamphlet using her opponent's name as well as her own: *Letters to Catharine E. Beecher in Reply to an Essay on Slavery and Abolitionism Addressed to A. E. Grimké.*[17]

In this pair of 1837 publications, as they disputed woman's appropriate role in the public controversy over the political issues of slavery, abolitionism, and racism, American spokeswomen openly debated the meaning of true womanhood. Beecher, who announced her *Essay* a response to Grimké's second *Appeal*, essentially sketched the figure of a domesticated angel as she argued that the spiritually superior woman was created to function within the private sphere. In an aside, she chided Grimké for using the biblical model of Queen Esther to justify women's public involvement, commenting that the Old Testament heroine became a petitioner only in a situation dire in the extreme.

Predictably, Grimké rebutted by arguing the dangerousness of the present moment. In her polemic, she reveals the origin of her ideas about gender oppression and connects them with her ideas about racial oppression: "The investigation of the rights of the slave has led me to a better understanding of my own."[18] Central to Grimké's discussion is the complexity of the emblemized supplicant. This figure suggests dialectically opposing notions: that to plead is to be powerless, unable to effect one's will except by influencing the actions of a powerful other; and that to plead is to voice one's concerns, to authenticate and assert oneself—that to speak for oneself is to express one's autonomy, one's power.

These distinctions were of particular importance in Grimké's America, where for a woman to supplicate was to conform to patriarchal patterns, but for her to articulate her concerns within the dialogue of political discourse was to move beyond gender proscriptions. Constitutional guarantees of the right to petition, a fundamental liberty specifically retained by the people of the United States, support the notion that to plead is to express one's power, and in *Letters to Catharine Beecher*, Grimké discusses petitioning as a political right, suggesting that those who cannot communicate freely are slaves: forbidden to articulate their ideas, or permitted to voice them only at another's whim, they lack direct access to an audience and are heard only insofar as their masters permit.

> The right of petition is the only political right that women have. . . . If, then,
> *we* are taxed without being represented, and governed by laws *we* have no voice
> in framing, then, surely, we ought to be permitted at least to remonstrate. . . .
> The *very least* that can be done is to give [women] the right of petition in all
> cases whatsoever; and without any abridgement. If not, they are mere slaves,
> known only through their masters.[19]

As she shifts her subject from "women" to "we" to "they," Grimké suggests that her own identity, as well as that of all women, is at stake. This
identity depends on taking significant action, and—denied other political
rights—the only significant act of which women are capable is petitioning.
Petitioning and thus affirming her own selfhood, Grimké urges other women
to follow. If they do not, she warns (and with the third person pronoun
dissociates herself completely), "they are mere slaves." And follow they did.
Hundreds of thousands of American women petitioned federal, state, and
local governments on the slaves' behalf over the next quarter century.[20]

In the *Letters to Catharine Beecher*, Angelina Grimké develops more fully
her earlier assertions about the appropriateness of woman's political involvement, filling in the outlines of her earlier sketch of a woman rising to her
feet. She still envisions woman created by God to reign as queen. But this
queen has been ruthlessly deposed.

> Woman was never given to man. She was created, like him, in the image of
> God, and crowned with glory and honor. . . . [O]n her brow, as well as on his,
> was placed the "diadem of beauty," and in her hand the sceptre of universal
> dominion. . . . Woman was the first transgressor, and the first victim of power.
> In all heathen nations, she has been the slave of man, and Christian nations
> have never acknowledged her rights. [Her present condition is] *a violation of
> human rights, a rank usurpation of power*, a violent seizure and confiscation of
> what is sacredly and inalienably hers.[21]

This figure of a deposed queen is a refinement of the enslaved self that
Grimké had inscribed years earlier in her diary. By referring to the Creation,
Grimké suggests the primary character of woman's oppression and implies
that all other systems of oppression, including slavery, are patterned on this.
Despite her exhilarative combative tone, as if recognizing their common
cause, she signed the last of her letters to Beecher, "Thy sister in the bonds
of a common sisterhood." Echoing the language of the biblical injunction of
the American double antislavery emblem, "Remember those in bonds as
bound with them," and retaining the dual readings of "bond" as connection

and as restraint, here she moves far beyond earlier significations. Revealing the deep connections between abolitionism and feminism, Grimké appropriates the language of bondage, which she had used to express her relationships with and responsibilities to slaves, and uses it to signify relationships among women and to voice the oppression women share. Historian Nancy Cott, commenting on a similar formulation used by Grimké's sister, Sarah, argues persuasively that the phrase must have been intentionally endowed "with the double meaning that womanhood bound women together even as it bound them down."[22]

As Angelina Grimké fulfilled speaking engagements throughout New England and met newspaper deadlines for her *Letters* in the summer of 1837, she privately tried out her new notions that linked women's condition to the condition of the slave. "I feel as if it is not the cause of the slave only which we plead but the cause of Woman as a responsible & moral being. . . . I do not know how I shall find language strong enough to express my indignation at the view [Beecher] takes of women's character & duty. . . . I verily believed in female subordination until very recently." And she revealed that for her, as for Beecher, womanhood was a cultural construct in which sensitivity was somehow gender specific: "I have no hope of converting C[atherine] because I fear she has not the heart of a woman."[23]

Angelina Grimké's appearance before the Legislative Committee of the Massachusetts legislature in February 1838 marked the high point of her public life. Six months before, she had privately characterized her pioneering attempts to "plead the cause of Woman" while pleading "the cause of the slave" as the efforts of a confused wanderer in a strange landscape. "What an untrodden path we have entered upon! Sometimes I feel almost bewildered, amazed, confounded, & wonder by what strange concatenation of events I came to be where I am & what I am."[24]

This uncertainty is not, however, apparent in Grimké's speech before the legislature. She brought with her twenty thousand signatures on a woman's antislavery petition, and, sensitive to her unique position as the first woman in the history of the nation to address a legislative body, she began her appeal with still another reference to Esther, the scriptural petitioner.[25] Although Grimké asserted that, like the biblical queen, she was appearing on "a mission of life and love," she did not stress the likenesses between her appeal and Esther's, as she had done earlier. Instead she concentrated on the differences. Now choosing to interpret supplication as powerlessness and implying that Esther was not actually a ruler but a sexual slave, "the mistress of her voluptuous lord," Grimké announced that she would not address the appetites of her male audience.

Repeating three times, "I stand before you," Grimké underscores the differences between Esther's supplicating pose and her own erect posture.[26] Grimké then supplants the model of the Old Testament female supplicant with a figure she characterizes as more appropriate to democratic nineteenth-century America: "In the age which is approaching . . . [woman] should be something more [than a queen]—she should be a citizen."

Grimké speaks in the first person as she fills in the outlines of this new political female identity.

> As a Southerner, as a repentant slaveholder, and a moral being I feel I owe it to the suffering slave, and to the deluded master, to my country and to the world to do all that I can to overturn a system of complicated crimes, built upon the broken hearts and prostrate bodies of my countrymen in chains and cemented by the blood and sweat and tears of my sisters in bonds.

Identifying herself in terms of her region and condition, as well as in terms of her relationship to her Creator and (in the last words of her sentence) to other women, she announces her duty as she now understands it. Grimké figures slavery, "a system of complicated crimes," as a material structure erected on and held together by the bodies of male slaves who are her countrymen and female slaves who are her "sisters in bonds." She announces her intention to overturn this system. In its place, she implies, she will substitute its opposite, a system of simple justice.

In this speech, Angelina Grimké envisions a new self—a self she had earlier been unable to name, unable even to imagine. Structured by the abolitionist emblems, this new female figure encompasses all of Grimké's earlier images. In her diary entry, like Chandler she had identified with the slave, seeing herself as imprisoned, weighted with chains, able only to weep. Then—first on her knees, later rising up on trembling limbs, still later reaching for her rights only to realize that they had been violently usurped—she had recognized herself as a queen deposed. But now she publicly announces herself a woman who, attempting to revolutionize an unjust world, achieves her own freedom in acting to end the oppression of others.

Gleefully reporting this speech to a friend, Grimké identifies herself anew as a self-emancipated slave. In her efforts to free others she has freed herself. "O! how my soul rejoices, yea exults in that emancipation which has been wrought out for Sister and myself. For many years I felt as if I was compelled to drag the chain and wear the collar on my struggling *spirit* as truly as the poor slave was on his body. . . . We Abolition Women are turning the world upside-down!"[27]

This triumphant figure of Justice as a self-liberated liberator represents a dynamic synthesis of the double figures of the antislavery emblem. Using the language of slavery to figure her own spiritual oppression in patriarchal society—the metaphorical chains she had dragged and the metaphorical iron collars she had worn—Grimké announces her emancipation. And in shifting to the first person plural, she celebrates the revolutionary liberation struggle of all women.

Self-liberating action is at the center of *Letters on the Equality of the Sexes and the Condition of Woman, Addressed to Mary S. Parker, President of the Boston Female Anti-Slavery Society.*[28] Sarah Grimké formulated this full-length theoretical counterpart to the feminist imagery that her sister Angelina had appropriated from the abolitionist emblems. Its original title, "Letters on the Province of Woman," recalls the spatial patriarchal terminology of "woman's sphere." When Sarah Grimké prepared her manuscript for publication as a pamphlet, however, she devised a three-part title that suggests a radically different perspective. Woman, she asserts, was created by God to rule as queen; after the fall in Eden, man made her his slave; now women must join together and assume their rightful role (which they share with men) in renovating the fallen world.

Sarah Grimké's notion that there was an original "equality of the sexes," and her conviction that in nineteenth-century America unjust oppression is the "condition of woman," are the grounding of a startling sentence that boils up from the surface of her earnest, labored prose. "All I ask of our Brethren is, that they will take their feet from off our necks, and permit us to stand upright on that ground which God designed us to occupy."[29] Perhaps recalling traditional designs emblemizing Despotism by showing slaves prostrated before an oriental ruler, Sarah Grimké hints that sexual bondage remains a reference point for the treatment of women, even by nineteenth-century American Brethren who claim to be Christians.

Sarah Grimké's formulation, like her sister's use of the language of bondage in relation to women who are legally free, charts the emergence of feminism from the abolitionist matrix. In common with many Americans of their generation, the Grimkés used scriptural language easily. Both sisters characteristically applied biblical formulations to social issues in their private correspondence before incorporating them into public speeches and writings. As the Grimkés expanded their discussions of the condition of slaves to include discussions of the condition of women, they continued to use the same discursive codes, but they connected them to new referends. In an 1829 diary entry by Angelina Grimké, a tyrant's foot is on the neck of the slave; in Sarah Grimké's 1838 polemic, that foot is male and the bowed neck is woman's. Similarly, in a diary entry made a year earlier, Angelina Grimké had referred to sin as a "root of bitterness," and in an 1832 letter she had used this biblical phrase to refer to slavery; in 1838, Sarah Grimké identifies the poison plant as "the mistaken notion of the inequality of the sexes."[30]

A single figure crouches behind Sarah Grimké's treatise and all of her sister's appeals. It is a woman weighed down by "chains with which man has bound us, galling to the spirit, though unseen by the eye." She is, however, neither the passive despairing victim nor the triumphant martyr that Angelina Grimké had sketched. This woman is not kneeling in supplication; she is prostrated because man is crushing her down. In Sarah Grimké's *Letters on the Equality of the Sexes* she is not shown alone; her debased form is contrasted with the figures of women who "arise in all the majesty of moral power, in all the dignity of immortal beings, and plant themselves side by side on the platform of human rights, with man."[31]

Sarah Grimké focuses on this erect elevated woman, a figure who would appear and reappear in feminist documents thereafter. She is God's moral creature who finally—despite congresses, legislators, churches, and ministers—is freeing herself of false ideologies, false religions, and a perverse interpretation of the Bible, is learning her true nature, and is beginning to act on this knowledge. Like most public arguments in nineteenth-century America, *Letters on the Equality of the Sexes* points to the Declaration of Independence and the Constitution; but its concern is millennial. While Angelina Grimké's writings and speeches increasingly addressed secular concerns, Sarah Grimké's approach remains solidly theological: her subject is woman's role as God's creature—her creation, her fall, and her work to redeem a fallen world.

Angelina Grimké's speeches and pamphlets contributed to the stock of female figures encoded in our national culture, and they paved the way for Sarah Grimké's feminist polemic, a milestone on the road to the woman's rights convention at Seneca Falls. Sarah Grimké's image of woman as God's active moral female creature became central to feminist writings in the

decades that followed. The sisters' application of antislavery discourse to the
condition of women was quickly taken up by others. In 1838 Eliza Davis,
corresponding secretary of the Providence, Rhode Island, Female Anti-
Slavery Society, wrote to the Second Convention of American Women Against
Slavery that "the iron shackle that drags heavily along the plains of the
South and the golden fetter hugged by so many of our sex, are both to be
broken!"[32] Not only pamphlets and prints, but also the dramatic oral culture
of the lyceum movement and Chautauqua spread the abolitionist-feminist
iconography of enchained supplicants, chain-breaking liberators, and self-
emancipated women throughout the North.

In smaller communities, the appearance of a prominent speaker was a
major event, and the presence of a speaker like Angelina Grimké had real
significance. Antislavery women flouted patriarchal restrictions concerning
the behavior of true women when they mounted the public platform to speak
before "promiscuous" audiences on the political issue of slavery and, in the
minds of many, were identified with whores, actresses, and other women
who were excluded from true womanhood. But the Grimkés and their followers claimed that they made this move in response to a moral imperative.
Hence, a new paradox: in the name of morality, out of the need to testify
against the sin of slavery, antislavery women deliberately violated patriarchal codes of female morality.

Two kinds of reactions to the Grimkés' appearances, and to the appearances of other women who gave political lectures in public, became standard. Abolitionist-feminists in the audience tended to frame their responses
in terms of the antislavery emblems. They did not, however, see the figure
on the platform as a woman struggling to free herself from chains imposed
by the patriarchy. Instead, envisioning her in terms of the heaven-sent
liberator of the double emblem, they characterized her as superhuman.
Even Sarah Grimké, who had herself mounted the public platform, used this
imagery to describe the appearance of a speaker confronting a mob: "She
arose amid the yells and shouts of the infuriated mob, the crash of windows
and the hurling of stones. She looked to me like an angelic being descended
amid the tempest of passion in all the dignity of conscious superiority."[33]
Sarah Grimké is describing an angel, but not an Angel in the House. Fixed
in a setting that is not private and domestic, but public and political, the
figure Grimké describes is an Angel in the Hall.

In accord with this perspective, audiences of antislavery women judged
the public appearances of abolitionist women speakers inspirational. L.
Maria Child's characterization of Angelina Grimké's speech before the legis-

lature as "a spectacle of the greatest moral sublimity I ever witnessed" testifies to the value they placed on these appearances. The admiring women created a support network for those among them who, against all their female training, dared expose themselves on the platform.[34] As late as 1850, a young Quaker woman who had recently spoken on woman's rights spelled out in a letter to abolitionist-feminist Amy Post the crucial significance of this female support:

> Did you ever when children think of doing some little act of kindness, performing an alloted task for your mother perhaps, without her knowledge, then to await with feelings of hope and fear for her approval or disapproval, then to be warmed and encouraged by her *approving* smile received with confidence in her ability to judge, scarce knowing which would relieve most, to laugh or cry—if so you know how I received thy graciously offered and accepted letter.[35]

Like their idolizing and nurturing supporters, critics of the platform speakers often responded less to their ideas than to their public presence. Both detractors and supporters saw the abolitionist-feminist speakers as larger than life, as more powerful than ordinary women. While their admirers praised them as angelic liberators, their critics condemned them as lewd nineteenth-century versions of the sinful women of Scripture, as diabolical. Reviled as "Devil-ina," Angelina Grimké was repeatedly characterized in the press as a loose woman. "Not at all abased in exhibiting herself in a position so unsuitable to her sex," she was seen as making "a bold dash among the Yankee law makers," shamelessly exhibiting herself "in search of a *lawful* protector, who will take her for better or worse for life."

The women's violation of codes restricting public female behavior caused hostile speculation about their willingness to violate sexual and racial codes restricting private female behavior, as well. To their critics, abolitionist-feminist women speakers were doubtless guilty of violating prohibitions against sexual activity outside marriage and against interracial sex. This would explain the newspaper comment that "The Misses Grimké have made speeches, wrote pamphlets, exhibited themselves in public, etc. for a long time, but have not found husbands yet. We suspect that they would prefer white children to black under certain circumstances, after all." And such hostility was not restricted to prominent targets like the Grimkés. One woman confided in 1841 to a well-known speaker that she, too, had "felt it was my duty to engage in some small measure in this work of reform," but that her friends "conclude that my senses are *all gone*. . . . I am *branded* with such names as *Elect. Lady, Comadore*, & willing to sleep with the *niggers* children to marry them &c &c."[36]

The controversy surrounding Angelina Grimké's public appearances before "promiscuous audiences" was not entirely new. At least three other women had preceded her on public political platforms in the United States—Frances Wright, Ernestine Rose, and Maria W. Stewart—and all had been subjected to abuse. Wright and Rose were Europeans who shared the dream of an egalitarian collectivist community with other advanced reformers on the continent. Their opponents claimed, as Grimké's would, that Wright and Rose behaved like sexual and racial deviants by appearing in public and characterized them in terms of Jezebel and the Whore of Babylon, while their supporters found their appearances spiritually uplifting. Although their audiences responded much like Angelina Grimké's, in their speeches and writings Wright and Rose expressed a libertarian, secular perspective an ocean removed from Grimké's evangelical Christianity.[37]

The American-born woman who preceded Grimké on the platform, however, was rooted in the matrix of Christian evangelism. In 1832–33, African-American Maria W. Stewart delivered at least four public lectures in Boston. Stewart's application of biblical thought and language to the social issues of slavery, racism, and sexism in America anticipated the evangelical rhetoric of Grimké and other female antislavery lecturers.

What was strikingly different about Maria W. Stewart was her race and her class. She was a freeborn black New Englander who, cheated out of her husband's estate after his death, earned her living as a domestic worker. Stewart was a Christian who had undergone a profound religious experience and consecrated herself to God's service. She addressed her first speech to the Boston Afric-American Female Intelligence Society. Then at Boston's Franklin Hall on 21 September 1832, Stewart became the first American woman on record to present a public lecture. A follower of the black militant David Walker, she delivered a secular message: "O, ye daughters of Africa, awake! awake! arise!" Stewart used biblical discourse and the abolitionist imagery of enchaining to present the situation of free, African-American domestics and day-laborers: "I consider our condition but little better than [slavery]. Yet, after all, me thinks there are no chains as galling as the chains of ignorance—no fetters so binding as those that bind the soul, and exclude it from the vast fund of useful and scientific knowledge." And she addressed the class and racial biases of white American women: "O, ye fairer sisters, whose hands are never soiled, whose nerves and muscles are never strained, go learn by experience! Had we the opportunity that you have had, to improve our moral and mental facilities, what would have hindered our intellects from being as bright, and our manners from being as dignified as yours?"[38]

Because there are no records of the responses of Stewart's Franklin Hall audience or of her later audience at African Masonic Hall, it is not known whether her supporters saw her as angelic and her detractors characterized her in terms of the fallen women of the Bible. But it is known that Stewart felt she faced serious opposition. Announcing that she was "sensible of exposing myself to calumny and reproach," she voiced her awareness of the perils of undertaking the role of a public female lecturer, standing "alone . . . exposed to the firey darts of the devil, and to the assaults of wicked men."[39]

In September, 1833, a year after Stewart faced her Franklin Hall audience, she acknowledged defeat. Yet in her "Farewell Address to her Friends in the City of Boston" she claimed her right as a black woman to a public role and, anticipating Angelina Grimké's strategy, cited Esther, among other biblical figures, as precedent for her actions. Further, in this speech Stewart adopted and reformulated the motto encircling the antislavery emblem, sounding a positive assertion that hints at Sojourner Truth's later transformation of its double inquiries: "What if I am a woman! is not the God of ancient times the God of these modern days? Did he not raise up Deborah, to be a mother, and a judge in Israel? Did not queen Esther save the lives of the Jews? And Mary Magdalene first declare the resurrection of Christ from the dead?" Presenting herself as God's moral female creature who, freed from falsehoods, is enacting her true nature by standing erect in the public sphere, Stewart anticipates the Grimkés' challenge of sexist and racist ideologies:

> Be no longer astonished, then, my brethren and friends, that God at this eventful period should raise up your own females to strive, by their example, both in public and private, to assist those who are endeavoring to stop the strong current of prejudice that flows so profusely against us at present. . . . What if such women as are here described should arise among our sable race? And it is not impossible.

Asserting her power of public speech as a divine gift and pleading with her reluctant audience to follow her lead, in her final words Stewart characterizes herself in the language of Isaiah: "the glorious declaration was about to be made applicable to me, that was made to God's ancient covenant people by the prophet, Comfort ye, comfort ye, my people: say unto her that her warfare is accomplished, and that her iniquities are pardoned."[40]

Garrison published Stewart's speeches, and it is reasonable to assume that the white Christian female abolitionists who read *The Liberator* were aware of her. But apparently either racism or class bias—or both—prevented them from identifying with Stewart. Nor did they identify with Wright or Rose. Their model was not the black Christian, the English-born libertarian, or the freethinking Polish Jew. The religious white female antislavery speakers who followed saw themselves walking in the footsteps of Angelina Grimké. Firmly fixed in their vision was the spectacle of Grimké's appearance at Pennsylvania Hall in 1838.

The hall itself had become an instant symbol. Built as a free-speech temple by Philadelphia abolitionists and booked to house the Second Convention of American Women Against Slavery, Pennsylvania Hall was condemned as a den of iniquity by the dominant white community. A sneering broadside depicts the lewdness critics found inherent in women's participation in public life (fig. 11).[41] "Abolition Hall" shows women lolling out of the building's upper windows as they might display themselves in the windows of a brothel. In the street below, interracial couples— and triples —stroll about with their varicolored offspring. A placard identifies these shocking violations of the mores of race and gender with abolition in general and in particular with David Paul Brown, a scheduled speaker at the inauguration of Pennsylvania Hall. Doubtless this image fueled the violence of the crowds that mobbed, then burned, the hall at its official opening.

While respectable white Philadelphia saw the building as an emblem of sexual and racial depravity, to antislavery feminists it was the site of Grimké's heroism. Speaking in the teeth of the mob, interrupted by shouts and breaking glass, she had made violence her subject. To the women, Grimké's presence, like her scriptural language flung in the face of the terror, created an unforgettable image of embattled heroic womanhood.

> Here it—hear it. . . . The spirit of slavery is *here* and has been roused to wrath. . . . Every man and every woman present may do something by showing that we fear not a mob, and, in the midst of threatenings and revilings, by opening our mouths for the dumb and pleading the cause of those who are ready to perish.
>
> Women of Philadelphia! Men who hold the rod over slaves, rule in the

Fig. 11. Zip Coon [pseud.], "Abolition Hall. The evening before the conflagration at the time more than 50,000 persons were glorifying in its destruction at Philadelphia May —1838" (ca. 1850s). Salt print of unrecorded lithograph.

councils of the nation: and they deny our right to petition and to remonstrate against abuses of our sex and of our kind. We have these rights, however, from our God. Only let us exercise them.[42]

Joining her on the platform that day was Maria Weston Chapman, polemicist, editor, organizer, and leader of the Boston Female Anti-Slavery Society, who was scheduled to make her first major speech. Like the other Boston women, Chapman had been mobbed before. At Pennsylvania Hall —slender, tall and blonde, her red shawl flaming against the drab and Quaker gray of the others—she tried to make herself heard.[43] But she lasted only a few minutes.

Although Chapman never again spoke in public, for another woman the Pennsylvania Hall mobbing sparked a lifetime on the public platform. Abby Kelley, who impulsively rose to her feet after Grimké's speech had ended, assumed the role Angelina Grimké had created and briefly played. For more than twenty years, Kelley (later Abby Kelley Foster) served as the foremost female antislavery lecturer in America. Like Grimké, she used the biblical language and imagery encoded in the antislavery emblems. Even in her impulsive first speech at Pennsylvania Hall, echoing the patterns Grimké

had established, Kelley presented herself as a supplicant: "It is the still
small voice within, which may not be withstood, that bids me open my
mouth for the dumb,—that bids me plead the cause of God's perishing
poor—ay, God's poor."[44]

Through the years that followed, Kelley spoke, as Grimké had, of powerless supplicants, of martyrs, of rising self-liberated women, of women in
chains. Like Grimké, Abby Kelley identified with the oppressed slave. She
wrote of this identification and of her struggle to express it, of her sense of
the inadequacy of words and the pressing need to create a new discourse to
convey all she felt:

> When I come to sit down in the cool of the day alone with none but God to hold
> communion with, and in the exercise of love to him, become myself the slave,
> that I may "remember him"—when at such a moment I feel the fetters wearing
> away at the flesh and grating on my bare ankle bone, when I feel the naked
> cords of my neck shrinking away from the rough edge of the iron collar, when
> my flesh quivers beneath the lash, till in anguish I feel portions of it cut from
> my back. . . . But the English language is not adequate to the task. . . . We
> must resort to the expedients of barbarous nations and express ourselves by
> significant signs, speaking through eloquent gesticulations. . . . We must do
> this until we can invent a language that is equal to the subject.

Like Grimké, Abby Kelley linked her own situation, and the cause of all
women, with the cause of the slave: "In striving to strike his irons off, we
found most surely that we were manacled ourselves." And like Grimké,
Abby Kelley asserted that her public acts testified to her own emancipation.
The first woman nominated to serve on a committee of the American Anti-
Slavery Society, Kelley voiced the significance of her public posture by
announcing, "I rise because I am not a slave."[45]

Kelley's language and images became by extension standard ways of
characterizing the oppression and liberation of women. Similarly, her admirers responded to her public presence in ways that had become standard.
Echoing Grimké's early vision of a female martyr who would save the nation,
Garrison called Kelley "the moral Joan of Arc of the world."[46]

Her detractors, like those of the earlier women speakers, interpreted her
speeches as sexual exhibitions (variously hypersexual, sexless, and perverse) and attacked her in biblical language reserved for harlots. When an
old woman, Abby Kelley still recalled the hurt she had felt decades earlier
when a clergyman had made her the text of his sermon on sexual immorality:

Mr. Hayes charged that another Jezebel had arizen, making high pretentions to philanthropy and Christianity, and with fascinations exceeding, even those of her scripture prototype, was aiming to entice and destroy this church. . . . I went to my chamber that night, but not to sleep. In agony of prayer and tears, my cry was "Oh! that my head were waters, and mine eyes a fountain of tears, that I might weep day and night, for the slain of the daughter of my people."[47]

Just as Angelina Grimké, speaking in Pennsylvania Hall, had inspired Abby Kelley to rise to her feet, so Kelley in turn moved Lucy Stone and other women to stand up and speak out. Quakers were of course prominent among them. As historian Nancy Hewitt has shown, the most radical among these Quaker women did not, however, follow the path to feminism that Angelina Grimké and others traced, "from domesticity to humanitarian reform via evangelical religion, and from evangelical crusades to feminism via a second conversion to unconventional Protestantism." Instead, drawing strength from their Quaker roots and from each other, these women "by-passed, for most of their lives, the basic elements of the new urban bourgeois gender system—the separation of spheres, the sex-consciousness of domesticity, and the idea of female moral and spiritual superiority."[48]

The Society of Friends, in accord with their belief in inspiration, officially recognized some females as preachers. The most important was Lucretia Mott, "reformer of reformers." Mott, a Hicksite Quaker, inspired all of the antislavery women and particularly those who braved the platform. But hers was a special case. Because she was an acknowledged Quaker preacher, the rationale for Mott's self-exposure on the platform was her Inner Light—not her status as one of God's rational creatures or as a citizen of the Republic. Years after Mott first preached, when the Grimké sisters spoke in public, they made a point of asserting their right to the platform not as Quaker ministers but as women and citizens.[49]

In 1851, at the Worcester Women's Rights Convention, Abby Kelley Foster faced a group undertaking a new mission. Standing before them, she appeared to represent an earlier epoch in the struggle. Speaking of their historic task, she evoked the abolitionist imagery of the barefoot supplicant: "I did not rise to make a speech—my life has been my speech. For fourteen years I have advocated this cause by my daily life. Bloody feet, Sisters, have worn smooth the path by which you have come up hither."[50]

It is generally assumed that the significance of the free female antislavery speakers was political, and certainly their contribution to the development of political feminism was important. Over the years, they reached extremely large audiences. During their 1837 tour alone, the Grimké sisters spoke in eighty-eight meetings to over forty thousand people, and wherever they spoke, new female antislavery societies were formed, and organized political work began.[51] But these pioneering female speakers were also important in other ways. The words and images that the abolitionist women appropriated from evangelical antislavery discourse to structure a feminist discourse — the visual and verbal imagery of enchained supplicants and chain-breaking liberators and the language of sisterhood — live on. The appearances of the antislavery women on the platform were praised as angelic and excoriated as diabolical, but in and through their public presence they dramatized the possibility of female freedom on a human level. Using the Woman and Sister as a model, the antislavery feminists created a version of true womanhood that for generations has structured the discussion of woman's role in America.

## CHAPTER THREE

# L. Maria Child

*Such as I am, I am here . . . refusing the shadow of a fetter on my free expression from any
man, or any body of men.*

> —*L. Maria Child*, National Anti-Slavery
> Standard[1]

The voices of the nineteenth-century American antislavery feminists were as
varied, and as various, as those of their activist great-great-granddaughters
a century later. L. Maria Child, perhaps the most important of the free white
female abolitionist writers, published a wide range of journalism, polemic,
poems, novels, and short fiction.[2] Child's recurrent references to chains and
enchaining demonstrate that the discourse of the antislavery emblems shaped
her nonfiction prose. In her journalism and polemic, Child presents herself
as a free woman who, engaging as her natural right in rational political
debate, finds herself threatened by chains because of her efforts to liberate
her enchained brothers and sisters. Angelina Grimké, using the language of
evangelical abolitionism, saw women as slaves and struggled for her freedom; Child, using the language of reasonable discourse, inscribes her
struggle to remain free.

   Child makes the Woman and Sister a literary subject in a few of her
fictional pieces. She is, however, better known for inventing the character of
the Tragic Mulatto—a slave woman of mixed race who wants to conform to
patriarchal definitions of true womanhood but is prevented from doing so by
the white patriarchy. If in the Grimkés' speeches and writings all of patriarchy's true women are slaves, in Child's fiction all slaves are patriarchy's true

women. Peopling her stories with the enchained supplicants and the chain-breaking liberators of the antislavery emblem, Child encoded the oppression of race, gender, and condition, and the struggle against this oppression, in a cast of characters and a series of plots centering on the sexual abuse of female slaves.

The contrast between the preface and the text of Child's most important book, the antislavery polemic *An Appeal in Favor of That Class of Americans Called Africans* (1833), embodies the contradictions involved in Child's projection of a voice that is at once political and female. *An Appeal*, first fruit of her conversion to Garrisonian abolitionism, combines a preface that is a woman's plea to be heard with a text that is a well-researched argument for immediate abolition voiced in the clear strong tones of a free female citizen of the Republic. The argument of *An Appeal* begins with historical and comparative analyses, discusses the economic and political significance of slavery in America, and examines the proposals to end slavery advanced by colonizationists (sending black people to Africa) and by abolitionists (freeing the slaves). Bluntly announcing to her white audience that "we must . . . clearly make up our minds whether they are or are not human beings," Child addresses the issue of race. This, like her willingness to address the sexual oppression of black women—the most taboo aspect of her taboo topic—testifies to an intellectual openness and a breadth of spirit reminiscent of Fanny Wright's rationalism; Child's twentieth-century editors have characterized her as "one of the most eighteenth-century of the nineteenth-century women reformers."[3]

Child's *An Appeal* helped initiate the national discussion of the immediate abolition of slavery. Its title echoes David Walker's revolutionary *Appeal to the Colored Citizens of the World* (1829) and doubtless influenced Grimké's later addresses to the Christian women of the South and to the women of the "nominally free states." It is also a link to the antislavery emblems. Opening Child's polemic, we are confronted by a frontispiece picturing a black woman kneeling in chains (one of the earliest American depictions of the female supplicant) and then by a title page on which Child inscribes herself a female supplicant pleading for the supplicant slave.[4] In contrast to the intellectual argument articulated by her text, Child's frontispiece and title page constitute emotional pleas of the sort commonly relegated to women in the nineteenth century.

Child shaped her preface into another plea. Revealing her awareness that her choice of subject violates strong gender taboos, she makes a direct appeal to her audience using the manner of women's fiction: "Reader, I beseech you not to throw down this volume as soon as you have glanced at the title." Presenting herself as a supplicant, in accord with the conventions of the antislavery emblem, Child pleads that we read her book to overcome our prejudice and permit ourselves to hear the appeal of truth; or—aiming lower—to repay the debt we owe her for having given us amusement (presumably with her novels), or for having instructed our children (evidently with her juveniles); or—still lower—to find a new excuse to sneer at abolitionism, a topic of conversation since the recent appearance of Garrison's *Liberator*; or—lowest of all—to satisfy our curiosity about what a woman, who is expected to restrict herself to private affairs, has to say about public matters. Then, in a quick reversal, she confidently asserts, "Read it, on any terms, and my purpose will be gained." In this preface, as in much of her later political writing, Child contributes to the construction of antislavery feminist discourse by knowingly manipulating the structures assigned to women in patriarchial culture in order to address issues judged inappropriate for women. The tensions resulting from Child's use of the available "woman's discourse" to enter a public political debate beyond "woman's sphere" undoubtedly prompted the famous comment, "she seemed always to be talking radicalism in a greenhouse."[5]

After *An Appeal*, and two years before the Grimkés' sensational speaking tour, which would focus the attention of abolitionists and the general public on the question of women's participation in political debate, Child published the two-volume *History of the Condition of Women, in Various Ages and Nations* (1835). The information that she amasses recalls the instructive first half of her earlier abolitionist polemic. But Child does not now advance proposals for the liberation of women, as earlier she had for the liberation of slaves. Instead of asserting woman's rights, she restricts herself to presenting a geographically organized chronology of woman's wrongs, starting with the biblical Middle East and ending with nineteenth-century North America. Child does, however, signal her sensitivity to connections between the condition of women and the condition of slaves by violating the organization of her book to insert a chapter on "Women in Slave-Holding Countries." Explaining that "slavery everywhere produces nearly the same effects on character," she maintains that by "not considering a large number of men, women, and children in the same light as other human beings," slavery turns "any form of society into a moral desert."[6]

Her preface to the *Condition of Women* reads very differently from that of *An Appeal*. In four sentences filled with denials and disclaimers that attest

to her awareness of the budding controversy over "women's rights" and "the
relation between the sexes," Child writes not as a supplicant pleading on
behalf of the oppressed, but as a source of information for others who might
argue woman's cause:

> This volume is not an essay upon woman's rights, or a philosophical investiga-
> tion of what is or ought to be the relation between the sexes. If any theories on
> this subject are contained in it, they are merely incidentally implied by the
> manner of stating historical facts. I have simply endeavored to give an accurate
> history of the condition of women in language sufficiently concise for popular
> use. Those who reflect on this highly interesting and important subject will
> find in the facts thus patiently collected much that will excite thought and
> many materials for argument.[7]

Part travelogue, part social history, and part anthropological study, the
*Condition of Women* signaled an important moment in the history of American feminism. Three years after its publication, Sarah Grimké took up
Child's challenge and, echoing her title and repeatedly citing her *Condition
of Women* as a source, appended a feminist polemic to a discussion of
woman's condition. In *Letters on the Equality of the Sexes and the Condition
of Women*, Sarah Grimké wrote what Child had not, an antisexist argument
to parallel Child's antislavery *An Appeal*.[8]

It was in the pages of the *National Anti-Slavery Standard* that Child wrote
as a woman asserting her right freely to engage in public debate despite the
threat of enchainment.[9] Appointed editor of the *Standard* in 1841, she
became the first woman in America to edit a newspaper directed to an issue
of public policy. In her first editorial, Child responded sharply to the charge
that her sex would bias her work. She used the chaining imagery of the
antislavery emblems to deny that she was enslaved and to affirm her independence from the American Anti-Slavery Society—and everyone else.
Writing that she has refused "the shadow of a fetter on my free expression,"
Child does not present herself, as Grimké had, as a self-emancipated
Woman and Sister who has broken her own chains. Instead, she suggests
that she sees herself threatened (although by a metaphorical, not a literal
chain); and in choosing the verb *refuse*, asserts her power to reject even this
"shadow of a fetter." In and through this act of choice, Child wills herself
free. Where Angelina Grimké, in her writings and speeches, had come to
see herself as enchained and, recognizing her own power, had inscribed that
power to free herself, Child, in a voice at once free and threatened, asserts
her power to withstand her would-be enslavers.[10]

Child exposed herself in print each week in the *Standard*, signing her editorials and seemingly taking for granted (and seemingly assuming that her audience took for granted) her right to participate in public debate. Sounding the clear reasonable voice she had used in *An Appeal*, Child addressed the most controversial issues of the day, urging her readers, both male and female, to act in the public sphere. Yet at the same time she expressed her awareness of the patriarchal restrictions on women's public debate, as she implicitly had in the frontispiece, title page, and preface of *An Appeal*. Child's complex manipulation of the language of womanhood and sisterhood in the pages of the *Standard* may be in part an effort to reach a broad "family" audience. Whatever the motive, her multileveled use of antislavery feminist discourse in the *Standard* is as inventive and as impressive as that heard in Angelina Grimké's speeches.

Child was determined to edit the paper according to the dictates of her own conscience. "While I have the entire responsibility for the paper," she privately wrote, "I must have the entire control."[11] But Child found herself pressured to open the pages of the *Standard* to factionalists among the abolitionists who were eager to air their disputes. During this period, when she writes that she is struggling to resist chains, she identifies one threatening tyrant not as the slavocracy or the patriarchy, but as an abolitionist who is "fettered in sectarian bigotry."[12] Because she feared driving away the common reader, Child systematically excluded material she thought factional—and thereby offended antislavery activists who were committed to reforms like nonresistance and women's rights.

Addressing "the woman question" in 1841, she wrote that she found this "vexed" issue "distasteful." Child explains that she chooses to fight for "the rights of others, rather than my own." "I prefer as quietly and noiselessly as possible, to *take* my freedom without disputing my claim to it." Duties and rights, she continues, appear "as reverse sides of the same thing; and to me, duty presents the lovelier aspect."[13] Here, again, her language is illuminating. As earlier she had written of refusing chains, now she writes of her preferences. Both formulations imply the power of choice; in both, Child presents herself as a free woman, however threatened.

The next year, in a piece called "Coincidence," Child considered "the general points of resemblance between the character and condition of women, and that of colored people." Asserting that "both with regard to women and slaves, men take away *rights*, and then make a great merit of granting *privileges*," she concluded that "physical force brought both of these classes into subjection; and moral power is bringing them both out of their false position."[14] Later, again considering race and gender, Child writes,

> In comparison with the Caucasian race, I have often said that they are what woman is in comparison with man. The comparison between women and the colored race *as classes* is striking. Both are exceedingly adhesive in their attachments; both, comparatively speaking, have a tendency to submission, and hence, both have been kept in subjection by physical force, and considered rather in the light of property, than as individuals. As the *intellectual* age passes toward the *moral* age, women and the colored race are both rising out of their long degradation.[15]

As Child was inscribing her own freedom of choice and tentatively exploring the complex issues that the abolitionist emblem encapsulated, free black antislavery feminists were similarly engaged. Maria W. Stewart's adaptation of its motto into the challenge, "What if I am a woman!" represents one instance. Another is Sarah Forten's brief poem:

> We are thy sisters; God has truly said,
> That of one blood the nations He has made.
> Oh! Christian woman in a Christian land,
> Canst thou unblushing read this great command?
> Suffer the wrongs which wring our inmost heart,
> To draw one throb of pity on thy part!
> Our skins may differ, but from thee we claim,
> A sister's privilege, and a sister's name.[16]

Published by the first Convention of American Women Against Slavery as an epigraph to Angelina Grimké's *Appeal to the Women of the Nominally Free States* in 1837, Forten's poem challenged the racism of northern white women. It presents a black Christian woman speaking in the name of all black women to an audience of white Christian American women. Forten's speaker sounds a positive response to the double inquiries of the antislavery emblem, but neither slavery nor patriarchal power is at issue. Instead, the speaker addresses the problem of white racism, the failure of her white female audience to acknowledge the primacy of gender over race.

But Forten also presents a solution in a witty play on connections between the pigmentation of the skin and the circulation of the blood. She writes that if the white reader, recognizing racism as a sin, becomes embarrassed and pities black women who suffer from discrimination, she will blush, her face will darken, and as she sympathizes her heart will throb and she will more closely resemble her dark-skinned, heart-wrung sister. Forten's final couplet makes a double demand: that her reader treat black women like sisters and that she acknowledge their kinship. Then, like her darker sisters, the white reader will be obeying God.

Forten was using the discourse of antislavery feminism to address the issue of racism. White antislavery feminists, however, chose to focus on patriarchy. Some of their writings can be found in *The Liberty Bell*, the annual giftbook that Maria Weston Chapman edited for the Boston Female Anti-Slavery Society. As early as 1839, Chapman had commented on the disputes within antislavery ranks caused by the Grimkés's lecturing. In light verse, she ridiculed their opponents, humorously pleading that a traditional patriarchal abolitionist brother learn to be more tolerant of "Grimké, Kelley, Weld" and their nontraditional antipatriarchal sisters:

> Oh would eternal Providence
> Enlarge his soul — increase his sense,
> To see that on this mole-hill earth,
> A congress and a sewing meeting,
> May each to like events give birth. . . .
>
> That FREEDOM is our only goal: —
> That every true and faithful soul
> Must choose its own means to effect it;
> And, be it ballot, be it fair,
> Or free produce, or monthly prayer,
> Bell, book, or candle, or what e'er,
> Grant others freedom to reject it.[17]

Three years later, *The Liberty Bell* published "Woman and Her Pastor," a poetic dialogue in which a woman's commitment to antislavery leads her to reject her minister's attempts to restrict her to the domestic sphere. The pastor counsels her not to express her deep distress at the evils of slavery in public:

> "Thy voice is too soft to be raised on high;
> And thy form too fair for the public eye."[18]

Instead, he cautions, she should pray in secret. When the woman explains that prayer only strengthens her "pure resolve" and nerves her "for each holy deed," he says that his advice is "for thy honor, thy fame." Nonetheless, the woman asserts her spiritual autonomy. She denounces him as "presumptuous" and, rehearsing the plight of the female slave, rejects the gender restrictions he is attempting to impose:

"Oh! tell me not of a woman's sphere,
When from day to day, and from year to year,
I see her forced o'er the blood-stain'd soil,
To the utmost stretch of her strength to toil."

At the end of the poem, the woman announces her determination to agitate in public against slavery:

"I will raise my voice, I will stretch my hand,
I will plead her cause with a guilty land."

In "Women's Work," an essay published in the same issue, Child's friend Eliza Lee Follen reviews "the whole catechism" questioning women's involvement in the slavery debate "and the whole list of stereotyped answers, which the sticklers for the prerogative of men are ready to give."[19] Follen argues that women are actually more able than men to address the slavery question, not because of any innate female qualities, but because, unlike men, they have not been corrupted by their social roles. She ends by stating: "The abolition of slavery is indeed woman's work. . . . Let neither fathers, nor brothers, nor husbands, nor false or weak friends keep us back from it."

Early in 1843, under pressure from abolitionist-feminists like Maria Weston Chapman and Abby Kelley Foster to "come out concerning the Rights of Women" as "a legitimate branch of the anti-slavery enterprise," Child finally focused directly on the relationship between feminism and abolitionism in the pages of the *Standard*. In "Women's Rights," she applies the discourse of the antislavery emblems to the condition of woman. Child likens the gallantry that profligates exhibit toward women to the indulgences slaveholders grant their slaves and deplores the practice of teaching woman, as slaves are taught, that her duty is "to man rather than to God . . . , the creature, rather than the Creator." She does not, however, endorse the Grimkés's assertion that woman's oppression is primary or their notion of a special relationship between women and slaves. Instead, Child argues that every kind of oppression expresses the conflict between moral and physical force. "I do not perceive . . . that the doctrine of Women's Rights, as it is called, has a more immediate connection with anti-slavery, than several other subjects."[20]

In the next two years, *The Liberty Bell* published letters and essays in which Lucretia Mott and Abby Kelley Foster outlined their views on women's role in the antislavery struggle.[21] Although written by women and directed toward a female audience, these pieces do not even mention that a woman who engages in public action defies patriarchal limits on female behavior. By 1845, these antislavery feminists, having long since created their own version of the true woman as Woman and Sister, were no longer debating their own legitimacy.

Child quit the *Standard* in 1843 in the face of insufficient financial support from the American Anti-Slavery Society and incessant criticism by individual abolitionists. In her farewell editorial, she again writes of feeling embattled and again reaffirms her freedom of choice, voicing her determination to maintain intellectual and political independence in defiance of those who would restrict her: "The freedom of my own spirit makes it absolutely necessary for me to retire."[22]

It is a comment on the sectarianism among the abolitionists that in this final editorial, Child evidently felt the need to defend "Letters from New York," her weekly columns that Thomas Wentworth Higginson later praised as a major achievement of nineteenth-century journalism: "the precursors of that modern school of newspaper correspondence, in which women have so large a share, and which has something of the charm of women's private letters, — a style of writing where description preponderates over the argument, and statistics make way for fancy and enthusiasm."[23] Written as personal commentary, the "Letters" are at their sharpest in the *Standard*, before Child collected them into an anthology, dropping some and softening others in hopes of reaching a wide audience. Even in their newspaper versions, many of the "Letters" invite James Russell Lowell's description of Child as a dear foolish watery reformer.[24] But Child's reminiscence in "Letters from New York: Number 33" about her experiences with antiabolitionist mobs is different. Here she presents a woman's first-person public narrative of an intense experience that was both personal and political.

In "Letter 33," as in the preface to *An Appeal*, Child uses the conventions restricting women's discourse to move beyond them.[25] She begins with a description of the sound of katydids, commenting that "a single note in the great hymn of Nature sometimes recalls the memories of years." This stylized opening, which appears utterly to conform to the conventions of "women's writing," introduces an utterly unconventional subject: her experiences running from antiabolitionist mobs in Boston and hiding from them in New York.

Child presents her reminiscence in tight prose. She recalls that in 1835 she and her husband had undertaken to provide safe passage for a prominent antislavery lecturer. They fled from Boston, which was torn by antiabolitionist riots, to New York, where riots were also threatened, finally finding refuge in Brooklyn. It was here that Child first heard the sound of katydids; she confused them with the shouts of a distant mob. Because their host's home was threatened with attack as an abolitionist safehouse, Child left. She knew no one in New York. In an atmosphere charged with violence, she rented a hotel room and hid. Recalling her distress, Child writes: "Never, before or since, have I experienced such utter desolation, as I did the few days I remained there. It seemed to me as if anti-slavery had cut me off from all the sympathies of my kind." By the end of this "Letter," Child has transformed her initial genteel reference to the katydids into a strong political and personal statement. In the clear voice of a woman embattled —not because of her private attachment to home and family, but because of her public commitment to a political cause—she writes, "To my mind the katy-dids will forever speak of mobs."

After the danger was over, Child expressed her fears of violence in a letter to a friend. The atmosphere in New York, she explained, had been whipped up by "a virulent little paper . . . buzzing about here, called The Anti-Abolitionist. Over it is a large wood cut, representing men and women, black and white, hugging and kissing each other; and on the table are decanters marked A.T.B.—which signifies Arthur Tappan's Burgandy." Her comment is intriguing because, while the masthead of the *Castigator and New York Anti-Abolitionist* pictures black and white men and women within a domestic setting, they are not "hugging and kissing each other" (fig. 12).[26] The cartoon certainly illustrates the notion that white women who defy gender restrictions and enter the public sphere to work against slavery also defy racial and sexual taboos in the private sphere. But why should Child, who had met innumerable times in domestic settings with black and white men and women, so describe it? Was the atmosphere in New York so charged that she could not see the woodcut accurately? Or was she merely reporting someone else's description of the masthead? One thing is clear: the picture was designed to stir up mobs against antislavery women like Child, and it did just that.

Seen from one angle of vision, the *Correspondence Between Lydia Maria Child and Governor Wise and Mrs. Mason, of Virginia* is Child's major contribution to the ongoing debate over definitions of true womanhood.[27] At issue is the question of a woman's responsibility in a public crisis; in this instance, the crisis precipitated by John Brown's attack on the United States arsenal at Harper's Ferry in 1859.

The events surrounding the *Correspondence* were extraordinary. Brown's

Fig. 12. Masthead of *Castigator and New York Anti-Abolitionist* (August 1835).

raid revitalized Child. She had withdrawn from political activity after her experiences on the *Standard*, but she quickly responded to the news from Harper's Ferry by writing to the wounded Brown, who was imprisoned awaiting trial. She enclosed her letter in a covering note to Governor Wise of Virginia; when after three days Wise responded, Brown's trial was almost over.[28] The governor apparently released this exchange of letters to the press. Brown himself answered her six days later, after he had been sentenced to death. Margaretta Mason (wife of the senator who had framed the 1850 Fugitive Slave Bill) evidently wrote to Child in response to the publication of Child's correspondence with Wise; Child wrote back to her after Brown had been executed and buried. Then, learning that the Virginia newspapers had printed Mason's letter, Child sent the entire correspondence to Horace Greeley, antislavery editor of the New York *Tribune*. The American Anti-Slavery Society published all eight letters as the *Correspondence*, and it became an abolitionist best-seller.

Child uses a broad range of discourse in her exchanges with her proslavery patriarchal opponent Governor Wise, writing as a powerless female supplicant, as a conventional true woman who sympathizes with the wounded prisoner, and as an assertive abolitionist leader addressing an opponent. In her exchanges with Brown, she writes as a sympathizing friend. When he asks that, instead of privately traveling south to nurse him, as she had proposed, she initiate a collective public fund-raising campaign to aid his destitute family, Child immediately complies by having his request published.[29]

The issue of female sympathy is touched on in Child's correspondence with Wise, and the question of public roles for women is implicit in her correspondence with Brown. But in Child's exchanges with Margaretta Mason, the debate over true womanhood becomes central. Mason makes this her subject, and she damns Child as a hypocrite, a female devil who mocks the Christian sympathy of true women by "attempting to soothe with sisterly and motherly care the hoary-headed murderer of Harper's Ferry." Mason echoes Wise's refusal to sympathize with Child's "sentiments of sympathy for Brown" and reiterates his accusation that Child's perverse sympathy, and that of other antislavery women like her, has caused Brown's actions. Mason denies that Child and other northern antislavery females are true women and reserves that identity for southern slave-holding females like herself. She contrasts the "ruthless ruin" that Child's perverted sympathy for terrorists inspires with the true sympathy she and the other southern women of her color and class show toward their "servants." Asking whether Child and the other antislavery females would sympathize with dying blacks, black women in childbirth, and destitute black children, "as we do," she proposes that Child learn true sympathy by ministering to her poor neighbors or by caring for the families of John Brown's victims.

A week after Brown's burial, three days after Mrs. Mason's husband was appointed head of the congressional committee investigating Brown's raid, Child responded. Calm, cheerful, and self-confident, she uses Margaretta Mason's angry letter as an opportunity to address southern women, as Angelina Grimké had done a generation earlier.[30] Child writes that she will not discuss Brown, but "the principle for which John Brown died." Quoting the Old and New Testaments, citing southern laws and newspapers, and referring to the testimony of fugitive slaves and former slaveholders —including the Grimkés—her letter sounds a mix of eighteenth-century puritanism and nineteenth-century progress.

Writing "in the name of all the women of New England," Child responds to Mason's taunts about her womanhood. She states that free northern women care for the sick and sew for the poor. Then—sharply rebutting her southern correspondent—Child suggests that the claim that slaveholding women sympathize with their slaves is hypocritical. She charges that if sympathy and benevolence constitute true womanhood, as Mason asserts, southern women are not true women because as slaveholders they profit from the sexual exploitation of their female slaves. It is northern women like herself, Child writes, who act as true women by acknowledging that, regardless of condition and color, all women are sisters: "I have never known an instance where the 'pangs of maternity' did not meet with requisite assistance; and here at the North, after we have helped the mothers, *we do not sell the babies.*"[31]

The sisterhood of black and white women and the sexual abuse of slave

women are central to much of Child's fiction. Her stories complement her
journalism and her polemics, where she writes as a woman who willingly
chooses to defy threats and to enter the public sphere on behalf of her
enslaved brothers and sisters. In her short fiction, Child characteristically
runs further risks. Here she presents forbidden subjects. Dramatizing issues
of sex, race, and power, she writes about relationships between tyrants and
supplicants, whites and blacks, men and women, masters and slaves. Her
stories dramatize one version of the discourse of abolitionist feminism by
repeatedly focusing on a female supplicant, a pleading oppressed dark
woman vulnerable to white violation, sexual bondage, and incest. Although
they do not often center on the figure of an engaged embattled woman like
Child herself, they do at times present a Woman and Sister who has entered
the public political sphere.

The antislavery females had been made a literary subject as early as
1835, when Child herself included a reference to "female societies for
benevolent purposes" in her *Condition of Women* and added an illustration
showing a philanthropic Ladies' Sewing Circle (fig. 13). One critic ridiculed
this picture because, he said, it shows elaborately coiffured women with
smirks on their faces. It is, however, of real interest. Several women are
shown seated doing needlework—not to beautify their homes or their families, but, as Child's text explains (and as the pointing finger of the figure at
the left signals), to raise money for a public cause. In addition, the papers
on the table (possibly minutes or petitions) suggest that the women are
literate and formally organized; the book held by the standing figure implies
that the goals of this female organization include self-development and
women's education, as well as philanthropy. The uncaged bird perched on
the hands of the woman on the right signals that these women are free.[32]

But such sympathetic portrayals of female activism were more than offset
by hostile views. As the attack on Pennsylvania Hall demonstrated, women
who entered the public sphere were routinely condemned as sexual nonconformists. Fanny Wright, for example, was graphically pictured as lewd
on a political broadside that was published after the mobbing of her lectures
at New York's Masonic Hall in 1838. In an attempt to discredit the Whigs by
associating them with Wright, blacks, and abolitionists, this broadside
pictures a black preacher exhorting from his pulpit. Wright, wearing a
low-cut gown and seated at a writing desk with a pen stuck between
her teeth, points to her right leg, which she is exposing by pulling up her
skirt. The text of the broadside includes a mock sermon by the preacher
(fig. 14).[33]

Fig. 13. Illustration in Lydia Maria Child, *Brief History of the Condition of Women* (1845), vol. 2, p. 271.

Parodying critics of the women activists, Chapman wrote a witty poem in which "The Lords of Creation" express their horror at females who have "leaped from 'their spheres.'"

> They've taken a notion to speak for themselves,
> And are wielding the tongue and the pen;
> They've mounted the rostrum; the termagant elves,
> And—oh horrid!—are talking to men!

But from these early days, women who braved the public platform were also the subject of adulatory verse in reform newspapers, giftbooks, and albums. In 1836, using her pseudonym, "Ada," Sarah Forten wrote a poem in praise of women who acted against slavery by publishing and speaking:

> . . . long as mothers' hearts are breaking
> Beneath the hammer of the auctioneer,
> And ruthless Avarice tears asunder bonds,
> That the fiat of the Almighty joined,
> So long should woman's melting voice be heard,
> In intercession strong and deep, that this
> Accused thing, this Achan in our camp
> May be removed.[34]

# THE
# PLOT EXPOSED!

## Or, Abolitionism, Fanny Wright,
## and the Whig Party!

☞ THE following SERMON, delivered at the African church in Church street, by the Rev. MOSES PARKES, a colored preacher from Canterbury, Conn., drew from MISS DESDAMONT the LETTER, exposing the PLOT, which led to her attempted expulsion from MASONIC HALL, and the DISGRACEFUL RIOT which followed.

Ainít dísplaíed for wbít es
De greasy heads ímus be,
Yet 'sertín by ablaím
From gen'rus debbil' ?
And when de bald face cat bím up,
Bild Arbo as de doral atno !

"What went him out for to see ? A nigger grinding corn." *Matt. ix.* 15.

Blubbed brudren, I shall divide my 'scorse ob dis mornin' under five extinct heads, and shall imediately, widout no circumstance, proceed to sprain and 'spostulate ein. In de fuss place, the 'postle in de text just read to your compression, asks, What *for* went him out to see ? and den, blubbed bredéren, comes de answer, plain as nose on nigger's face, a NIGGER GRINDING CORN But what de debble he gríb' de corn for, perhaps some nigger, full of de gracious thirst ob biblical knowledge, may ask. I'll tell you, blubbed brudren, and here I want you to pay 'ticlar 'tention to the profundity of my speech, 'cause its the pith of de marrow—he grin' it for to make de meal, and de meal he make into johnny cakes, and dese he eat all up hesef, and giv de rest to de dam whites dat planted and hoed de 'corn. Ah, brudren, in dose bressed 'cripter days de niggers was gentlemen—what you grunin' at you dam brack nigger —in dose days niggers was de only genꞌmen besides hogs. Who dar deny it ? Who dar ?— Let me see de brack man dat *dar* disperse and exfluncifly de sacred character of his grorous posterors that lived like gen꞊men on de ribber Nile ! Show me his brack profile. Ah brudren, I see you star, and roll up de eye, and squirt de 'backer juice, but its God's truth. De WHITE MAN was de SLAVE den, he plant de corn, and de rice, and de sugar cane, and de cotton. I 'spose you tink no cotton den. How you know ? How you tink da make de mummies widout cotton ? How you tink de men and women da widout cotton for dar shirts ? But blubbed hearers, I must hasten to de end of dis 'scoorse. Dis is neder here nor dare. What tink you ? what do you tink, I say, of dis bubbub bout FANNY WRIGHT and de ABOLITIONISTS? Bress my soul, da say she's turned WHIG, and gone to Masonic Hall, and dat we brack Ablitionists must turn too. What tink of dat, eh ? what tink of dat, I say ? What your seven senses, sleepy niggers ? Wake up, and tell me how you like to be sold like Sud-

ern slaves or brack sheep by dis white Jezbeel dat de WHIGS have BOUGHT? Who guv her leave to sell niggers to de hoco pocos ? who DAR? Did your Uese Gumbo ? your Leut Samcry ? you Cato Johnsing ? you Peter Gusa ? Ah you all grabítate your heads and say NO! And I did'nt noder. Blubbed brudren, dare is worser tings goin on now-a-days dan de grindin' mention in de text. De 'pressions of de whites is ponderously grabitating on de head of de brack man. De fountains of de great deep is risin up, and scatterin desecration ober de froe nigger. Let us, as Gaffer says in de play of Wenus Deserved—let us UNCOVER dis 'fernal POT dat de whigs and FANNY GOOSEMONT have been bilin' our dinners in. I 'spose you tink its full ob 'roast beef, and plum pud'n, de nice goose, and de pork and cabbage—ah, niggers, I sees yer tick lips water and yer big eyes snap when you conceive de aptness of my 'lusions—but dares none of dese tings dare—nuffin but dem stinkin CAT's MEAT. Dats what de whigs and dare new 'ly been cooking for us niggers. I wonder they aint 'fraid de funders of gor-a-mity 'll rise in its awful preponderositty and strike 'em down, down, down to de bottom of de bottomless pit, what de smoke of dare groom 'll scent for eber and eber, and de debble wid his pitchfork 'll toss 'em about till he break ebery dam bone in dare body. Brudren, let us 'tick to OLE TAMMANY like a woodchuck to an apple tree. Fight for de good ole kase of democracy, for wherever we be, niggers is niggers still. Don 'I say in de face of dis sollum and bery 'tentive 'sembly. Amen.

### LET US BRAY !

De Cryer will now sing de Benediction Hymn.

Lor', carmïas us wïd dy lovening,
Fïll our mouds wïd 'socker juice,
Let us all our ends compression,
Squirt it on de whïte man's boots !
O refresh us
Wïd de luxky 'tocker juice !

Tœks we guv, and mystication,
For do prenur precivus tïme,
Wïmm de jest of abolitïon,
Tïck us deep in ebery crime,
Dat sïx when mem,
Gin us fïner de dreffel sïgn !

And now may de grease ob gor-a-mity be scatter ober ebory dam nigger present in dis 'sembly dis day. May it 'tick deep in yer bery wicked hearts, and be wid you fru de day and night, and cubber your head like de half when de grorious sunshine rise in de mornin. May it 'company yer to you birmous commoberal beds, so dat de prowlin white man cant creep in and sturb yer nooptal bliss wid his dam lingo, jus as de Debil did to mudder Eve in de gardum ob Eden. Amen.

A report of this discourse having reached the ear of Fanny Wright, that lady immediately wrote the following letter to Mr. Parkes :

Masonic Hall, Thursday, Oct. 11, 1838.

Rev. Sir—I have just been informed that in a sermon which you delivered last Sunday, you was pleased to make an allusion to me, in the course of some remarks on abolitionism, whigism, &c. I shall not stop at present to discourse on the propriety of mixing such subjects with the religious services of the Sabbath, or the indelicacy of dragging a lady's name into politics on any occasion—especially one who, like myself, seeks no notoriety ; but shall proceed at once to the charge which you have more than insinuated against me, namely, that I have SOLD MYSELF TO THE WHIGS, and am endeavoring to sell my friends the ABOLITIONISTS to the same party. I plead not guilty to this wholesale charge. It is true that I have gone over to the whigs, but I deny that I have been bought. No man or set of men can buy me or my principles. I trust I am above even the thought of the venal purchaser of other mens' consciences ; for it is my opinion that if one crime is more than another deserving of scorn it is that of a freeman selling his vote for a few pieces of dirty silver, be they ten or thirty. No sir, I left Tammany because she's a dirty bitch, and I did'nt want any thing more to do with her.

But, although I disclaim all participation in the affair, I must admit that there *is* a plot in existence the object of which is to transfer the abolitionists in a body to our party. A——— T——b, B——B. S———n, on the one part, and A——— C———k and G———n L—, on the other, are the commissioners who have been appointed to consummate the bargain and carry its provisions into effect. Of this plot I had no knowledge until applied to by M— C—k to assist the commissioners with my advice and influence. This request was accompanied by many expressions flattering to myself personally, and to the cause in which I have been so long and so arduously engaged. But I indignantly spurned the offer, and told him that, although I was heart and soul with the whigs, and willing to do all I could individually and above-board to advance their cause, yet I would never dirty my hands with any affair which had bargain and corruption for its basis. He left me in a rage, and I heard nothing more of the plot until you saw fit to allude to it ; nor do I care whether it succeeds or not. I have affairs enough to attend to, without meddling with matters which more properly belong to the sterner sex, as they are called.

With sentiments of respect,
FANNY WIGHT DESDAMONT.

Fig. 14. *The Plot Exposed* [1838].

Another anonymous poet lauded Chandler, Lydia Sigourney, the Grimkés, Child, and Mary Parker as she celebrated the English abolitionist Elizabeth Heyrick for ending British slavery:

> She spoke, the galling fetter falls:
> Kindled the beacon liberty!
> And sorrowing thousands disenthrals!"[35]

Still others urged more women to mount the platform:

> Speak! for the wronged and trampled slave,
> Until the tyrant's heart shall feel—
> Speak! till the strong are roused to save,
> And startled Freedom bursts her grave.
>
> . . . . . . . . . . . . . . . . . . . . . .
>
> Lift up thy woman voice, and pour
> Thy stern rebuke from shore to shore—[36]

They praised Lucretia Mott's lectures:

> Thy human heart still uttereth back its voice
> To all the sore oppressed in utter need.
> And God's down-trodden poor do still rejoice
> In thy deep, choring tone and kindly deed.[37]

They celebrated Maria Weston Chapman's bravery confronting the mob:

> So send thy voice of pleading forth—
> Oh, woman! Till its thunder
> Shall strike the trembling mount of sin
> And rend its top asunder.[38]

And an Ohio housewife likened Abby Kelley Foster not to an Angel in the House, but an Angel in the Hall:

> Forth from the ark of happiness and love,
> Stifling the feelings of a wife and mother,
> Thou journeyest like the Patriarch's faithful dove,
> In pity for the sorrow of another.
>
> Pleading for her condemned in chains to mourn,
> Driven to her unpaid labors, scourged and gory,
> Whose helpless babes are from her bosom torn,
> Beneath our country's stars and stripes of glory!

> Thou askest no reward, but it will come!
> The wreath of amaranth shall yet be given
> When thou at last shalt reach a peaceful home,
> Upon the right and stormless shore of heaven.[39]

The abolitionist poet John Greenleaf Whittier repeatedly paid tribute to women who braved the platform. He commemorated their courage in the face of the 1835 mob:

> Unshrinking from the storm,
> Well have you borne your part,
> With WOMAN'S fragile form
> But more than manhood's heart![40]

And he attacked the framers of the Pastoral Letter of 1837 for attempting to suppress the Grimké sisters' speeches. Calling them men "who scorn the thrilling tale / Of Carolina's high-souled daughters," Whittier pronounced his hope that the women be strengthened

> With Miriam's voice, and Judith's hand,
> And Deborah's song, for triumph given![41]

By the 1850s antislavery feminists and their supporters were presenting women like themselves in fiction. In *Clotel* (1853), black activist William Wells Brown sketched a young southern woman, Miss Georgiana Peck, who had been influenced by abolitionists and feminists while being educated in the North. Upon returning south, Georgiana converts her suitor to abolitionism, emancipates her slaves, and moves them north. (Although Georgiana successfully acts out Grimké's advice to southern women, she never moves beyond the domestic sphere, as the Grimkés had done.)[42]

In 1856, Lydia Maria Child serialized a novel about bloody Kansas. Among her characters is Kate, a Massachusetts-born antislavery woman who has emigrated to Lawrence, where proslavery and antislavery forces confront each other over gun barrels. Kate provides her family not only with emotional strength to sustain their struggle against proslavery forces, but also with physical protection. By smuggling gunpowder under her full skirts, Kate helps supply the antislavery settlement with ammunition needed for their defense. When proslavery marauders rape a Lawrence woman, Kate gets a gun and organizes her women friends into a shooting club. At the story's climax, proslavery men burn freesoil Lawrence, and Kate arms herself and returns to save what she can. Perhaps in deference to Child's

Garrisonian pacifism, she does not shoot. But she verbally defies the drunken male ruffians, boldly announcing that although they have burned the newspaper, they have not destroyed antislavery in Lawrence. When she predicts that the abolitionist *Herald* "will sound across the prairies yet," they respond admiringly, "What a hell of a woman!"[43]

Three years later, the free black antislavery feminist Frances Ellen Watkins Harper published her short fiction "The Two Offers" in the New York *Anglo-African Magazine*. Harper's character, Jeanette, dramatizes the possibility of a viable alternative to marriage. Jeanette's cousin vascillates between two suitors, chooses one, is victimized by him, and dies, but Jeanette does not marry. She becomes a writer. Spurred by her cousin's pathetic death, Jeanette attempts to fulfill what she conceives as her "high and holy mission": working to end slavery. Harper writes that although Jeanette "was an old maid," her life demonstrates that happiness consists in "the full development and right culture of our whole natures." Challenging the patriarchal notion that a woman can be fulfilled only in marriage, "The Two Offers" judges the life of an "old maid" writer and reformer more satisfactory than that of a victimized wife.[44]

In 1869, the abolitionist-feminist lecturer Anna Dickinson published *What Answer?*, a novel addressing the issue of white racism and miscegenation. The book presents a young woman who denounces slavery from the public platform. Instead of appearing unsexed or oversexed, as in hostile characterizations, Dickinson's female orator is beautiful and desirable. The hero is smitten when he hears her deliver the commencement speech at her school. She has chosen slavery as her subject, and he had anticipated listening to "a pretty lady-like essay." Instead, he sat

> astounded at what he saw and heard. Her face—this schoolgirl's face—grew pallid, her eyes mournful, her voice and manner sublime, as she summoned this monster to the bar of God's justice and the humanity of the world; as she arraigned it; as she brought witness after witness to testify against it; as she proved its horrible atrocities and monstrous barbaries; as she went on to the close, and, lifting hand and face and voice together, thrilled out, "I look backward into the dim, distant past, but it is one night of oppression and despair; I turn to the present, but I hear naught save the mother's broken-hearted shriek, the infant's wail, the groan wrung from the strong man in agony; and I look forward into the future, but the night grows darker, the shadows deeper and longer, the tempest wilder, and involuntarily I cry out, 'How long, O God, how long?'"[45]

According to the critic Leslie Fielder, Child was the first American writer to fictionalize miscegenation. Her most important explorations of this potent American theme are not, however, in her earliest novel *Hobomok* (1824), where she showed a befuddled white woman briefly choosing a Native American husband, but in her later stories of sexual relationships between Anglo-Americans and African-Americans.[46] In these stories, Child portrays American slavery, a labor system in a capitalist economy, using the familial discourse that proponents of the "patriarchal institution" had adopted. Her antislavery stories resemble antebellum plantation fiction in privatizing public economic and political issues, reducing them to a domestic scale. But Child's stories resemble the narratives of fugitive slaves in interpreting as political these private dramas of relationships involving parents, children, and siblings and in viewing them as instances of institutionalized tyranny and the struggle against it.

In this antislavery fiction, Child conflates race and sex, emphasizing the similarities between women and blacks that she had earlier explored in the *Standard*. Focusing on the enchained powerless female victim of the antislavery emblems, she dramatizes a racist society in which the quintessential slave is a victimized woman. Child defines the victimization as sexual and refines the racial specificity of this figure as mulatto.[47]

The strategy of giving her female victim a mixed racial heritage enables Child to dramatize the historic sexual abuse of black women: it took two generations of interracial sex to produce a "quadroon," three for an "octoroon." But as critics have pointed out, this strategy also feeds the white racism of those in Child's audience incapable of identifying with a black woman.

The implications of Child's characterization are complex. Nina Baym has defined "woman's fiction" in antebellum America as a literature written by females for a female audience, that chronicled "'the trials and triumphs' . . . of a heroine who, beset with hardships, finds within herself the qualities of intelligence, will, resourcefulness, and courage sufficient to overcome them." Instead of following this pattern, Child's antislavery stories repeat the earlier conventions of the literature of seduction, which presented woman as sexual prey. As Baym points out, from the perspective of that prey, that is, "from a woman's point of view, this is a demoralized literature."[48] What are the consequences of Child's choice of seduction literature as a model for her tales of nonwhite women? One answer is that it permitted her white female readers to identify with the victim by gender while distancing themselves by race and thus to avoid confronting a racial ideology that denies the full humanity of nonwhite women.

Child invented a series of plots involving the Tragic Mulatto, a figure she first presented as Rosalie in "The Quadroons."[49] Rosalie is pious, obedient, and domestic, hopelessly struggling to be pure, and notable for her beauty, sensitivity, and moral excellence. Like the patriarchal model of the true woman, she feels that her identity exists only in and through her relationship with the man she loves. But Rosalie's sense of selfhood is grounded not in the love of just any man; it is grounded in the love of a white man. Her manners, aristocratic sensibilities, and polished language identify her as a model of patriarchal true womanhood; but her mixed racial heritage prevents her from achieving marriage, the traditional true woman's only goal. Rosalie persists in her piety and in her devotion to the white man with whom she is sexually involved, although her love, because unsanctioned, is impure. Obedient, yet denied the joys of true domesticity, Rosalie is doomed never to be a wife; her life is blighted, and she dies.[50]

A model of patriarchy's true womanhood—except for the crucial fact that her sexual relationship is not sanctioned by marriage—the Tragic Mulatto appears at first glance a nonwhite variant of Child's other female victims of love. In "Elizabeth Wilson," "Hilda Silvering," and "Rosenglory," which were anthologized along with "The Quadroons" in *Fact and Fiction* (1847), Child presented sympathetic stories of white sexual victims of male perfidy.[51] But unlike the free white characters, the Tragic Mulatto is forbidden by law from conforming to the sexual patterns mandated by the patriarchy for true womanhood. The pathos of the Tragic Mulatto rests in the contradiction between her sincere efforts to adhere to the patriarchal definition of true womanhood and the patriarchy's insistence that she violate this norm. Sometimes, ignorant of her condition and abandoned by her white lover, the Tragic Mulatto discovers she is a slave—and dies. Sometimes, ignorant of her race, thinking herself foreign (often French), and abandoned by her white lover, she discovers that she is black—and dies. Occasionally, however, her white lover overcomes the barriers of slavery and racism and flees with her (usually to France).[52]

In 1826, responding to the complex sexual and racial tensions peculiar to the United States in the early nineteenth century, James Fenimore Cooper had introduced an interracial pair of sisters into American fiction in *The Last of the Mohicans*. Cooper located the sisters, Cora and Alice, within the context of American racism, but not within the context of American slavery. Despite her mixed heritage, Cora is a free woman protected by a powerful white father; she is no man's legal prey. Cora competes with her white sister, Alice, for the affection of a white man, but he is not a slaveholding southern libertine who keeps one sister in sexual bondage and marries the other. In the 1840s, however, alongside essays in which the antislavery women attempted to redefine true womanhood, antislavery giftbooks like *The Liberty Bell* published tales ringing variations on the pathetic life of the Tragic Mulatto. Child's "Slavery's Pleasant Homes," not *The Last of the Mohicans*, spoke to the concerns of the free women readers of the *Liberty Bell* who were wrestling with their duty to female slaves.[53]

"Slavery's Pleasant Homes" addresses the issues signified by the antislavery emblems that structured the discourse of the abolitionist feminists, dramatizing their contention that no women are free in a slave society. In this story, an illegitimate slave and her white mistress are half sisters. Despite these differences of race and condition, they love each other. Although not rivals for the master's attention, both are his sexual objects and ultimately his victims. The enslaved mulatto sister is powerless to deny him her body; the white sister, although his wife, is powerless to command his exclusive sexual attention or to prevent him from molesting the Tragic Mulatto.

Writers following Child adopted her Tragic Mulatto character, and some added the second, chain-breaking female of the double emblem. Characteristically, when these writers include a female liberator, her efforts end in failure. As a woman, she must depend on a man to enforce her will in the courts, and he betrays her. The protagonist of Mattie Griffith's *Madge Vertner* (1859), for example, dies believing in the men to whom she has entrusted the emancipation of her slaves. But she is deceived. Legally powerless in a patriarchal society, the failed female liberator can break neither her black sister's chains nor her own.[54]

The repeated appearance of a cast of female characters (sometimes literally sisters) including a free platform speaker, a victimized Tragic Mulatto, and a female liberator (successful or failed) attests to the vitality of antislavery feminist iconography. In stories structured by the abolitionist emblems, Child and other free antislavery women encoded their ongoing imaginative efforts to affirm their identities as Women and Sisters: as God's moral female creatures and as sisters to enslaved blacks.

Their fiction featuring the Tragic Mulatto dramatizes a complex series of variations on the emblemized figure. Its focus on a victimized female slave obviously embodies a critique of slavery, but because of the Tragic Mulatto's mixed racial heritage this can be interpreted either as a critique or as an endorsement of white racism. Certainly, it appears to endorse the patriarchal ideology of true womanhood in relation to women of color. But because

the Tragic Mulatto is a victim of male sexual violence, she also dramatizes
the Grimkés' contention that the oppression of slavery is modeled on the
oppression of woman. Her predicament—as patriarchy's true woman who is
forbidden to achieve the only goal patriarchy permits her—can be read as a
comment on the lack of opportunities for all women.

When these stories include a white female who vies with the Tragic
Mulatto for the attention of a white male, or when they include a failed
female liberator, they dramatize the notion that a society that enslaves any
women also inevitably oppresses those women it calls free. With this reading, fictional relationships between a Tragic Mulatto and her white sister
signify the idea that, under slavery, the nominally free status of the pampered white mistress is inexorably connected to the naked oppression of her
black female slave. The fiction of the Tragic Mulatto is a construct that is at
once a criticism of, and a contribution to, contemporary racist and sexist
ideologies. Historically, it has been instrumental in feeding our national
obsession with interracial sex—which, as W. E. B. Du Bois noted, is what
white Americans mean by "the race problem."[55]

Child included the staples of the miscegenation-slavery theme in her
last novel, written after Emancipation. *A Romance of the Republic* includes
not one but two Tragic Mulattoes, sisters who believe themselves French and
free but discover that they are blacks and slaves.[56] The older sister, duped
into a false marriage with a master-lover whom she adores and whose son
she bears, competes with his white bride for his attention. The female
liberator is a middle-aged white Boston Brahmin who helps the younger
sister escape, adopts her, and aids in the rescue of a black mother and
children. To these now-standard story lines involving women, Child adds a
baby-switch involving a pair of half brothers who are master and slave.[57]

Substantiating Child's claim that she was becoming more radical as she
grew older, the *Romance* presents miscegenation as a solution to the American racial dilemma. For decades, abolitionists accused by white racist
opponents of promoting "amalgamation" (interracial sex) had denied that
they advocated intermarriage as a policy. Countering, antislavery women
had charged that white males exploited black women sexually. They circulated petitions against antimiscegenation laws that refused the protection of
marriage to black women who were sexually involved with white men and
denied legitimacy to their children.[58]

Written during Reconstruction, Child's *Romance* has as its subject the

creation of a free multiracial American population by miscegenation on a
large scale. The numerous interracial pairings—involving brothers and
sisters, tyrants and victims, rescuers and rescued, haters and lovers—are
designed to dramatize the collective national experience. Child's account of
power struggles, over three generations, among men and women, southern-
ers and northerners, whites and blacks, and masters and slaves, culminates
in the vision of a happy interracial American family. Signifying this, Child
updates the double antislavery emblem as she describes a tableau presented
by members of the third generation after the Civil War:

> Under festoons of the American flag, surmounted by the eagle, stood Eulilia
> [blue-eyed white-skinned granddaughter of a slave] in ribbons of red, white,
> and blue, with a circle of stars above her head. One hand upheld the shield of
> the Union, and in the other the scales of Justice were evenly poised. By her
> side stood Rosen Blumen [her cousin, daughter of a German immigrant]
> holding in one hand a gilded pole surmounted by a liberty cap, while her other
> hand rested protectingly on the head of Tulee's Benny [a black child] who was
> kneeling and looking up in Thanksgiving.[59]

As in pre-Emancipation versions of the double emblem, this assignment
of the role of liberator to the light-skinned girl and the role of grateful,
kneeling ex-slave to the dark child suggests an endorsement of white superiority that contradicts egalitarian claims. Although the good white characters
in Child's *Romance* are differentiated from the bad by their attitude toward
slavery, among nonwhite characters the crucial distinctions are racial. Mulattoes, quadroons, and octoroons are attractive and intelligent. When enslaved,
they act to become free; when free, they work hard and are upwardly
mobile. In contrast, the blacks want freedom, but they lack the initiative to
struggle for it. The device of switching black and white babies seems
designed to dramatize the arbitrariness of racial categories in America. But
while Child exposes the conventional character of distinctions between
whites and blacks with light skins, she makes little of the differences
between the situation of the white master who discovers himself black and
that of the black slave who learns he is white. The cultural and psychological complexities of American racism that Mark Twain would explore in
*Pudd'nhead Wilson* are completely ignored. Although proposing miscegenation as the solution to the American race problem, *A Romance of the
Republic* colors the multiracial American family not from white to black, but
only from white to beige.

In her polemics and journalism, for decades Child inscribed herself a free woman in a land of chains. Yet in 1870, in a private letter, she wrote that all her adult life she had felt that she, too, was enslaved:

> For forty years, I have keenly felt the cramping effects of my limitations as a woman, and I have submitted to them under a perpetual and indignant protest. . . . I have walked in fetters thus far, and my pilgrimage is drawing to a close.[60]

The tension between the voices that Child manipulated in her nonfiction prose—between the tones of the female supplicant and the tones of the woman who wills herself free—suggests the difficulties she herself faced writing as a woman claiming space in the public arena.

Child was a complicated woman negotiating complicated times; her public and private writings merit a full-scale study, particularly in relation to her complex and shifting responses to issues of race, slavery, and gender. Child did not center her fiction on a woman like herself, a woman who chooses to exercise her freedom to defend the rights of others and, in consequence, feels herself threatened, but who for years denies that this threat signifies that she is not free. Nor did she center it on a woman like Grimké, who announced herself a slave and argued that women are slaves who must break their own chains. Instead, Child used the structures of antislavery feminist discourse to create fictions suggesting that female slaves are patriarchal true women, and she popularized the Tragic Mulatto, a light-skinned version of the black female supplicant who is prevented by slavery from complying with patriarchal definitions of true womanhood. By focusing on the sexual victimization of this figure, Child presented the spectacle of the white patriarchy forbidding a nonwhite slave woman from conforming to the norms that it mandated for free white women. Yet these writings, in which she dramatized the sexual oppression of a light-skinned slave, implicitly endorsed for the Tragic Mulatto the restrictive patriarchal ideology of true womanhood—an ideology that Child rejected for herself. With the invention of the Tragic Mulatto, one branch of antislavery feminist discourse became race specific.

CHAPTER FOUR
# Sojourner Truth and Harriet Jacobs

*I had a woman's pride, and a mother's love for my children. . . . My master had power on his side; I had a determined will. There is might in each.*

          *—Harriet Jacobs[1]*

*I am a self-made woman.*

          *—Sojourner Truth[2]*

Enslaved women were the cause. Their presence had jolted free women, forcing them to examine the condition of slaves in relation to their own situation, to take seriously the double inquiry, Am I Not a Woman and a Sister? As free black and white antislavery feminists used the discourse deriving from antislavery emblems to explore issues of race and gender as well as of condition, they recreated themselves as liberated Women and Sisters. Concurrently, black ex-slaves were also using these emblems as they created their own structures of true womanhood and inscribed themselves the subjects of their own discourse.

Not surprisingly, determining the authenticity of the speeches and writings of ex-slaves presents problems. Because Sojourner Truth was illiterate, her words have come down to us—if at all—as transcribed by others. The varied ways that her language has been rendered suggest the enormous influence of her transcribers in shaping the texts we have today.[3] Harriet Jacobs's sensational slave narrative, *Incidents in the Life of a Slave Girl: Written by Herself*, which was accepted in her day as her own work, became

77

in our century a questionable text assigned to L. Maria Child, who was named on the title page as editor. Only now that Jacobs has been established as the author of *Incidents* can it be examined seriously as the narrative of a black woman who had been held in slavery.[4] Sojourner Truth's speeches—however mutilated in transcription—and Harriet Jacobs's book —however shaped to appeal to her target audience of free white women —bring us as close as we can come to the words of African-American women held in slavery.[5]

Angelina Grimké's central insight was that the antislavery emblem figured the condition of free women. She believed that in a patriarchal America where slavery was institutionalized, all women were in a sense slaves. Grimké had focused on her own shock of recognition, on her sense that she was figuratively an enslaved and enchained victim. L. Maria Child had written fiction identifying a powerless female victim as representative of all slaves. But the enchained oppressed women who inhabit the sentences of Sojourner Truth and Harriet Jacobs were seen differently.

Sojourner Truth and Harriet Jacobs understood the difference between being legally chattel and legally free. Excluded from the patriarchal definition of true womanhood because of their race and their condition, they approached this definition not as a category of nature, but as a cultural construct that functioned to justify their oppression. Their life experience in a system that denied their very humanity enabled them to penetrate the myths obscuring the political implications of the patriarchal ideology of true womanhood. They developed a definitive critique of that ideology that constituted a unique challenge to it.

The life experience of Jacobs and Truth also enabled them to unmask the racial implications of alternative models of the true woman as Woman and Sister. Free antislavery feminists found it liberating to relate the antislavery emblem to their own condition. Angelina Grimké, applying the terms of this emblem to her own life, had been able to recognize and acknowledge her oppression and to begin her struggle for self-emancipation. The abolitionist discourse encoded in the antislavery emblems structured the free antislavery feminists' discourse and dramatized their oppression as women in a patriarchal society.

But by conflating the oppression of women who were enslaved and the oppression of women who were free, by collapsing the literal enslavement of (conventionally) black women into the figurative enslavement that they felt they suffered, white free antislavery feminists obscured the crucial differences between the experience of women who were held as chattel and their own experience. Confusion resulted. On one hand, the free women misinterpreted the situation of slave women, and on the other, they misinterpreted their own: they were not, after all, literally in irons. Their appropriation of the emblems of antislavery discourse masked the very real differences between the oppression of black slave women and free white women in America —and the very real differences in the character of the struggle against these oppressions.[6]

The speeches and writings of black women who had been held in slavery testify that they did not, however, confuse the experience of free women with their experience as female slaves. Nor did they confuse the free women's struggle for self-liberation from a metaphorical slavery with their own struggle for self-liberation from slavery. For them, the discourse of antislavery feminism became not liberating but confining when it colored the self-liberated Woman and Sister white and reassigned the role of the passive victim, which the patriarchy traditionally had reserved for white women, to women who were black.

Transforming themselves from the objects of the discourse of others into the subjects of their own discourse, these women who had been held in slavery refined the antislavery feminists' definitions of womanhood.[7] Jacobs, like Grimké, recounts in her writings the initial shock of awareness that came when she realized that she was a slave. Instead of expending energy on surprise and focusing on her recognition of powerlessness, however, she centers on ways to counter her oppression. Where Grimké had attempted to devise a new definition of womanhood to express her needs and goals, Sojourner Truth uses her everyday experience as the norm. These former slaves present themselves not as powerless, but as powerful; not as passive, but as active. Characterizing their situation as a war, they present themselves engaged in struggles for freedom, and they successfully invent new identities and new communities, emerging as self-liberated liberating women, tried by fire.[8] On paper, they create what Henry David Thoreau had demanded of every writer: "a simple and sincere account of their own lives."[9] Inscribing themselves as black women who have survived through struggle, they use the first person to discuss their female humanity, their womanhood, and to articulate their efforts to expand female siblingship into a political sisterhood of black and white women. They urge this sisterhood to follow their lead into the public arena to oppose slavery, racism, and patriarchy. Recasting the free antislavery feminists' motto Am I Not a Woman and a Sister? into an even more potent text, these female survivors of slavery compress its formal double inquiries into a vernacular question that functions as an assertion: "A'n't I a woman?"

In her *Narrative*, Sojourner Truth repeatedly addresses the issue of selfhood in her discussions of names. Born Isabella, a slave, she was legally property. In 1827, the year before emancipation in New York, she escaped from her owner, found refuge with the nearby Van Wageners, and assumed their name. As Isabella Van Wagener, she initiated the legal proceedings that rescued her son from Alabama, supported her youngest children working as a domestic in New York City, bore public witness as a mystic on the streets of Manhattan, and joined a religious commune. Then in 1843, the Spirit commanded her to travel and preach, and she announced herself Sojourner Truth.

Her speech at the 1851 Akron Women's Rights Convention articulates her awareness of her power.[10] In a noisy atmosphere in which hostile white ministers, who were trying to take over the meeting, spouted biblical strictures against females participating in public life, a number of the convention participants opposed giving a black woman the floor. They feared being identified "with abolition and niggers." The chair had to plead for silence as Sojourner Truth stood, tall and black, to deliver a speech that redefined womanhood. Her subject was power: the lack of power that men ascribe to womankind and the presence of her own power and the power of all women.

With a manner her audience called magical, she countered the ideas of the white male representatives of the clerical establishment: "That man over there says that women need to be helped into carriages, and lifted over ditches, and to have the best place everywhere. . . . Nobody ever helps me into carriages, or over mud puddles, or gives me any best place!" Instead, she proposed a redefinition of womanhood based on her own experience. In doing so, she transformed the formal antislavery inquiry circling the abolitionist emblem into a revolutionary chorus: "A'n't I a woman?"

Standing before the white audience of fearful white women and hostile white men, she commanded, "Look at me!" Directing their eyes—not to the breasts and hips with which the patriarchy defines womanhood—but to her arm, she defined herself as an oppressed producer: "I have ploughed, and planted, and gathered into barns, and no man could head me! And a'n't I a woman? I could work as much and eat as much as a man—when I could get it—and bear de lash as well! And a'n't I a woman?" She next characterized herself as an oppressed reproducer, a mother whose children had been used as commodities: "I have borne thirteen children, and seen them most all sold off to slavery." And she defined herself as God's creature, as a suffering Christian: "when I cried out with my mother's grief, none but Jesus heard me! And a'n't I a woman?"

In asserting that not only the white male slavocracy, but also women like the white self-proclaimed feminists present had been deaf to her grief, Sojourner Truth exposed the racism that historically has plagued movements for social change in America. Then, in an off-handed demonstration of her considerable intellectual powers, she dismissed the argument that human rights are dependent on merit. "What's [intellect] . . . got to do with woman's right's or nigger's rights? If my cup won't hold but a pint, and yours holds a quart, wouldn't you be mean not to let me have my little half-measure full?"[11] Denegrating her clerical opponent, she countered his biblical arguments against women's rights: "Then that little man in black there, he says women can't have as much rights as men, because Christ wasn't a woman! Where did your Christ come from? Where did your Christ come from? From God and a woman! Man had nothing to do with him." Finally, she warned male usurpers to beware women's revolutionary power: "If the first woman God ever made was strong enough to turn the world upside down all alone, these women together ought to be able to turn it back, and get it right side up again! And now they is asking to do it, the men better let them."

Frances Gage, who later published Sojourner Truth's speech among other reminiscences of the convention, wrote that it had "subdued the mobbish spirit of the day." But Gage demonstrated that she had not learned the black woman's lesson: that all women must reject the characterizations with which patriarchal culture defined them and must redefine themselves. Instead, writing that Sojourner Truth had "taken us up in her strong arms and carried us safely over the slough of difficulty," Gage evoked the figures of the double antislavery emblem. But, reversing its racial roles, she cast the black woman as a powerful rescuer and herself and the other white women at the convention as powerless rescued female victims.

Ironically, the definition of womanhood so clearly voiced by Sojourner Truth at the Akron Woman's Rights Convention was contradicted by the most influential contemporary essay on her life, Harriet Beecher Stowe's *Atlantic Monthly* article "The Libyan Sibyl."[12] Stowe's Libyan Sibyl is passive. She possesses knowledge but cannot act on it; further, because her language cannot readily be understood, no one else can use her knowledge as the basis for effective action. Where the former slave Isabella had invented and assumed the persona of Sojourner Truth, a woman who traveled to bear witness to all who would listen, Stowe created a creature that is passive, mysterious, and inhuman. Where the black woman had redefined herself, using her own experience as the norm against which to gauge other definitions of womanhood, Stowe's Sibyl suggests instead the figures shown on the double antislavery emblem. She is seen alternatively as an emotional kneeling black supplicant who "seemed to impersonate the fervor of Ethiopia, wild, savage, hunted of all nations, but burning after God in her tropic heart, and stretching her scarred hands toward the glory to be revealed."[13] Or she is characterized as the powerful rescuer of weak genteel white females: "One felt as if the dark, strange woman were quite able to take up the invalid in her bosom, and bear her as a lamb, both physically and spiritually."[14] In reversing the races of rescuer and rescued on the antislavery emblem, Stowe established the rhetorical posture toward Sojourner Truth that Gage would later adopt. She did not, however, present this black rescuer as heroic, as Gage would do. Instead, characterizing Sojourner Truth as one of those "nobly and grandly formed human beings, that have come to us cramped, scarred, maimed, out of the prison-house of bondage," she claims that one can only speculate, "[h]ow grand and queenly a woman she might have been."[15] Stowe's "Libyan Sibyl" is not an enchained queen, but a mutilate.

Nevertheless, Stowe's essay is important. Not only does it present a perverse characterization of Sojourner Truth, but it also identifies the former slave as the inspiration for William Wetmore Story's sculpture *The Libyan Sibyl*. Stowe writes that the artist created the *Sibyl* after hearing her describe an encounter with Sojourner Truth. She recalls that when she related the incident to Story in Rome in 1857 he asked her to repeat it, and that in 1860, when she again visited his studio, he said he wanted to hear it once more and immediately began a clay sketch of the *Libyan Sibyl* (fig. 15).[16]

Story's *Sibyl* is seated. With her right leg crossed over her left and her right elbow on her knee, she leans forward and rests her chin on the palm of her partially closed right hand. Her left hand obscures a closed scroll. Her body is half draped, and her wavy hair is elaborately braided. The headdress that she wears suggests her relationship to Jupiter's oracle; it is decorated with the tetragrammaton that names the Almighty and with two interlocking triangles. (Although these geometric forms have come to signify the Jewish faith, in Story's day they were used to represent the Seal of Solomon and to signal interrelationships between spirit and nature.) Her earrings and necklace are appropriate for an early Nubian woman, and her pendant repeats the Seal of Solomon.[17]

Fig. 15. William Wetmore Story, *The Libyan Sibyl* (1861).

In late June 1860, Story wrote that his next subject would be "Africa facing her future"; in December he reported that he was beginning his "African sibyl." That winter and spring, as in America the compromises over slavery crumbled, southern states seceded, and northern abolitionists pressed for Emancipation, in Italy Story worked on the sculpture he called his "anti-slavery sermon in stone." Writing from his studio in Rome, he spelled out the sculpture's political significance in a letter to his friend the antislavery congressman Charles Sumner:

> I have taken the pure Coptic head and figure, the great massive sphinx-face, full-lipped, long-eyed, low-browed and lowering, and the largely-developed limbs of the African. . . . It is a very massive figure, big-shouldered, large-bosomed, with nothing of the Venus in it, but, as far as I could make it, luxuriant and heroic. She is looking out of her black eyes into futurity and sees the terrible fate of her race. This is the theme of the figure—Slavery on the horizon, and I made her head as melancholy and severe as possible.[18]

Story's American audience understood. In the Emancipation year of 1863, *Harper's* characterized his sculpture as dramatizing "the genius of a race obscurely strong, mysterious in history, confronting the future with a majestic resolution which compels reply," and commented that "it is our peculiar interest in the African race at this time which nationalizes Story's statue of *The Libyan Sibyl*."[19]

Story posed his sibyl in an attitude commonly assigned to defeated barbarians in Roman art. His decision invites the viewer to consider parallels between the American enslavement of Africans and the Roman enslavement of defeated peoples—including the inhabitants of Britain and Jerusalem.[20] Nineteenth-century English antislavery graphics repeatedly pictured a black woman seated under a tree. This figure derives from *Judea Capta*, a biblical type based on Isaiah's prophecy of the punishment of the daughter of Zion, "and she being desolate shall sit upon the ground" (3:26). In America, this type had been invested with special significance since the seventeenth century, when Cotton Mather likened the people of New England to the Jews in Babylonian captivity. Referring to the Roman medal struck to commemorate the triumph over the Jews, showing Judea as a woman seated under a palm tree with her head in her hand, Mather had written: "If poor New-England were to be shown upon her old coin [depicting a pine tree], we might show her *Leaning* against her thunderstruck Pine tree, Desolate, sitting upon the Ground."[21]

In addition to recalling the iconic Roman coin of *Judea Capta* (fig. 16), the pose that Story chose for the *Libyan Sibyl* echoes a tradition derived from Dürer's *Melancholy*. Two aspects of Dürer's work, Erwin Panofsky explains, suggest Africa: The pose of the head and hand occur in ancient Egyptian art, and Melancholy was traditionally depicted with "a swarthy 'earth-like'

Fig. 16. Roman coin (A.D. 69–79).

complexion which under certain circumstances can deepen to actual blackness." Panofsky writes that Dürer's characterization, which was mytholo-
gized by Vasari and emblematized by Rippa, influenced art and thought for
three hundred years.[22] Clearly, mourning figures in early nineteenth-century
America echoed its posture, as does John A. Baralet's "Sacred to the
Memory of Washington" (fig. 17). Below the upper section of this engraving
of the apotheosis of George Washington, the seated figure of a sorrowing
America appears at the center, head in hand.[23]

But Story's *Libyan Sibyl* also addressed contemporary American politics.
Although working abroad, Story was well aware of the slavery issue. An
acquaintance of L. Maria Child, he had published five sonnets in Maria
Weston Chapman's *Liberty Bell*, and both Charles Sumner and Theodore

Fig. 17. John J. Barralet, *Sacred to the Memory of Washington* (ca. 1800).

Parker were visitors at his Rome studio.[24] Although Story's *Libyan Sibyl* was
not intended as a portrait of Sojourner Truth, it seems clear that Stowe's
description had suggested a focus for the artist's antislavery concerns.

Both Story's *Sibyl* and Isabella's creation Sojourner Truth are identifiably
African women, powerful in body, knowledge, and spirit. But they are in
many ways antithetical—most obviously, of course, in color. The ex-slave
was a black woman; Story's African is carved of whitest marble. Where the

*Sibyl* suggests motherhood by exposing a bared full breast (which in artistic iconography of the period suggests the continent of Africa as nurturer of mankind), Sojourner Truth had bared her arm to define herself as a worker.

Perhaps more important is the difference in the way the *Sibyl* and Sojourner Truth respond to their special circumstances. The fervent ex-slave testified that voices had commanded her to travel and speak to effect social change, and that she had obeyed them. Story's mythic female appears to have heard such voices, or to be waiting intently for them, or perhaps to listen to them even now—but she is incapable of either speech or action. Brooding and passive, the sculptured *Sibyl* is unable to alter her own destiny or that of anyone else. Sojourner Truth, although illiterate, arranged for a narrative of her life to be written and published, and she journeyed about selling her *Book of Life*. The *Sibyl*, however, deliberately closes her scroll and thrusts it aside, negating the possibility that anyone at all might share her knowledge and use it to effect change. Story's powerful sculpture recalls Dürer's Melancholy in presenting as its subject a "thinking being in perplexity" fixed on "a problem which cannot be solved."[25] Like Stowe's essay, it contradicts the black woman's projection of active purposeful womanhood.

Sojourner Truth articulated her autonomy in all major ways but one. Conspicuously absent from her speeches, her *Narrative*, and her *Book of Life* is any discussion of sexuality. Forbidden to female speakers and writers in America throughout the nineteenth century and most of the twentieth, this tabooed subject is central to Harriet Jacobs's pseudonymous slave narrative, *Incidents in the Life of a Slave Girl*.[26]

*Incidents* counters racist endorsements of slavery, and racist condemnations of it, by presenting Linda Brent, a narrator who assumes responsibility for her own actions.[27] In and through her first-person discourse, Jacobs's pseudonymous narrator demonstrates that she is one of God's moral creatures. She focuses on her struggle against her oppression as a sexual object and as a mother. Like Sojourner Truth, Jacobs's narrator was excluded from traditional definitions of true womanhood because of her color—which, to racist white Americans, identified her as less than human, as a female whose enslaved condition was a natural consequence of her inferior race. Like other female slaves identified as her mother's daughter and forbidden the legal status of wife, Brent was required to obey neither a father nor a husband, but an owner.

In childhood the light-skinned Linda Brent, whose mother died young, was gently treated by her first mistress and taught to read and sew; later, in her second mistress's household, she was raised among the children in the family. But she was a slave nonetheless, and she quickly learned, "that which commands admiration in the white woman only hastens the degradation of the female slave" (p. 28). During adolescence, Linda is denied the treatment of a true woman. Instead of her sexual "purity" being insisted upon, she is made to understand that her virginity will not be tolerated.

Her lecherous middle-aged master, whom she calls Dr. Flint, forbids her to marry the young black man she loves and demands that she instead submit to him. His jealous wife, instead of rushing to her defense, treats her as a sexual rival. Linda Brent feels threatened and isolated. Too embarrassed to confide in her grandmother (a freed woman who was her major emotional support), desperate to deny her master's claim that she must comply with his demands, and determined to exert some control over her sexual experience, she tries to utilize the sexuality her master covets as a defense against him. Brent involves herself in a secret liaison with a young white neighbor. When her master orders her to move into the house where she is to live as his concubine, she announces that she is pregnant. As she anticipated, Dr. Flint feels cheated of her virginity and no longer wants her.

Pregnancy outside wedlock presented a serious problem in nineteenth-century American life and fiction. Its treatment in *Incidents*, however, is unusual. Popularly, the cult of motherhood enshrined the relationship of a mother and child only if the mother was first a wife; in popular fiction, pregnant girls found their way to the riverbank and drowned themselves and their unborn babes.[28] Although Linda Brent presents her sexual history as a confession, she counters this condemnation of unwed motherhood: initially she views her pregnancy not as a problem but as a solution, thinking it will save her from further sexual harassment by her master. Later, by repeatedly characterizing her baby as a "tie to life," she implicitly criticizes the notion that extramarital sex and illegitimacy involve sin and death.[29] Brent writes that she lives for her beloved children and that her determined efforts to win them freedom and a home give her existence meaning.

*Incidents* embodies a major critique of white patriarchal sexual ideology and practice in nineteenth-century America.[30] Although, like Child's fiction, the book divides women into blacks and whites, slaves and slaveholders, it is not fruitful to search here for characters modeled on the passive chained female supplicant or on the chain-breaking liberator of the double anti-slavery emblems.[31] Instead, like Sojourner Truth's speech in Akron, Jacobs's

book centers on the figure of a woman struggling to break her chains—
the figure that emerged in Grimké's later writings. But here, the struggling
woman is literally a slave, and she is black.

From the beginning, Jacobs's narrator identifies herself in terms of family
relationships, as a sister, daughter, niece, granddaughter, but most impor-
tantly as a mother; motherhood is central to *Incidents*. Linda Brent tells her
story against a background of violence in which slave mothers, sexually
abused by their masters and targets of their jealous mistresses, suffer giving
birth, or are sold away from their families as punishment for having given
birth, or die in childbirth. The evils of slavery are dramatized as the sexual
abuse of women and the torture of mothers. The sketch of the childless
cook, Betty, suggests that for a woman maternity is a prerequisite for full
humanity; women black or white—Linda Brent, Grandmother, Aunt Nancy,
Mrs. Flint—are all defined by the ways in which they respond to motherhood.

Following her son's birth, Linda Brent presents herself as a slave mother.
After her second child is born, she writes that this identification becomes
even stronger. "When they told me my new-born babe was a girl, my heart
was heavier than it had ever been before. Slavery is terrible for men; but it is
far more terrible for women. . . . Superadded to the burden common to all,
*they* have wrongs, and sufferings, and mortifications peculiarly their own"
(p. 77).

Brent's role model is her grandmother. She is the first of four generations
of "white slaves" in the family, but none of these women suggests either the
pathetic supplicant of the emblem or the passive, victimized, adoring Tragic
Mulatto of Child's fiction. Instead of preaching passivity and self-destructive
romantic love, Grandmother teaches Linda the doctrine of active, nurturing
motherhood: "Stand by your own children, and suffer with them till death"
(p. 91).

*Incidents* shows Grandmother nurturing three generations.[32] Sustained by
Christianity, she has preserved her family through hard work, diplomacy,
goodwill, and a little cash. Although a former slave, Grandmother enjoys
unusual status in the town. Freed in childhood, then captured and reenslaved,
all her adult life she has attempted to free her children and provide them
with a home by working within the system. While held in slavery, Grandmother obtained permission to earn money after hours. She saved every
penny, arranged for her own purchase and emancipation, and managed to
buy a house. Working as a baker, Grandmother persists in her attempts to
purchase her children's freedom, but she is successful in buying only her
older son. Grandmother is powerless to save her youngest child from torture

when he is caught after running away, and she cannot redeem her only surviving daughter, who dies Dr. Flint's slave. In order to identify the device of the enchained female with Grandmother, one must construe the supplicant's pleas, as Angelina Grimké did, as a protest.

Brent shares her grandmother's goals but uses new tactics to realize them. In early adolescence she was sent to live in Dr. Flint's house where she was subjected to sexual harassment and abruptly learned what it meant to be a female slave. By the time she was fourteen, she writes, "The war of my life had begun; and though one of God's most powerless creatures, I resolved never to be conquered" (p. 19). Brent battles Flint. In girlhood she vowed, "I would do any thing, every thing, for the sake of defeating him" (p. 53). Later, faced with his threats against her children, she swears she will stop him. She fears, however, that if she follows Grandmother's law-abiding path, her children, like Grandmother's, will never be free. When she learns that her master has ordered the children to the plantation to be "broke in," she decides to run away (p. 53). Her hope is that Dr. Flint will be unable to catch her, will find the children so troublesome that he will sell them, and that their father will buy them all.

Brent's plan is partially successful. Although Dr. Flint refuses to sell her, he does sell the children, and covertly, through a third party, their father does manage to purchase them. He allows them to live with Grandmother. The runaway Brent is sheltered by friends and neighbors, then concealed in a tiny attic in Grandmother's house. When, after years in hiding, she finally concludes that the children's father does not intend to free them as he had promised, she decides that she must act herself. Using her cramped den as a warroom, Brent wages a successful campaign of liberation. To lighten the surveillance of her family, she convinces Dr. Flint that she is no longer in the area by writing letters and arranging for them to be mailed from the North. She even gains vengeful pleasure watching Dr. Flint falsify the contents of her letters when he reads them to Grandmother.

A community that is largely a sisterhood of mothers supports Linda Brent in her insurgency. Most important is Grandmother. Although condemning Brent's decision to establish a sexual liaison, the old woman had pitied her and had taken her in when the jealous Mrs. Flint, sensing Flint's interest in his adolescent slave, had ordered her out of the house. After Brent's children were born, Grandmother had feared the consequences of attempting an escape and advised her against running away. But when the "slavegirl" became a fugitive nevertheless, Grandmother risked everything—her possessions, her house, even her own freedom—to hide her.

Almost as important as Grandmother is Aunt Nancy. Chronically over-worked, "slowly murdered" by the selfish demands of Mrs. Flint, her mistress, she is unable to bear a healthy child. Jacobs's narrator presents Aunt Nancy as a bereaved slave mother who transforms her mourning into militancy. In the early years, she acts a mother's part by trying to protect Brent from Dr. Flint. When Brent goes into hiding, Aunt Nancy encourages her in her dangerous course. "She sent me word never to yield. She said if I persevered I might, perhaps, gain the freedom of my children; and even if I perished doing it, that was better than to leave them to groan under the same persecutions that had blighted my own life" (p. 144).

This maternal sisterhood in *Incidents* embraces generations of mothers and daughters and is contrasted with a failed community that is also based on motherhood. Although black mothers honor their bonds with their mistresses' daughters, whom they had nursed in infancy, their white beneficiaries reject both them and their children. The betrayal of black women by the whites they have nurtured is most forcefully figured in a gothic anecdote encoding the underlying hatred between mistress and slave. Brent writes of a slave "mammy" who steals into the room where her cruel mistress lies dead and strikes the corpse—only to be sold off to Georgia after her tiny ward, a little girl just learning to talk, reports the incident. White women's betrayal of their black "milk sisters" is dramatized by Mrs. Flint's abuse of Aunt Nancy. In infancy, she had supplanted Nancy at Grandmother's breast; after growing up, she blighted Aunt Nancy's motherhood. Because of this cruelty to her "milk sister," Brent characterizes Mrs. Flint as an antiwoman, even though she has been a mother many times. It comes as no surprise when, instead of protecting Brent, Mrs. Flint attacks her as a sexual rival.

Brent contrasts the lives of black and white sisters in a set piece:

> I once saw two beautiful children playing together. One was a fair white child; the other was her slave, and also her sister. . . . The fair child grew up to be a still fairer woman. . . . Scarcely one day of her life had been clouded when the sun rose on her happy bridal morning.
>
> How had those years dealt with her slave sister, the playmate of her childhood? She, also, was very beautiful; but the flowers and sunshine of love were not for her. She drank the cup of sin, and shame, and misery, whereof her persecuted race are compelled to drink. (P. 29)

Jacobs's Brent repeatedly pairs female slaves and slaveholders, but nowhere does she show a slave and a mistress who can sustain affection for each other. Although Brent had loved her first mistress, she felt betrayed because when the woman died she did not free her; she loved her second mistress when both were children, but before reaching adulthood she knew Miss Emily as her enemy.

Even in this perverse and violent atmosphere, however, *Incidents* shows some white women acknowledging the bonds of sisterhood and motherhood, and honoring them over and above those of race and class. The narrator expects and anticipates the sisterhood of other black women and reserves her scorn for those who may betray her, but she is surprised again and again when white women help. Miss Fanny buys Grandmother at auction and sets her free; Grandmother's lady friend tries to stop Dr. Flint from harassing Brent; a female slaveholder hides Brent after she runs away; Brent's New York employer gives over her baby to Brent's care so that she can escape to New England in the guise of a traveling nursemaid instead of as a fugitive.

*Incidents* was written and published to foster a community of women who would act to oppose slavery. In her preface, Jacobs's Linda Brent announces that she wants "to arouse the women of the North to a realizing sense of the condition of two millions of women at the South, still in bondage, suffering what I suffered, and most of them far worse" (p. 1). L. Maria Child was equally explicit in her introduction, explaining that she was bringing out this outrageous book on a scandalous topic "with the hope of arousing conscientious and reflecting women at the North to a sense of their duty in the exertion of moral influence on the question of Slavery, on all possible occasions" (p. 4). Both the author and the editor of *Incidents* urge their female readers to move beyond the private sphere and to emulate their example by engaging in the public debate on slavery and racism. Informed not by "the cult of domesticity" or "domestic feminism" but by political feminism, *Incidents* is an attempt to move women to political action.[33]

*Incidents* embodies the conflict between patriarchal definitions of true womanhood and the definition advanced by the antislavery feminists. The book is double, linking Linda Brent's confessions as what the patriarchy called a "fallen woman" with her heroic account of her successful struggle as a slave mother. Although the language and rhythms of the Bible resonate throughout the text, its contradictory lines of action are narrated in different literary styles. When confessing her sexual history, Linda Brent utilizes the euphemisms and the elaborate sentence structures characteristic of genteel discourse, which, conflating class and gender, the patriarchy assigned to true women. "O, ye happy women, whose purity has been sheltered from childhood, who have been free to choose the objects of your affection, whose homes are protected by law, do not judge the poor desolate slave girl too severely!" (p. 54). When writing as a heroic slave mother, however, Brent gives more precise information, her vocabulary is simpler, and her narration is more direct. "Alone in my cell, where no eye but God's could see me, I wept bitter tears. How earnestly I prayed to him to restore me to my children, and enable me to be a useful woman and a good mother!" (p. 133). This doubleness of style is perhaps a consequence of Jacobs's anxiety about her sensational subject matter. Her northern antislavery feminist friend, Amy Post, testifies to the author's reluctance to reveal her sexual history. Post quotes Jacobs as saying, "You know a woman can whisper her cruel wrongs in the ear of a dear friend much easier than she can record them for the world to read" (pp. 203–4). Searching for a way to tell her tale of sexual oppression, Jacobs appears to have chosen fictional models that focused on women's sexual experience but presented it in elevated, elaborate, oblique forms. The genre of the slave narrative, in contrast, provided her with a literary discourse that included many models—some of which were clear and direct—to express her successful struggle for freedom.

Confessing her sexual history, Linda Brent defines her reader as a woman who endorses patriarchal patterns and believes that females must not engage in sex outside of marriage. Pleading with this reader not to judge her too harshly, the narrator plays the role of a supplicant and, apologizing for her transgressions from this standard, apparently endorses it.

> Pity me, and pardon me, O virtuous reader! You never knew what it is to be a slave; to be entirely unprotected by law or custom; to have the laws reduce you to the condition of a chattel, entirely subject to the will of another. You never exhausted your ingenuity in avoiding the snares, and eluding the power of a hated tyrant; you never shuddered at the sound of his footsteps, and trembled within hearing of his voice.

Yet by repeating "you never," the narrator also invites a reading that emphasizes the reader's ignorance of the circumstances and minimizes her fitness as a judge. In accord with this, at the conclusion of the passage, instead of awaiting her reader's verdict Linda Brent assumes a judge's role and pronounces judgment on herself. "I know I did wrong. No one can feel it more sensibly than I do. The painful and humiliating memory will haunt me to my dying day."[34]

Later, Linda Brent negates any possible resemblance between herself and the figure of a passive victim by recalling that her motivations for establishing the sexual liaison with the father of her children were "revenge . . . calculations of interest . . . flattered vanity . . . and sincere gratitude for kindness." Further, she says that "I knew nothing would enrage Dr. Flint so much as to know that I favored another; and it was something to triumph over my tyrant even in that small way" (p. 55). Brent assumes full responsibility for transgressing patriarchal standards and involving herself in the long-standing relationship that produced her two children. "I will not try to screen myself behind the plea of compulsion from a master; for it was not so. Neither can I plead ignorance or thoughtlessness. . . . I knew what I did, and I did it with deliberate calculation" (p. 54).

Then, in what appears to be a major reversal, she uses the present tense to assert an alternative standard of female sexual behavior: "Still, in looking back, calmly, on the events of my life, I feel that the slave woman ought not to be judged by the same standard as others" (p. 56). By proposing that patriarchal strictures on women's behavior are not applicable to slave women, Brent reveals these strictures as arbitrary and conventional, not natural and inevitable. This makes possible a discussion of alternative sexual standards for women. It is a long step from her statement to the proposition that free women, to the extent that they are coerced by men, should also be spared condemnation for untraditional sexual behavior. And it is another long step to the proposition that if enslaved women should not be judged solely in terms of their sexual behavior, but on a variety of grounds (as men are), then free women should also be judged on multiple grounds. Yet, in politicizing her sexual experience and in moving toward these logical extensions of Brent's brief statement, *Incidents* moves beyond the limits of nineteenth-century polite discourse and toward modern feminism.

It is not surprising that Jacobs's narrator did not extend to free women her reevaluation of female sexual behavior or that she could not consistently reject her condemnation as a woman who had deviated from accepted sexual patterns. In her rebellion against slavery, she was bolstered by a fully developed ideology of antislavery and antiracism that was endorsed by much of her functional community. But there was no comparable articulation of an antisexist ideology in nineteenth-century America to support her challenge to patriarchal views of women's sexual behavior. When Jacobs wrote, free women who were feminists were promoting an end to the double standard by urging that men, like women, remain virginal before marriage and monoga-mous afterward. Some reformers such as Child, who publicized the plight of prostitutes and other sexually nonconforming women, condemned the patri-archy for punishing its female victims.[35] Abolitionists denounced the sexual abuse of slave women and exposed the hypocrisy of the southern patriarchy, which demanded that free women conform to the model of virginity before marriage and monogamy afterward while simultaneously denying slave women either virginity or legal marriage. Brent's condemnation by her grandmother suggests that a slave woman who transgressed patriarchal norms was vulnerable to censure even within the black community.

Because Linda Brent does not sustain and develop her assertion of sexual autonomy, the conflict over her sexual behavior remains dramatically unresolved until near the end of *Incidents*. In a chapter called "The Confession," Brent reveals her sexual history to her young daughter and receives full and complete acceptance. This exoneration solves the problem caused by her grandmother's initial harsh judgment and reestablishes the generational community of black women.

The narrator handles her struggle for freedom differently. Discussing emancipation, she addresses an audience that she assumes shares her conviction that mothers are entitled to use any and every means to free their children. Nevertheless, Brent writes that years after escaping to the North, she rejected the offer of her employer, Mrs. Bruce, to purchase her.

> The more my mind had become enlightened, the more difficult it was for me to consider myself an article of property; and to pay money to those who had so grievously oppressed me seemed like taking from my sufferings the glory of triumph. I wrote to Mrs. Bruce, thanking her, but saying that being sold from one owner to another seemed too much like slavery; that such a great obligation could not be easily cancelled; and that I preferred to go to my brother in California. (P. 199)

Despite Brent's wishes, Mrs. Bruce purchases and frees her, and her children are finally safe. The narrator, however, expresses relief—not triumph. Further, it appears that the successful realization of freedom, her primary goal, may have negated the possibility of achieving her secondary objective, a home for her children. The means by which Brent is emancipated apparently place her under such a "great obligation" to Mrs. Bruce that she feels she cannot leave to establish her own home, though she still longs "for a hearthstone of my own . . . for my children's sake more than for my own" (p. 201).

Thus suddenly, after establishing Linda Brent as a self-liberated liberator, in its final pages *Incidents* suggests the pattern of the double antislavery emblem in which the activity of the white female emancipator renders the black woman passive. In a letter that Post quoted in the appendix of *Incidents*, Jacobs expressed the frustration she felt after being freed by purchase: "I served for my liberty as faithfully as Jacob served for Rachel. At the end, he had large possessions; but I was robbed of my victory; I was obliged to resign my crown, to rid myself of a tyrant" (p. 204). Deeply disappointed, yet feeling that "since I have no fear of my name coming before those whom I have lived in dread of I cannot be happy without trying to be useful in some way," Jacobs wrote her book to further the antislavery cause.[36] Like other slave narrators, she gained her triumph in and through the process of recreating herself as the subject of her own discourse.

In *Incidents*, by redefining womanhood in terms of her own life, a "slave mother" directly challenged white patriarchal notions that denied her the status of a true woman. By shaping her sexual and maternal experience into autobiography, Jacobs's Linda Brent articulates structures of female individuality and female community that counter patriarchal definitions of true womanhood. In the process, she also challenges an easy acceptance of the notion that, in nineteenth-century patriarchal racist America, the condition of a free white woman could be equated with the condition of a black slave woman. The black female slave narrator of *Incidents* addresses herself to an audience of free white women readers precisely because their lives are so different from hers that she feels compelled to tell them her story.

Jacobs's narrative and Sojourner Truth's speeches sharpened the antebellum debate over definitions of true womanhood by presenting a critique of patriarchal definitions that restricted true womanhood to free white women. They also presented a critique of those antislavery-feminist definitions that envisioned free white women as the potential liberators of oppressed passive black slaves or that, alternatively, collapsed the oppression of black slave women into the oppression of free white women and presumed to speak for the slave. Inscribing their life experience within the antislavery-feminist discourse structured by the antislavery tokens, these former slaves translated the figure of the Woman and Sister into the vernacular. In doing so, they reinvented womanhood.[37]

# PART THREE

# Woman and Emblem
# in Stone and Story

## CHAPTER FIVE

# Hiram Powers's
# *The Greek Slave*

*To the feeling heart and discerning eye, all slave girls are GREEK, and all slave masters TURKS, wicked cruel and hateful, be their names Haman, Selin, James, Judas or Henry; their County Algiers or Alabama, Congo or Carolina, the same.*
—The North Star[1]

*To call it either Venus, or Eve, or Nymph, or anything but what it is, would, we think be a blunder . . . , it is the Greek Slave, and nothing else. Yes, it is something else—a most touching emblem of Woman.*
—New York Tribune[2]

The speeches and writings of Sojourner Truth and Harriet Jacobs present the fullest antebellum challenge to the patriarchal definition of true womanhood and the fullest antebellum development of the Woman and Sister, the version of womanhood that the antislavery feminists advanced. Modeling themselves on their English counterparts, the black and white abolitionist women replicated the image of the kneeling female supplicant so diligently that, over the years, it proliferated throughout the North. Both as a commercial printer's device and as a folk motif, this partially nude female in chains was incorporated into the shared cultural codes available to artists and writers. Predictably, in the decades before the Civil War, the iconography of the antislavery feminists also became incorporated into works acclaimed as high art.

The antislavery feminists had encoded the image of the enchained female to signify both woman's oppression and her struggle against that oppression. Despite their differing interpretations of this image, female activists all used it to persuade women to move into the public sphere and to join the movement against slavery and sexism. Once their icon had become popular, however, the antislavery women could not control its interpretation. When the image of a woman in chains appears in works of elite culture produced by white males, as in Hiram Powers's *The Greek Slave* (1841–43) and Nathaniel Hawthorne's *The Scarlet Letter* (1850), it still encodes woman's oppression. But while the chains that signal injustice remain, the identity of the woman has changed. She is no longer black, nor is she a white woman who lives in nineteenth-century America. These women in chains carry meanings that contradict those assigned by the antislavery feminists. Instead of signifying that woman should engage in public action to end her oppression, in elite texts the icon of an enchained female signifies that the appropriate womanly response to tyranny is resignation.

Hiram Powers's *Greek Slave*, the most popular American sculpture of the nineteenth century, incorporates the chains and the nudity of the antislavery emblem (fig. 18). It displays these attributes, however, in connection with the figure of a woman who is not black but dazzlingly white, not an African sold in America but a Greek exposed in a Turkish slave market half a world away from American slavery.

Connections between the enslavement of Christian women by Muhammedan Turks in Greece and the enslavement of African women by Christian Americans were routinely made by the abolitionists. As early as 1827, L. Maria Child had used the sale of Greek women and girls as the subject of a children's story. In *Condition of Women*, she denounced the enslavement of all women everywhere, condemning the American "marriage market" by likening it to the sale of Circassian women in Turkish markets. Sarah Grimké had glossed a reference in her *Letters* about African-American women "bought and sold in our slave markets, to gratify the brutal lust of those who bear the name of Christians" with a note on the Turkish sale of Greek women. Ernestine Rose, speaking at a woman's rights convention, had quoted John Randolph's comment to white Virginia women who sat sewing for Greek relief while a slave coffle passed by, "Ladies, the Greeks are at your doors."[3] Other abolitionist women, publishing poems in antislavery gift books, used the example of Greece to spur northern women to work harder for the abolition of slavery in America.

Fig. 18. Hiram Powers, *The Greek Slave* (1841–1847).

Greece, Greece cries to you, from her slumbering ashes,
And tells you to cherish the freedom she lost—
To save your oppressed from their wo-twining lashes,
To calm the dark billows Oppression has tossed![4]

Long after completing the *Greek Slave*, Powers wrote that he first conceived of his subject in response to the Turkish victory over Greece. His
earliest direct reference to the *Greek Slave* was in an 1841 letter where,
decades after the Greek defeat, he described two new projects:

> The one to represent a Greek slave and the other a fisher boy. . . . The former
> is of a young girl, and nude—with her hands bound and in such a position as
> to conceal a portion of the figure thereby rendering the exposure of nakedness
> less exceptional to our American fastidiousness. The feet also will be bound—to
> a fixture and the face turned to one side, and downwards with an expression of
> modesty and Christian resignation. That she is a Christian will be inferred by
> a cross, suspended by a chain around her neck and hanging resting on her
> bosom. I said a young girl but the form will express puberty.[5]

As Powers worked on this sculpture over the next two years, he referred to
it alternately as a "Greek slave" and as a "captive." During this time, he
modified his original design. While the work was in progress, a visitor to his
studio described the *Slave* with her "hands folded before her"—a gesture
that recalls the abolitionists' supplicant. His finished sculpture, however,
recalls the pose of the Venus Pudica. Her hands are not folded, she is not
bound hand and foot, nor does she have a chain around her neck suspending
a cross. Instead, the attributes of Powers's subject—cross, locket, Greek
hat, and draperies—lie on the pedestal where she rests her right hand. Not
her folded hands, but heavy link chains, the attribute of her unseen (implicitly male, implicitly Turkish) owner, are interposed between the viewer and
that "portion of the figure" Powers knew Americans would fear to view
unobstructed.[6]

Hiram Powers's *Greek Slave* has been much discussed by art historians as
the first female nude to win the acceptance of American audiences. The
sculpture secularizes the images of martyrdom and saintly suffering traditional in European art. But Powers, characterized as "every inch an American" even after thirty years abroad, was also influenced by American popular culture. Both his *Greek Slave* and his *America*, a later work, were
influenced by abolitionist iconography.[7] Powers's female slave displays the
Christian faith, the nudity, and the chains of the antislavery emblem.

Powers was thoroughly familiar with the slavery controversy. He left Vermont to move west at the age of nineteen and from 1818 to 1837 lived in Cincinnati, Ohio, on the border between slavery and freedom. Although he worked in Washington, D.C., and Boston before going abroad in 1837, his correspondence testifies that his home was always Cincinnati.[8] During the decades that Powers lived there, the slavery issue was tearing the Queen City apart. Two years after he arrived, the first Cincinnati census counted 9,642 inhabitants, about 2 percent of whom were black. When the city was incorporated nine years later, the entire population had more than doubled and the black population had multiplied tenfold. According to Carter G. Woodson, from 1826 until 1840 "Negroes were a real issue in Cincinnati."[9]

Because the Queen City was on the free side of the river, the slave trade was not part of local commerce, and one of its most dramatic aspects—the buying and selling of women—was not a part of the local scene. The internal slave trade, however, was visible. In 1833, an editorial in a local newspaper entitled "Unrighteous Traffic" describes passing the wharf and encountering a steamboat carrying "a cargo of negroes, of all ages and sexes, amounting to 150 in number." It then details the process whereby "a drove" of slaves is bought, transported "in irons if necessary for safekeeping," and marketed "in the lower counties."[10]

But it was not even necessary to walk along the riverbank to see evidences of slavery in Hiram Powers's Cincinnati. The results of the efforts of blacks to escape from the South were visible in the increasing number of African-Americans on the streets and in the ubiquitous advertisements for fugitives. In 1827, a local type foundry issued a series of designs for sale to printers that graphically testifies to the presence of fugitive slaves and slave catchers in Cincinnati (fig. 19). The variety and number of these cuts which were produced over time suggest a ready market among printers whose customers wanted to advertise for a runaway or to announce a fugitive's capture.[11]

During Powers's last years in Cincinnati, tensions over slavery and race erupted into public violence. Some white residents, worried both about the presence of fugitive slaves and about the mushrooming free black population (whose legal status was unclear), formed a chapter of the Colonization Society and worked to send blacks to Africa. Others organized abolitionist groups, a few in concert with the black community.

Still others rioted. Early in the summer of 1829, an effort was made to enforce the Black Laws directing African-Americans to register and present their certificates of freedom within thirty days or to leave the city. In August, mobs of white youths invaded black homes, and the black community

Fig. 19. *Specimen of Printing Type, from the Foundry of O. & H. Wells* (Cincinnati, 1827); and *Specimen of Modern and Light Face Printing Types and Ornaments, Cast at the Cincinnati Type Foundry,* 1834.

armed itself. As a consequence of the threats and the violence that followed, more than eleven hundred black residents—more than half the black population—left Cincinnati.

In 1832, the surviving African-American community opened a school to educate its children, who were excluded from public schools when the city was incorporated. Two years later, under the leadership of evangelical abolitionist Theodore Weld—later the husband of Angelina Grimké—the young men of Cincinnati's Lane Theological Seminary debated the slavery question, constituted themselves an abolitionist society, and began working with African-American leaders to establish a night school for black people.[12]

Joining the Lane students were the "Cincinnati sisters," three women who had come west to Cincinnati's "little Africa" in response to an abolitionist appeal in *The New York Evangelist*. Phebe Mathews, Emeline Bishop, and Susan Lowe were enthusiastic about the black women and children they taught in day schools, Sabbath schools, and sewing societies. Ostracized by most white Cincinnatians and sheltered by the black community, these white abolitionist women felt that they were creating their own "little bethel." The Cincinnati sisters were evangelical Christians who worked for their students' literacy and prayed for their salvation. Their letters testify to the inspiration they found in their students' struggles against slavery, racism, and poverty. They strongly condemned the racism of critics who "feel so bad if perchance we lay our hands on a curly head, or kiss a coloured face." In addition to teaching, Mathews, Bishop, and Lowe became activists in the local abolitionist organization.[13]

The Cincinnati Anti-Slavery Society was attacked from the start. Lines between abolitionists and their opponents sharpened in 1836 when former slaveholder James Birney established an antislavery newspaper in the Queen City. Rioters attacked Cincinnati's black community, and early in July they destroyed Birney's press. Although the paper resumed publication immediately, on the night of July 30 it was mobbed again, and this time white abolitionists' homes were attacked. Over the next week, the black community was invaded repeatedly.[14] Although the Cincinnati sisters were forced to retreat to the antislavery enclave at nearby Oberlin, the violence did not close their schools.

Nor did violence end the involvement of women in the slavery dispute. In 1837, Cincinnati saw the sensational fugitive slave case of Matilda Lawrence. Lawrence, "an octoroon and therefore nearly white, of striking beauty and most engaging manners," was the daughter of a rich Missouri planter who took her with him to visit New York. Traveling not as his slave but as a member of his family, she was treated "with all the deference due the daughter of a rich southern planter." Lawrence learned that since she had been brought into a free state by her master, she could legally remain there and claim her freedom. She told her master-father this and begged him to emancipate her, promising that if he did she would return to Kentucky and stay with him. Instead, alarmed by her demands, he decided to return south at once. At Cincinnati, Matilda Lawrence escaped. Protected by local black and white abolitionists, she lived in Birney's house for almost a year before being seized as a fugitive. Although defended in court by Salmon P. Chase, Lawrence was remanded into slavery.[15]

A few years earlier, the city had been the focus of another social controversy involving women: their appearance on the public platform. It was in the Queen City that on succeeding Sundays in 1829 Frances Wright delivered the first of her unprecedented series of public lectures. Despite attacks by the entire local clergy, Wright's talks on Free Inquiry proved so popular that she repeated them at the local theater. There is no record that the young Hiram Powers attended or experienced the excitement that Frances Trollope felt at seeing a woman displayed in public. To Trollope, Wright's appearance resembled a classic marble sculpture:

> It is impossible to imagine any thing more striking . . . Her tall and majestic figure, the deep and almost solemn expression of her eyes, the simple contour of her finely formed head, unadorned, except by its own natural ringlets; her garment of plain white muslin . . . hung around her in folds that recalled the drapery of a Grecian statue.[16]

In 1837, when Hiram Powers and his family went to Italy, they left a city that had experienced public controversy over women's role and had been torn by violence over slavery. Although Powers's years abroad stretched into decades, he never lost touch with home. His letters chart his changing views on slavery and abolition—a shifting perspective that he shared with many of his fellow Cincinnatians. Initially, Powers opposed the extension of slavery but believed that "while the Constitution exists, the South has the sole right to legislate upon the matter of slavery within its own limits." A supporter of the Missouri Compromise, he feared that "such fanatics as Garrison" would destroy the Union.[17]

As the crisis grew, however, Powers's politics shifted. In 1859, he summarized his changing views:

> The Sumner case. The breaking of the Missouri Compromise, the atrocious frontier proceedings in Kansas, the Dred Scott decision, all southern measures of encroachment have brought this about and as if Providence intended an issue of the slavery question. . . . Millions of our people were friendly to the South until forced to resist slavery extension. They were content to let it be where it already exists, but not content to see the fair reserves of public lands

for their posterity peopled with negroes! They did not want slavery every where and in every thing.[18]

Powers rejoiced at Lincoln's election: "I have never been an abolitionist, but if it must come to this—I too—am one. It is a necessity that the Union shall be preserved." The dramatic events that changed Powers's mind led large numbers of other Americans to rethink their attitudes toward slavery. Over this period, although few Cincinnatians joined the abolitionists, the dialogue that the Garrisonians sparked led a majority of them to oppose the extension of slavery.[19]

In Powers's Cincinnati, the center of popular culture was the Western Museum, where he worked from 1829 to 1834. Founded with high intellectual and aesthetic hopes, this institution soon entered a "hokum phase" suggestive of the backwoods culture Mark Twain's Duke and Dauphin laid on their audiences. The museum holdings reflect the ubiquitousness of the slavery issue: Powers's comic figure of a black freezing in a lake in hell, one of the sensational "Infernal Regions" waxworks, demonstrates that, during his Cincinnati years, the artist participated freely in the white racism endemic in American popular culture. The museum also featured a painting of a female Circassian slave, evidence of an awareness, in Powers's Cincinnati, of female bondage in the Middle East.[20]

The official interpretation of Powers's *Greek Slave* was elaborately presented in a pamphlet issued to accompany its exhibitions: the sculpture signified Christian resignation.

> The ostensible subject is merely a Grecian maiden, made captive by the Turks and exposed at Constantinople, for sale. The cross and locket, visible amid the drapery, indicate that she is a Christian, and beloved. But this simple phase by no means completes the meaning of the statue. It represents a being superior to suffering, and raised above degradation by inward purity and force of character. Thus the *Greek Slave* is an emblem of all trial to which humanity is subject, and may be regarded as a type of resignation, uncompromising virtue, or sublime patience.[21]

The sophisticated *Democratic Review* endorsed this reading: "In the chastened and beautiful resignation of the face and figure, the artist has embodied the highest idea of a Christian slave."[22] Around the *Greek Slave*'s attributes —the locket, cross, fringed draperies, and hat—viewers and commentators devised a rich scenario. An excerpt from the New York *Tribune* is representative: "She is thinking not of herself; she is recalling the struggling country she has left behind her . . . , the lover of whose fate on the battle field she is still ignorant."[23]

The *Greek Slave*'s pose was much discussed. It was noted that the head is turned aside, away from the chains and away from viewers. A minister remarked that "she stands with one hand extended in modest self-defense, like the Venus di Medici."[24] Hostile critics—of whom there were few—did not propose another interpretation, but instead argued that the *Greek Slave* did not adequately express its elevated subject. Some found the hands, in fact the entire carriage of the figure, relaxed and at ease, the passionless expression inappropriate for the stressful situation depicted. Judging the face too much in repose, they objected to Powers's decision to give the *Greek Slave* "an air of total unconsciousness."[25]

Hundreds of commentators agreed, however, that the sculpture should not be discussed on aesthetic grounds, but in terms of morality. As Rev. Orville Dewey wrote, in a promotional piece designed to forestall clerical criticism of Powers's naked lady, "There ought to be some reason for exposure *besides* beauty. . . . The highest point in all art . . . (is) to make the spiritual reign over the corporeal; to sink form in ideality. In this particular case, to make the appeal to the soul entirely control the appeal to sense."[26] Most American critics dealt with the statue's nudity by denying it. Facing this totally undraped full-length female figure, they wrote that they saw not her body, but her spirit; that the *Greek Slave*—whose whiteness, too, they interpreted not as mainly aesthetic but as moral—was clothed in a "robe, of purity."[27]

To nineteenth-century Americans, Powers's female nude nevertheless raised the moral issue of how it could decently be viewed. This meant deciding whether women should be allowed to see the sculpture in the presence of men. Despite considerable controversy during the first two years the *Greek Slave* was exhibited, the sculpture was viewed by "promiscuous" audiences of men and women; later audiences were segregated by sex. Arguments over viewing arrangements were particularly bitter in Cincinnati, where Rev. Lyman Beecher led the fight against promiscuous audiences. The flavor of the controversy is suggested by a local headline, "The Greek Slave vs. Modesty!" and by the fact that Nicholas Longworth, Powers's first patron and lifelong friend, refused to attend a private promiscuous showing.[28]

No matter what exhibition arrangements were made, some detractors charged that the *Greek Slave* was indecent because it did not actually express spirituality. According to the *Ladies' Repository*, these critics claimed that "if the chain on her arm . . . were removed, the Greek Slave might be taken for a nymph, or a beautiful woman, preparing for a bath, pausing to muse, in abstraction, on some serious or absent fact."[29] The Boston *Harbinger* agreed: "Remove the chains, and would any spectator . . . be able, to form any distant guess of the special design of the artist? Would any one . . . surmise that it was designed to represent a slave? . . . From the chain alone do we learn that she is a slave."[30] And the *Western Christian Advocate* lamented: "Take off that chain—present no fiction of its being a helpless slave, and what remains but a licentious exhibition?"[31] To these commentators, the only attribute of Powers's nude that suggested his ostensible subject was her chain.

The connection between Powers's enchained female and American slavery was the subject of much comment. Antiabolitionist newspapers characteristically used exhibitions of the *Greek Slave* as occasions to ridicule local antislavery efforts. The New York *Saturday Emporium* mocked: "We have not heard that a single *habeas corpus* has been obtained for her release, though we are certain that the attorney for the Anti-Slavery Society has examined the subject."[32] This satiric concern was echoed in the Cincinnati *Citizen's Advertiser*, which laughingly deplored the fact that in this "city of philanthropists, even of abolitionists," no one had tried to liberate the *Greek Slave*.[33]

The antislavery press, in turn, used showings of the *Greek Slave* as opportunities for propaganda. The *Christian Enquirer* wrote: "It is an impersonation of SLAVERY. This creature, exhibited for sale in the slave market, is a counterpart of thousands of living women. . . . Would that the Greek Slave, as she passes through various portions of our country, might be endowed with power to teach, to arouse, to purify public opinion."[34] Birney's newspaper, which had moved from Cincinnati to Washington, D.C., criticized white women whose racism prevented them from sympathizing with African-American slaves. Describing a visit to the exhibition, it deplored

> the wondrous hardness of that nature which can weep at the sight of an insensiate piece of marble which imagines a helpless virgin chained in the marketplace of brutal lust, and still more brutal cupidity, and yet listens unmoved to the awful story of the American Slave.
>
> There were fair breasts that heaved with genuine sympathy beneath the magic power of the great artist, that have never yet breathed a sigh for their sable sisters at the South![35]

Others implicitly acknowledged the connections between Powers's subject and American slavery by making racial jokes about the contrast between the whiteness of the sculpture and the blackness of African-American slaves. New York congressman Caleb Lyon rhymed:

> A Carolinian, fresh from his plantation
> Gazed till o'ercome with quite a perspiration—
> His brains were racked—something was not right—
> He's never seen a slave girl half so white. [36]

And Minor Kellogg, who was arranging exhibitions of the *Greek Slave*, wrote to Powers that in Baltimore

> A strapping fellow came in and walked up to the statue with an expression of astonishment. After looking for a time steadily at the statue, [he] turned to the boy and asked, "Is this a slave?" "Yes, Sir." After looking for a moment in silence, says, "Why! it ain't black!!" "No," said the boy. "It is a Greek slave and the Greeks are white." "Ah, well," said the man with a self-satisfied expression, "I thought there was some English in her."[37]

The notion that Powers's subject "is of no color or country," that the *Greek Slave* signifies every slave, was forcefully stated in a letter Frederick Douglass published in *The North Star*. Tightly linking Powers's sculpture to abolitionist discourse, this comment interprets the statue in terms of the abolitionists' encoding of the emblem of the enchained supplicant:

> This beautiful and lovely creature . . . [teaches the soul] to detest that depravity in man . . . in the act of ENCHAINING, and degrading to the brute level a being of which this magnificent piece of statuary is but a cold and lifeless resemblance.
>
> We . . . burn with hatred of the cruel TURK who does thus violate the sacred rights of human nature; and places his own diabolical self between GOD and his creature. . . . A human soul in chains; our sister with all her affections aspirations and high capacities, *sold* to the bestial TURK, whoever he may be, and he designs to cast her down from her god-given estate, into the dominion of *things*.[38]

Some viewers, however, read Powers's enchained figure not in reference to African slavery in America but in relation to various aspects of womanhood. Powers himself recalled that, while a boy in Vermont, he had been "haunted in dreams by a white figure of a woman—white as snow from head to foot and standing upon some sort of pedestal." He "could not get near to it for the water which seemed deep and running . . . my desire was always intense to come nearer." Although this fantasy would seem to suggest his first sculpture, an *Eve*, he repeatedly connected it with the *Greek Slave*, sometimes called an Eve in chains.[39] To post-Freudian readers, Powers's recollection suggests the sexual significance his nude may have held for him and for his nineteenth-century audiences.

At first glance, the placement of the *Greek Slave*'s chains, like that of her hands, appears to protect her. But because the chains are her master's property, instead of barring her sexual violation, they virtually guarantee it. This message had profound significance in nineteenth-century America. Viewing Powers's sculpture, American audiences saw a woman facing a fate that many really did judge worse than death.

Noting that nineteenth-century commentaries repeatedly refer to the figure's passivity, and that nineteenth-century sexual etiquette demanded passivity of women, Linda Hyman has suggested that the *Greek Slave* was the subject of erotic Victorian fantasies.[40] Hyman points to a male viewer who wrote: "Loud-talking men are hushed into silence at what they themselves wonder; those who come to speak learned and utter ecstasies of dilettantism sink into corners alone that they may silently gaze in pleasing penance for their audacity."[41] And she quotes the musings of a female viewer:

> The history of her fallen country, her Greek home, her Greek lover, her Greek friends, her capture, her exposure in the public marketplace; the freezing of every drop of her young blood beneath the libidinous gaze of shameless traffickers in beauty; the breaking up of the deep waters of her heart; their calm settling down over the hopeless ruins, flowed noiselessly into the rapt ear of our mind. Voices from a group near roused us from our stupor, when we found *we had been in this spell for five hours.*[42]

The subjectivity and intensity of these comments suggests that, viewing the *Greek Slave*, both men and women may have responded in terms of their sexual concerns. If this is true, doubtless Powers's nude in chains presented —life-sized and in three dimensions—the sexual bondage that the anti-slavery emblem encoded.

To some the *Greek Slave* represented ideal womanhood. A male poet versified Powers's creation as

> The embodiment of all a poet ever,
> In his holiest reveries of Woman,
> Saw, or musing sung![43]

But Lucy Stone, who had begun lecturing for the American Anti-Slavery
Society, saw the *Greek Slave* as representative of woman's degraded condition. Recalling the force of her insight—which replicated Angelina Grimké's
earlier sense of identification with the supplicant slave—Stone later wrote:

> I went to see [the *Greek Slave*] one morning. No other person was present.
> There it stood in the silence, with fettered hands and half-averted face—so
> emblematic of woman. I remember how the hot tears came to my eyes at the
> thought of millions of women who must be freed. At the evening meeting I
> poured all my heart out about it. At the close, the Reverend Samuel May . . .
> admonished me that, however true, it was out of place in an antislavery meet-
> ing. . . . After thinking a little, I said, "Well, Mr. May, I was a woman before I
> was an abolitionist. I must speak for the women."[44]

Stone subsequently split her lectures between antislavery and feminism.

The New York *Tribune*, too, in an interpretation recalling the triple
vision of womanhood that Sarah Grimké had earlier proposed in *Letters on
the Equality of the Sexes*, read the *Greek Slave* as a critique of woman's
oppression:

> In the Eve, which is not yet finished, Mr. Powers has made a mother of
> humanity; the Greek Slave represents her after the Fall has set its brand upon
> the race, suffering the chains of slavery and the brutal violence of her captors;
> when will the sculptor embody in marble Woman such as she is destined to be
> in the days of the Redemption, when the ransomed of the Lord shall return
> with everlasting joy upon their heads, and sorrow and sighing shall flee away?[45]

While Powers's countrymen flocked to see the *Greek Slave* and discuss its
significance, in Florence the artist began work on a new project. Hopeful of
creating a sculpture that would win acceptance as America's "national
statue," he designed a triumphant Liberty.[46] Powers had difficulty representing the Despotism his heroic figure had vanquished, however, because of
the widespread acceptance of abolitionist iconography, where chains signified slavery and broken chains signified emancipation.

Describing his new work-in-progress, in 1848 Powers wrote that his subject was

> a strapping lass . . . lightly draped down to just above the knees—her arms
> bare and her posture erect, holding on her finger ends, with the left hand, and
> high above her shoulder the emblem cap—below which and beneath her left

foot (which is advanced in front), appears a diadem — emblem (at least in this case) of despotic power. . . .

The effect of the whole is as one confidently addressing a multitude.[47]

Over the next seven years, Powers reworked his design. As he revised his opinions of the revolutions that were shaking Europe, he changed the symbols representing Liberty, transforming his "strapping lass" from a Liberty of republican insurrection into a Liberty of republican institutions. He changed the emblems representing Despotism as he revised his views of the sharpening slavery controversy at home.

Reconceived as *America*, in its surviving form, a plaster model in the collection of the National Museum of America Art, Powers's sculpture is partially nude and slightly larger than life size (fig. 20). A loose classical drapery hangs from a thin strap over her left shoulder, is caught around her hips, and falls to her right ankle before looping in deep folds over the fasces (a bundle of rods signaling the authority of classical Rome); surmounted with a laurel wreath, these form her support. Her wavy hair is pulled back, and her head is crowned with a diadem bearing thirteen stars. Standing with her weight on her right foot, her right arm resting lightly on the wreath, she thrusts her left foot forward to crush the emblem of Despotism under the heel of her classical sandal. She raises her left arm above her head with her open fingers extending upward and looks forward with calmness and confidence. This version differs from earlier ones because here the Liberty Cap has been omitted and the wreath and crown have been added. Apparently, except for the emblem of Despotism, this plaster is like the finished marble, which was destroyed by fire in 1865.[48]

Offering a rationale for making his *America* female, Powers defined womanhood in terms of the spiritual values that the patriarchy assigned to women. Earlier he had written that "peace, meekness, love, modesty and self denial distinguish a woman from the . . . masculine." Now he explained that

> Perhaps by associating the beauties and advantages of our government with the form and attributes (as far as I have been able to represent them) of woman, the hearts of our woman-loving and woman-respecting people might be inspired with . . . love for our institutions, and the wisest and finest government upon the earth.[49]

Despite this endorsement of traditional gender patterns, by adopting the *adlocutio* gesture associated with classical orators, Powers inevitably sug-

Fig. 20. Hiram Powers, *America* (or) *Liberty* (1848–1850).

gested the upheaval the antislavery feminists were causing as they followed Fanny Wright's lead and mounted the public platform.[50] Powers was aware of American feminism. Apparently ambivalent about "the woman question," he wrote to one friend charging that women dominate men and ridiculing their entrance into public life; to another, he acknowledged the legitimacy and seriousness of feminist demands: "Much can be done and ought to be done no doubt, and I hope it will be done to place womankind upon proper footing with us."[51]

Powers changed his mind repeatedly about how to represent the Despotism that *America* crushed underfoot. In 1848, he decided that it should be a diadem. Then, worried that this choice might offend the English, and reasoning that he should not foreclose the possibility of attracting a British patron, he reexamined this decision. In 1850, he considered using broken chains but feared that the abolitionists had appropriated this symbol for their exclusive use. Powers wanted to choose an attribute that the public could understand, but he also wanted to distance his sculpture from the antislavery movement: "I shall substitute a scepter for the diadem . . . and I would add chains under it and the foot if I thought it would not be noticed as having some relation to slavery in America—indeed if I could venture to do so, I would place chains only under the foot, for chains would fully express the sentiment intended."[52]

It is understandable that before Emancipation, when the United States remained among the shrinking group of nations still tolerating slavery, artists found it almost impossible to create a national iconography expressing the idea of America as a land of liberty. For decades, the abolitionists had been addressing both verbally and visually the contradiction between these significations of America. One antislavery illustration, designed "to demonstrate the hypocrisy and villainy of professing to be votaries of Liberty, while, at the same time, we encourage . . . the most ignoble slavery," showed a "Goddess, in a melancholy attitude" flanked by symbols of America and Liberty, "looking majestically sad at the African Slaves" (fig. 21).[53] A poem read:

> Hail! 'tis the Sovreign Genius of our land;
> A splendid banner waves in her right hand,
> Bedecked with many brilliant stars of gold;
> And as the light and graceful curls unfold,
> We see emblazoned, as it floats on high,
> The glorious words of Freedom! Liberty! . . .

Fig. 21. Frontispiece for Thomas Branigan, *Penitential Tyrant* (1807).

And now, our eyes to the dark side we turn,
Where, deep in shadow, clearly we discern
The left hand holds a strong and heavy chain,
Attached to which, is dragged a lengthened train
Of wretched beings, doomed for life to sigh,
And raise to Heaven the sad and bitter cry
Of Bondage! Bondage! Slavery!

Assuming the time-honored role of supplicant, the poet pleads that slavery be abolished so that America can rightfully appear as the exemplar of liberty:

We would not mar the beauty of thy form,
We would not mutilate thy powerful arm;
But rather supplicating, bend the knee,
Beg thee to drop the chain, and set the captive free,
Then would the mighty Genius of our land,
In full and glorious perfection stand.[54]

A *Liberty Bell* poem, written in response to rumors in the press about Powers's work-in-progress, addressed the artist directly. "To Powers, the Sculptor: Upon Hearing that He Was Employed on a Statue of California and One of America" treats the problem of attempting to create a statue of America that signifies Liberty while slavery remains institutionalized. The poet's advice to Powers is that he should delay:

Hold back thy work, bright son of Genius, hold!
Let not the spotless statue come too soon!
. . . . . . . . . . . . . . . . . . . . . . . .
Hold back America! or give her true,
Clasping the viper to her deep-stung heart!
Oh hold her back till her warped soul renew
Its virgin faith, — then give her pure, oh Art![55]

Still searching for a patron, still uncertain about how to represent vanquished Despotism, Powers did hold *America* back. In 1853, the carving was complete except for a space under the left heel of the figure. Powers proposed incorporating broken chains into his design and, writing to Longworth in Cincinnati, attempted to make a distinction between the meaning of chains and manacles. Acknowledging that broken manacles had become accepted as the symbol of African emancipation, he asserted that broken chains had no such signification: "Do not start! They are not manacles—no allusion to the 'Peculiar Institution' but simply an emblem of despotism or tyranny."[56]

After the Kansas-Nebraska Act had effectively repealed the Compromise of 1850 and opened the way for the extension of slavery, however, Powers expressed his fury by verbally adopting abolitionist imagery.

> How would it do to make a new statue of "America" . . . the principal figure holding on high a banner with the words, All are born free and equal and in the other a cat-o-nine tails. The other figure—a "nigger" kneeling at her feet and imploring for mercy. The hand cuffs and chains could all be done in marble and the effect would be beautiful. The pedestal should be a sugar hogshead standing on a bale of cotton.

Bitterly, he proposed another alternative: "How would it do to make a new statue of *America*, the principal figure . . . hugging to her bosom a mass of fetters."[57]

Powers finally won a federal commission in 1855. Although *America* was not named as the work the government would purchase, he promptly carved chains beneath the foot of his "national statue." When news of his design became public, however, it was attacked in the press as abolitionist propaganda: "Does a half-naked female figure . . . with one hand pointing upwards, and one foot trampling on the symbol of emancipated Slavery, truthfully, historically typify America?"[58]

In three years of complex and bitter negotiations, the federal government neither definitively accepted nor absolutely rejected *America*. Powers was convinced that this vacillation resulted from his decision to represent Tyranny with a chain. "If chains (tyranny) cannot with propriety be placed under the foot of an allegorical figure of a Republic, then the emblem can never be used with propriety—and let us say—there is no such thing as tyranny—or if there is—we must not allude to it—by any word or emblem —lest we offend our Southern brethren."[59]

He had begun to revise his ideas about the threat to the Union. In another savage parody, Powers expressed his newly acquired conviction that slavery, and not the abolitionists, threatened the nation. Presenting multiple interpretations of his sculpture, he began with his initial notion that *America* represents liberty. Powers then echoed abolitionist critiques, caricaturing his *Greek Slave* as he envisioned *America* a slave-holding tyrant. "I could see another allegory of my country—America flourishing aloft the cat-o-nine tails and the bludgeon, leaning upon a whipping post, and trampling upon the cap of Liberty!" Recalling both the *Greek Slave* and Wedgwood's enchained supplicant, Powers went on to describe *America* as enslaved and enchained: "My first conception of America now lies prostrate in my studio. . . . In a few more years . . . the chains now under her foot may be welded upon her arms, and she herself—prostrate and helpless may be the corpse of freedom and exposed to the mockery of all the despots of the world."[60]

When Buchanan won the 1856 election, Powers fulfilled his government contract by sending other examples of his work to Washington. Still lacking a buyer for *America*, still hoping that she would be acknowledged our "national statue" at last, until Emancipation he maintained that her broken chains symbolized solely the national struggle for independence. Then, in 1865, Powers wrote that the broken chain represented her triumphs over both despotisms: British rule and slavery.

> America with the broken chains of slavery under foot, the Union unbroken and crowned with victory and herself thanking God for all. . . . It represents our country with her foot on slavery, broken and destroyed forever. It is quite true that I did not comprehend our slave system purposely in the design. The broken chains referred to the way in which we got our national liberty. But the statue herself fully comprehends both.[61]

Powers's triumphant *America* suggests the third version of womankind that Sarah Grimké had envisioned and that the New York *Tribune* had called for after seeing the *Greek Slave*: A "marble Woman such as she is destined to be in the days of the Redemption, when the ransomed of the Lord shall return with everlasting joy upon their heads, and sorrow and sighing shall flee away."[62] But *America* is a sculpture Powers's fellow Americans never saw. It did not decorate the Capitol as he had dreamed, nor was it displayed in England or continental Europe. What nineteenth-century Americans saw and remembered was not Powers's triumphant chain-breaking woman, but his female slave in chains.

Public responses to the *Greek Slave*, which was featured at the London Crystal Palace Exhibition in 1851, must have exacerbated Powers's difficulties choosing a symbol of Despotism for his *America*. The British audiences at the Crystal Palace apparently accepted the abolitionist encoding that identified link chains with slavery and broken chains with Emancipation; certainly the popular press forced acknowledgment of the connections between the *Greek Slave* and American slavery.

The London humor magazine *Punch*, noting that the American exhibition

SAMPLE OF AMERICAN MANUFACTURE.

Fig. 22. Illustration in *Punch, or the London Charivari* 20 (January-June 1851), p. 209.

at the Crystal Palace featured an eagle, first printed a sketch that recalls both Wedgwood's supplicant and the double emblem commemorating British emancipation (fig. 22). It shows kneeling slaves in chains facing a whip-wielding eagle-headed overseer; a black male and female stand shackled in the background. An accompanying article discusses the relationship between the *Greek Slave*, the focal point of the American exhibit, and slavery in the United States: "We have the Greek Captive in dead stone —why not the Virginia Slave in living ebony? . . . Let America hire a black or two to stand in manacles, as American manufacture protected by the American eagle."[63]

*Punch* then published the image that irrevocably links Powers's *Greek Slave* to the emblem of the female supplicant: John Tenniel's cartoon "The Virginian Slave, Intended as a Companion to Powers' 'Greek Slave'" (fig. 23). The "Virginian Slave" mirrors the black skin, the African features, the clasped hands, the imploring upward glance, the seminudity, even the ankle irons and the elongated links of chain that characterize the design of the abolitionists' female supplicant. She does not kneel in profile, however, but stands in a three-quarter view that reverses the posture of the *Greek Slave*. Although lowered, her hands are folded like those of the supplicant, and like the supplicant, she is partially draped. But instead of Greek artifacts, her supporting post is draped with an American flag. Decorated with whips and chains, her pedestal bears the words "E Pluribus Unum."[64] Visually, "The Virginian Slave" connects traditional British and American

**THE VIRGINIAN SLAVE.**

INTENDED AS A COMPANION TO POWER'S "GREEK SLAVE."

Fig. 23. Illustration in *Punch, or the London Charivari* 20 (January–June 1851), p. 236.

antislavery iconography with Hiram Powers's sculpture. Politically, it condemns as hypocritical both the American celebration of the *Greek Slave* as a
moral statement dissociated from the issue of American slavery and the
claim that America is a land of liberty.

Publication of Tenniel's cartoon provided African-American abolitionists
in London with the occasion for a public demonstration. The *Liberator*
reports that on a day when the queen attended the Crystal Palace, the black
activist William Wells Brown laid *Punch*'s "Virginian Slave" in front of
Powers's sculpture, announcing loudly: "As an American fugitive slave, I
place this 'Virginia Slave' by the side of the 'Greek Slave,' as its most fitting
companion."[65] Appropriately, a fugitive slave woman participated in this
demonstration. The light-skinned Ellen Craft had made a sensational escape
from Georgia with her dark-skinned husband William by masquerading as a
young planter while he played her servant. After arriving safely in Boston,
the couple appeared together on the lecture platform. According to one
commentator, Ellen Craft's "very particular account" of their dramatic escape
"was told in so simple and artless a manner as must have carried conviction
to the mind of everyone present." After passage of the 1850 Fugitive Slave
Law, the Crafts fled abroad. One of the few fugitive slave women in England,
Ellen Craft sparked popular interest; her portrait in male attire appeared in
*The Illustrated London News* and later decorated the Crafts's slave narrative.
At the Crystal Palace, she promenaded all day on the arm of a white male
reformer. This arrangement, Garrison's British correspondent explains, "was
purposely made in order that . . . it might be shown that we regarded . . .
[the fugitives] as our equals, and honored them for their heroic escape from
Slavery."[66]

All five full-length, full-size versions of the *Greek Slave* that Powers's
studio completed before Emancipation are bound by link chains. Powers
persisted in carving these chains despite the wishes of his first patron, who
had written "that a fac-similie in works of art is not desirable" and requested
that in subsequent versions of the *Greek Slave* he "omit the chains, or if not
omit them altogether, . . . substitute some kind of cord." Powers's persistence appears odd in light of what his later correspondence recorded: he
knew that link chains had not been used on Greek women in Turkish slave
markets. In accepting a commission for yet another *Greek Slave* in 1869,
however, Powers implied that although he was aware that the chains hanging
from the wrists of the five versions of the *Greek Slave* were not historically
correct, he felt that they were legitimate aesthetically. He wrote that this
sixth slave, however, would be different: "I regard the substitution of the

regular *manacles* for the rather ornamental than real chain in former repeti-
tions of the 'Greek Slave' as a decided advantage, since it distinguishes it
from all the others, and is really more to the purpose."[67] By then, his
troubles with *America* apparently had taught him that to the public mind at
home, link chains signified slavery. His reference to the ornamental quality
of the chains of the earlier versions of the *Greek Slave* may refer to their
conformity to this artistic convention, as well as to the decorativeness of the
carved links.

The *Greek Slave*, Powers's most famous work, signifies slavery by using
the iconography that the abolitionists had popularized. But while it incorporates the nudity, the piety, and the chains of the supplicant slave emblem,
the *Greek Slave* presents a version of womanhood that counters the model of
the Woman and Sister advanced by the antislavery feminists. Angelina
Grimké, concluding that traditional passive women were slaves, interpreted
the emblemized supplicant as active; L. Maria Child, exploring the idea that
slaves resembled traditionally passive women, wrote fiction presenting a
slave woman of mixed race in the role of traditional supplicant and a free
white woman like herself in the role of the active liberator figured on the
double emblem; Sojourner Truth and Harriet Jacobs, recognizing white
patriarchal definitions as exclusionary and repressive, redefined womanhood on the ground of their own experiences as active self-liberating liberators. All of these women presented themselves as actively combating tyranny. The antislavery feminists read the supplicant slave emblems as
encouraging women to overthrow the despotisms of slavery, racism, and
sexism through public struggle, and in their discourse they endlessly replicated the emblems in an effort to win adherents to their cause.

In contrast, Powers's female slave was interpreted by everyone who saw
her as a victim, variously identified as a slave or as a woman who, through
Christian resignation, transcended the tyranny of slavery or of patriarchy.
From this perspective, Hiram Powers's *Greek Slave* appears a companion
piece to Harriet Beecher Stowe's Uncle Tom. Like the white Americans who
were to celebrate Tom's Christian resignation as a black man's most appropriate response to his oppression, the popular writer Grace Greenwood, who
saw Powers's *Greek Slave* as an "embodiment of womanhood triumphant in
sorrow and in degradation," celebrated her Christian resignation. "Oh, joy
in the midst of her desolation, the will of her tyrant cannot subjugate her
love, his base chain is not upon her spirit!!"[68] But Elizabeth Barrett Browning condemned it. Her sonnet "Hiram Powers' *Greek Slave*," the most

important critique of the passivity of Powers's enchained captive, addresses the appropriateness of resignation as a response to oppression.[69] Barrett Browning's poem begins with a static situation. Noting the belief that "ideal beauty cannot enter the house of anguish," her speaker describes that beauty, "An alien image with enshackled hands / Called the Greek Slave," who stands outside, "On the threshold." Although "shadowed" by her proximity to "the house of anguish," her "passionless perfection" is not "darkened"; the entire tableau appears, the poet writes, as if the artist intended to "confront man's crimes in different lands / With man's ideal sense."

Using a series of verbs in the imperative voice, the poet then calls for an art that can "Pierce to the centre . . . and break up . . . / The serfdom of this world." She urges the "fair stone" to "Appeal . . . against man's wrong!" to "catch up in thy divine face . . . grief"—and not only "East grief" (the sorrow of the enslaved Greeks) but "west" grief (the sorrow of the Africans enslaved in America); to "strike and shame the strong, / By thunders of white silence, overthrown."

In this carefully constructed sonnet, the octave poses the problem presented by the juxtaposition of "ideal beauty" and "the house of anguish"; in the sestet, this is resolved by the claim that an active beauty resulting from an impassioned art can overthrow oppression. Asserting the value of activity, this poem implicitly condemns the Christian resignation of Powers's *Greek Slave.* Urging instead a vital political art, Barrett Browning—who opposed slavery and had published in Chapman's *Liberty Bell*—presents a critique of Powers's sculptural celebration of woman's passivity in the face of oppression.[70]

Hiram Powers's *Greek Slave* displays the iconography of the antislavery feminists but reencodes it. His statue was praised for showing an enchained woman submitting her body, elevating her spirit, and, turning inward, practicing Christian resignation on earth, certain of a reward in heaven. Whether Powers's sculpture was interpreted as a quintessential slave or as a quintessential woman, it was generally understood to valorize a response to oppression that opposed the activism urged by the free black and white antislavery feminists. Although its nudity challenged one group of American gender conventions, by fundamentally reversing the signification of the iconography of the antislavery feminists, Powers's *Greek Slave* pressed that powerful iconography into the service of patriarchal discourse.

# CHAPTER SIX
# Nathaniel Hawthorne's
# *The Scarlet Letter*

*Picture . . . Hawthorne's grand woman, in all her native dignity, standing calm and
self-poised.*

— *Elizabeth Cady Stanton*[1]

Perhaps the most complex and influential literary work that uses the antislavery women's iconography to reject their ideology is *The Scarlet Letter.*[2]
Tracing the abolitionists' discursive codes in literary works is, obviously,
different from tracing them in sculptural icons. In Hawthorne's romance, the
emblem of the antislavery women functions as a subtext to Hester Prynne's
emblem.

The narrator of *The Scarlet Letter* addresses, and invites his audience to
address, the issue of signification by overtly playing with the meanings of
Hesters's "A." Intended to brand her as an adultress, after seven years it
means *able* to a portion of Boston's population. Hester herself, the narrator
tells us, has been encoded to signify "woman's frailty and sinful passion,"
and at times this is how she understands herself (p. 79). But behind these
shifting interpretations of Hester and her emblem lie the shifting interpretations of the emblem of the female slave. Dramatizing the notion that womanhood is not a natural but a conventional construct — as Sojourner Truth,
Harriet Jacobs, and the other female slaves excluded from this category

testified—Hawthorne's book begins by presenting a woman publicly exposed, a figure made familiar by the abolitionists. Hester Prynne's ordeal on the scaffold, and the events that follow, signal her exclusion from the category of true womanhood. Although its focus later shifts, _The Scarlet Letter_ recurrently presents the structures of the antislavery women's discourse. Repeatedly addressing the concerns of the antislavery women, the book explores Hester's ideas, and those of the narrator, in relation to her identity (her womanhood) and her membership in the community (her sisterhood).

In _The Scarlet Letter_, as in the speeches, writings, and images of the antislavery feminists, enchaining and exposure signify woman's oppression. Hawthorne, however, does not use them as a signal that woman should mount a public effort for self-liberation. Although his book ends with a kind of restoration of Hester as a Woman and a Sister, she does not achieve this identity by asserting the antislavery feminists' ideology or by struggling for her rights in the public sphere. Instead, learning that she should accept her lot, confident that someday, somehow, things will change for the better, Hester conforms at last to patriarchal definitions of womanhood. _The Scarlet Letter_ is, on one level, a critique of patriarchal ideologies and structures, but it is a critique that seriously considers the new feminist definitions of womanhood and, rejecting them, replicates traditional imagery and endorses patriarchal notions. Hawthorne's narrator openly discusses the reencoding of both the embroidered emblem and of Hester herself. But the presence of the emblem of the enchained female slave, which functions as a subtext of Hawthorne's emblem, is never mentioned; its reencoding is covert.

Recently, studies of Hawthorne's life and of the selfhood that he expressed in his writings have explored beyond the walls of his legendary "dismal and squalid chamber" at Salem. They have, for example, established that, like other white Americans of his place and time, he had everyday contact with African-Americans and that, in addition to sharing the common awareness of the slavery question, he was more than routinely familiar with Cuban slavery and something of an expert concerning African colonization and the slave trade.[3]

As a writer of fiction, Hawthorne chose to center his work on moral issues; repeatedly, on one level, his subject was psychological slavery. Although the antislavery activists were denouncing slavery as a tyranny of both flesh and spirit—and his brother-in-law Horace Mann was condemning slavery on the floor of Congress as a system in which "man claims authority over the body, mind, and soul of his fellowmen"—Hawthorne never did connect slavery with the bondage that was his chosen subject. He never did identify the "unpardonable sin" that obsessed him with "the American national sin" that the Garrisonians were denouncing.[4] Where Hiram Powers had distanced an enchained white woman in space and called her a *Greek Slave*, Nathaniel Hawthorne distanced an enchained white woman in time and called her Hester Prynne.

Hawthorne was, of course, familiar with the abolitionists. Even conservative Salem, although not a Garrisonian center like Boston, had its share of antislavery controversy. His black townswomen had been first in the nation to organize a female antislavery society, and they later joined an interracial organization that sent delegates to all three Conventions of American Women Against Slavery. At the 1839 convention, Clarissa C. Lawrence, a black Salem delegate, took the floor to point out that she, and other blacks, "meet the monster prejudice *every where*." She urged the white delegates, "Place yourselves, dear friends, in our stead." Four years earlier, racist, antiabolitionist white Salemites had mobbed an antislavery meeting planned for Howard Street Church. When the Grimkés had come to town in 1837, however, local antislavery women successfully scheduled four full days of activities. Angelina Grimké wrote that she and her sister spoke at the Friends' Meeting House, met with "colored members of the Seaman's and Moral Reform Society," addressed an audience of more than a thousand at the Howard Street Meeting House, and talked with children and adults at the "colored Sabbath School."[5]

Although Sophia Peabody, the townswoman Hawthorne would later marry, represented just the sort of person that the abolitionist activists were trying to influence, she did not involve herself in the female antislavery movement in Salem or elsewhere. Long before her marriage, the invalided Sophia had lived for a year and a half on a Cuban sugar plantation. In the "Cuba Journals" (letters she and her sister Mary, her companion, had written home to Salem), the Peabody sisters recorded their experiences and impressions of slavery. They commented on the overwhelming black presence and on the picturesqueness of the Africans at play, on the oppressiveness of slave labor, on the brutality of the system, on the sexual exploitation of slave women, and even on the practice of infanticide. This Cuban experience motivated Mary Peabody to become an active abolitionist, but it prompted Sophia to decide not even to think about slavery. Dwelling on this subject, she wrote, "would certainly counteract the beneficent influences" of her Cuban visit; and her faith in God reassured her "that he makes up to every being the measure of happiness which he loses thro' the instrumentality of others. I try to realize how much shorter time is, than eternity and then endeavour to lose myself in other subjects of thought."[6]

Back in Boston, before her marriage, Sophia Peabody was part of a grouping that included Maria White, who converted her fiancé James Russell Lowell to abolitionism, and the Sturgis sisters, members, as was White, of the Female Anti-Slavery Society. At the bookstore of her sister Elizabeth, she met with other "advanced" women to attend Margaret Fuller's Conversations and discuss topics such as art, ethics, great men—and Woman. After marrying Hawthorne and moving to Concord, her circle included the Alcotts and Lydian Emerson, members of the local Society. But Sophia Peabody Hawthorne distanced herself from abolitionism. She expressed her hostility to women's antislavery activities when, during her pregnancy, she wrote to her mother that she planned to engage "the ladies of the antislavery society" to sew a layette because "I have no manner of scruple about making them take as little as possible; while I could not think of not giving full and ample price to a poor person, or a seamstress by profession."[7]

She rejected not only the work of the female abolitionists, but also the feminist ideas Margaret Fuller voiced in "The Great Lawsuit," the most important statement on the "woman question" to follow Sarah Grimké's *Letters on the Equality of the Sexes*. Commenting to her mother about Fuller's polemic, Sophia Peabody Hawthorne writes that Fuller fails to understand that "Had there never been false and profane marriages, there would not only be no commotion about woman's rights, but it would be Heaven here at once. Even before I was married, however, I could never feel the slightest interest in this movement [women's rights]."[8] Sophia Peabody Hawthorne then voiced her disapproval of women who, following in the Grimkés' footsteps, brave the public sphere and speak from the platform: "it was always a shock to me to have women mount the rostrum. Home, I think, is the greatest arena for women."[9]

Years later, she indignantly responded when her sister Elizabeth Peabody, who had written an antislavery pamphlet, mailed it to the Hawthornes' young daughter, Una. Attacking radicals like the abolitionists and the feminists who advocated breaking oppressive laws in the name of a higher law, Sophia Peabody Hawthorne wrote, "I consider it a very dangerous and demoralizing doctrine and have always called it 'transcendental slang.'" Announcing that she had not shown the pamphlet to Una and that she would not, she stated that she was familiar with reports of slave sales and did not believe her sister's accusations that slave women were routinely subjected to sexual abuse: "And you would display before . . . [my daughter's] great, innocent eyes a naked slave girl on a block at auction (which I am sure is an exaggeration for I have read of those auctions often and even the worst facts are never so bad as absolute nudity)."[10] This correspondence reveals that Sophia Peabody Hawthorne followed neither Angelina Grimké's advice to act against slavery nor Catharine Beecher's advice to influence men to take action against it.

Some of the Hawthornes' neighbors, however, were deeply involved in antislavery feminist activities. In Salem in the spring of 1848—shortly after Hawthorne's persistence had won him an appointment as surveyor of the Custom House and the family had moved from Concord back to their home town—the first women's rights petitions in Massachusetts were circulated. For six years, with the help of Phebe King of Danvers, Mary Upton Ferrin drafted, circulated, and submitted petitions. Literally standing in Angelina Grimké's footsteps, in 1850 she addressed a committee of the Massachusetts legislature. Using what was by now a staple of feminist rhetoric, Ferrin likened the condition of woman to that of the slave. Although widely ridiculed, Ferrin was encouraged by a local minister turned politician, Rev. Charles W. Upham—the same man who led the local Whig attack against Hawthorne's federal appointment in 1849. Aiding him was Phebe King's son Daniel, a U.S. congressman. Salem politics dictated that feminism's strongest supporters were Hawthorne's bitterest political enemies.[11]

The reformers made consistent gains in their efforts to bring the slavery question home to New England throughout the years of Hawthorne's literary apprenticeship. They succeeded in alerting everyone to the 1835 attack on the antislavery women, and many agreed with Angelina Grimké that the mobbed women were martyrs. This was the term that the British writer Harriet Martineau, who had met the members of the Boston Female Anti-Slavery Society, used to describe them in the *London and Westminster Review.* Attacked in the newspapers for endorsing the women's antislavery principles, Martineau cut short her American excursion shortly after the riot. Four years later, when the women were again mobbed in Philadelphia, reform Boston gossiped about Maria Weston Chapman's collapse after her failed attempt to speak at Pennsylvania Hall—her voice drowned out by the mob surrounding the building and her red shawl flaming against the Quaker gray worn by the besieged abolitionists trapped within.[12]

Other well-publicized incidents involved abolitionist efforts to rescue fugitive slaves. In 1845, Jonathan Walker, a white Massachusetts sea captain, was arrested and jailed in Florida for aiding fugitives. Convicted,

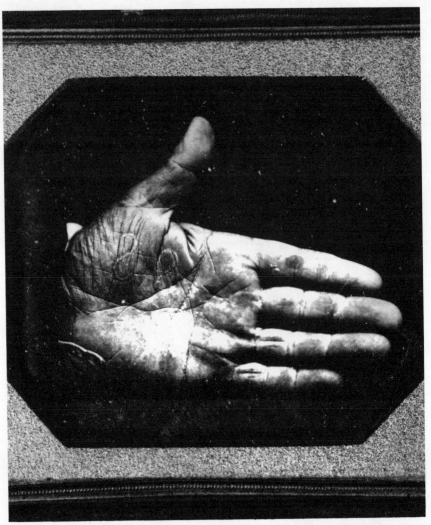

Fig. 24. *The Branded Hand of Captain Jonathan Walker* (ca. 1845).

Walker was punished by being enchained, displayed on the pillory, and branded on the hand with the letters *SS* (slave stealer). Back home, he went on the antislavery lecture circuit, recounting his harrowing experience and displaying his "branded hand," which was daguerrotyped by Southworth and Hawes (fig. 24). Walker's ordeal inspired John Greenleaf Whittier to write a poem that elevates the brand by likening it to armorial hatchments and reversing its signification from negative to positive, from "slave stealer" to "salvation to the slave." In 1848, the slave emblem was transformed into a living tableau by the capture of the schooner *Pearl*. Mary and Emily

Edmondson, two young black sisters, had been seized when the schooner
was caught transporting a group of fugitive slaves to freedom. To raise money
for their manumission, Henry Ward Beecher invited his congregation to
attend a mock slave auction where the audience could simultaneously experience the delights of beneficence by helping emancipate slaves while expe-
riencing the delights of sin by bidding for females standing on the block.
The widely publicized Plymouth Church "auction" of the Edmondsons
—and later, of other fugitive slave women and girls—caused a sensation.
The Edmondsons' would-be rescuers, however, were not so fortunate as
Beecher's "slaves." After a celebrated trial, Captain Edward Sayer and Mate
Daniel Drayton were convicted. Sentenced to heavy fines they could not pay,
the men spent four years in jail before being pardoned.[13]

Two of these sensational events personally involved members of Sophia
Peabody Hawthorne's family. In 1835, Hawthorne's future sister-in-law Elizabeth Peabody had been a guest in the house where Martineau was staying
and had burned the Boston newspapers to spare the Englishwoman the
embarrassment of reading their attacks. Martineau later wrote that Peabody
had begged her to modify her antislavery sentiments in order to retrieve at
least a degree of respectability. When Martineau refused, her American
tour collapsed. In the case of the *Pearl*, Hawthorne's brother-in-law Horace
Mann defended Sayers and Drayton in court. As a literate New Englander,
Hawthorne would doubtless have been aware of these highly publicized
incidents; as Sophia Peabody's husband, he had direct knowledge of two of
them.[14]

Hawthorne knew the reformers well. He did not like them much. An 1835
journal entry testifies to his lack of sympathy for them and for their causes:

> A sketch to be given of a modern reformer—a type of the extreme doctrines on
> the subject of slaves, cold-water, and all that. He goes about the street
> haranging most eloquently, and is on the point of making many converts, when
> his labors are suddenly interrupted by the appearance of a keeper of a mad-
> house, where he has escaped. Much may be made of this idea.[15]

After his brief stay at Brook Farm, Hawthorne sketched the reformers in
more than a half-dozen short pieces. "Earth's Holocaust," which condemns
them most fully, presents a vision of ultimate destruction not uncommon in
his time, and commonplace in our own. Here the world is destroyed not by
accident or by oppressors desperate to maintain their power, but by reformers whose attacks on social corruption ultimately consume mankind's most
valuable achievements.[16]

Women's rights reformers appeared repeatedly in Hawthorne's writings years before he created in Zenobia of the *Blithedale Romance* a fictional feminist who betrays both her sister and herself. As early as 1830, he published a biographical piece so unsympathetic to Anne Hutchinson that it mandates a careful examination of his apparent approval of her in *The Scarlet Letter*. In this early work, Hawthorne's narrator states that he is repelled by women who make themselves intellectually visible—even by writing for publication: "There is a delicacy . . . that perceives, or fancies, a sort of impropriety in the display of a woman's natal mind to the gaze of the world, with indications by which its inmost secrets may be searched out."[17]

In "The Gentle Boy" (1832), Hawthorne cast as a woman the most prominent Quaker exemplar of "unbridled fanaticism." Ilbrahim's mother, Catherine, "neglectful of the holiest trust which can be committed to a woman," abandons her son in response to her driving need to testify against persecution (and to experience it).[18] In "A New Adam and Eve" (1843), Hawthorne follows a pair of newly created innocents through nineteenth-century Boston. Entering the legislature, Adam seats Eve in the speaker's chair, and the narrator comments that "he thus exemplifies Man's intellect, moderated by Woman's tenderness and moral sense! Were such the legislation of the world, there would be no need of State Houses, Capitols, Halls of Parliament." These words, although appearing to endorse political feminism, also enunciate a gendered ideology that assigns intellect to males and morality and emotion to females.[19]

The opposition to feminism is more direct in "The Hall of Fantasy," also published in 1843. Despite a disclaimer, by identifying only Abigail Folsom among the reformers, Hawthorne's narrator suggests that women who defy tradition are insane. (Famous for speechifying at antislavery meetings, Folsom was generally considered quite mad; Emerson called her "the flea of the conventions.") Female reformers concerned with women's rights are openly criticized in Hawthorne's "A Christmas Banquet" (1844). Here the narrator includes among his misfits an ideological feminist who has "driven herself to the verge of madness by dark broodings on the wrongs of her sex, and its exclusion from a proper field of action."[20]

In light of this hostility to feminist reformers, it is surprising that in *The Scarlet Letter* the first view of Hester standing on the pillory recalls the antislavery feminists and their emblem of the Woman and Sister. Of course, Hawthorne's terms are different from theirs: he identifies a different cast of characters and locates them within a different temporal framework.

Yet the women we have been examining had repeatedly related their struggle for self-definition to similar struggles in the seventeenth century, the period Hawthorne chose for his romance. Responding to the clerical attack against women's participation in public life, in *Letters on the Equality of the Sexes* Sarah Grimké had likened the Puritan persecution of "witches" to the abuse heaped on her and the other antislavery feminists. Grimké predicted that in a freer future, "the sentiments contained in the Pastoral Letter will be referred to with as much astonishment as . . . that judges should have sat on the trials of witches, and solemnly condemned nineteen persons and one dog to death for witchcraft."[21] Similarly, Abby Kelley Foster, appearing before hostile audiences, had routinely discussed the martyrdom that Mary Dyer and others had suffered at the hands of the New England Puritans in relation to the hostility directed against her for deviating from established norms: "A century ago my Quaker ancestors were acquainted with the Deacons of New England. Their backs were stripped and whipped until the skin was torn off, and their ears were cut off, and they were sometimes even put to death. . . . I have no doubt you would commit similar barbarities upon my person if you thought public sentiment would allow it."[22]

*The Scarlet Letter* encodes not only connections between repression in seventeenth-century Boston and in nineteenth-century Salem—between the public punishment of Hester Prynne and the exposure and "beheading" of the "Custom House" narrator—it also encodes the public attacks on the antislavery women, Hawthorne's contemporaries.[23] One of their central icons is displayed in the opening scene: the figure of a woman forcibly exposed in public. Although Hester is not marked by an iron chain but by a piece of needlework, recurrent references to the scarlet letter as a brand force the connections between the embroidered symbol and the instruments of slavery. Later, presenting abolitionist iconography in its fullness, the narrator irrevocably links Hester, his seventeenth-century adultress, to the antislavery feminists, his contemporaries, by using their image of an enchained woman to describe Hester's condition in Boston: "The chain that bound her . . . was of iron links and galling to her inmost soul" (p. 80).

Perhaps the opening view of Hester on the scaffold of the pillory seemed familiar to the antislavery feminists among Hawthorne's earliest readers. Some might have reacted to the color of Hester's embroidery by recalling the red shawl of Maria Weston Chapman at Pennsylvania Hall; others perhaps associated Hester's symbolic branding with Jonathan Walker's barbarous punishment. Certainly Elizabeth Cady Stanton was responding to the feminist subtext of *The Scarlet Letter* when she evoked Hester as "Hawthorne's . . . grand woman, in all her native dignity, standing calm and self-poised through long years of dreary isolation from all her kind."[24] This regal conquered female figure is best depicted, in nineteenth-century American sculpture, by Harriet Hosmer's *Zenobia*. Shown exhibited as a trophy by the Roman emperor Aurelian and wearing the chains of her conquerers, Hosmer's Queen of Palmyra submits to public display (fig. 25).[25] In Hawthorne's writings, however (despite her name), it is not the disappointed suicide—the Zenobia of *Blithedale*—but the defiant adultress, Hester of *The Scarlet Letter*, who embodies the energy of the captive queen.

When the sculptor Howard Roberts created his full-length figure of Hester, he, too, incorporated the abolitionists' iconography of link chains (fig. 26). Like Hawthorne's creation, Roberts's Hester stands at once fully disclosed and completely unrevealed. Although she is forcibly displayed before us, her gaze does not meet ours. She is not nude but fully clothed. Her left arm cradles her sleeping baby, whose head rests against a large badge ornamented with a capital *A* on Hester's breast. Roberts's Hester does not try to hide either the letter or the babe. Like Hawthorne's creation, she is apparently concentrating on some painful reality, and her posture and expression suggest strain. Standing on rough wooden boards, she rests her right hand on a wooden post, and below that hand, Roberts carved the two hanging links of chain. These links connect his pilloried Puritan with Powers's *Greek Slave* and Hosmer's *Zenobia*—and all of them with antislavery iconography.[26]

From the moment Hawthorne's Hester emerges from prison, her regal impression underscored both by her person, "tall, with a figure of perfect elegance, on a large scale," and by her manner, "characterized by a certain state and dignity," she is presented in terms of the conquered queen (p. 53). The description of the letter branding her emphasizes this identification. "Glittering like a . . . jewel" (p. 202), it is characterized as an ornament appropriate for "dames of a court" (p. 81), as "fitting decoration" (p. 53) for royalty. In response to the magnificence of her badge and her regal presence, those unfamiliar with Puritan customs judge Hester "a great lady in the land" (p. 104), "a personage of high dignity among her people" (p. 246). Like Hosmer's *Zenobia*, who wears her manacles as if they were bracelets, and named for Esther, the captive biblical queen whose defiant courage the antislavery women admired, Hawthorne's Hester wears her embroidered brand like conquered royalty.[27]

*The Scarlet Letter* is linked to the discourse of the antislavery women not only by these iconographic motifs, but also by its central concerns. In

Fig. 25. Harriet Hosmer, *Zenobia in Chains* (1859).

Fig. 26. Howard Roberts, *Hester Prynne* (1872).

*Letters on the Equality of the Sexes*, Sarah Grimké had argued that after the fall in Eden woman was the first victim. Although the action of Hawthorne's book takes place in America, almost with his first words the narrator characterizes this new world as fallen. Describing Hester's appearance on the pillory, he notes that while "a Papist" "might have seen in this beautiful . . . woman with the infant at her bosom, an object to remind him of the image of Divine Maternity," she actually resembles Mary only "by contrast." Hester, we are told, is not like that second sinless Eve, but the first, and it is as a type of fallen woman, he tells us, that she is condemned to be identified by the people. Hawthorne's opening pages present a repressive new society practicing institutionalized violence against a woman.

The first scaffold scene showing Hester, her infant in her arms, displayed in public as punishment for the crime of adultery, of course focuses a number of issues. The problem Hawthorne's Puritan theocracy addresses (a problem central in nineteenth-century American fiction) is that the family on the scaffold is incomplete. This woman lacks a husband; this child lacks a father. The solution to this problem, the emergence of the absent male figure, like the solution to the problem of Arthur Dimmesdale, the polluted priest, is figured in the three scaffold scenes as the story unfolds.

But this initial view of Hester on the scaffold also dramatizes the issues that the antislavery women were addressing. *The Scarlet Letter*, no less than *Uncle Tom's Cabin*, published three years later, portrays an American society where publicly, officially, and institutionally, one of God's reasoning creatures is transformed into a thing; and where, privately, one individual tyrannizes over another in this world and threatens his salvation in the next. Here a human being is branded, displayed before the community, and dehumanized. It is perhaps not surprising that, written as the abolitionists labored to convince Americans that slavery was the national sin and as the feminists intensified their characterization of woman's condition as slavery, *The Scarlet Letter* dramatizes the problem of the institutional violation of an individual, the problem central to the notion of slavery, in the person of a woman. Hawthorne's intermittent use of the discourse of the antislavery women to present the twin issues of Hester's dehumanization and her isolation—which relate to the issues of womanhood and sisterhood the antislavery women were raising—results in a series of images that periodically push against the static symmetry of the scaffold scenes.

At the beginning of the book, the drama in Hawthorne's Market Place is heightened because the community condemning Hester is shown as monolithic. While Native Americans are present, here their society is not seen as an alternative to Boston (although Hester will later suggest this to Arthur). Further, as Hawthorne knew, in addition to the Native Americans and transplanted Europeans his narrator shows in the Market Place, the population of seventeenth-century New England had included another group: the Africans. By obliterating this historic black presence, Hawthorne's narrator helps guarantee Hester's absolute isolation.[28]

He does, of course, suggest a black community of a kind. *The Scarlet Letter* presents a classic displacement: color is the sign not of race, but of grace—and of its absence. Black skin is seen as blackened soul. Instead of presenting an African-American alternative to white Boston, it hints at a diabolical reversal. This satanic conspiracy, like establishment Boston, is male-dominated; it is ruled by the Black Man whose purpose seems to be to enslave others—particularly women. (That he wants their bodies as well as their souls is suggested by Hester's statement to Pearl that the Black Man is the child's father. It is tempting to play with connections between dark unpredictable Pearl and the untamed exotic dark females of American nineteenth-century letters. Subtexts concerning women and the sinfulness of female sexuality on the one hand, and blacks and the sinfulness of black sexuality on the other, lend added significance to the nineteenth-century phrase coupling "women and Negroes.")

Members of this subversive group live in the town, but their activities in the forest suggest the international slave trade with the colors of the participants reversed: the names of whites are signed in a book belonging to the Black Man, and whites are branded with the Black Man's mark. They suggest, too, white reports of black Africans—of wild dancing in the woods.[29] Although this diabolical society is never taken seriously, when "black" is read as describing skin color and not moral status, the text of *The Scarlet Letter* reveals the obsessive concern with blacks and blackness, with the presence of a dangerous dark group within society's midst, that is characteristic of American political discourse in the last decades before Emancipation.

By choosing to obliterate the historic black presence and by choosing not to show Native American culture as an alternative to the society of white Boston, Hawthorne's narrator helps guarantee Hester's absolute isolation. With the negation of these potential alternative communities, her ostracism will be complete if the women—the one group within Boston society who might possibly sympathize with her—endorse Hester's official condemnation.

The opening pages of *The Scarlet Letter* dramatize these women rejecting their common sisterhood with Hester. Demonstrating that they have thoroughly internalized the patriarchal values of the community, the women in the Market Place judge Hester's punishment not as too harsh but as too lenient. Even while condemning the criminal more severely than do the male officials of the colony, however, they implicitly acknowledge that although they do not recognize Hester as one of themselves, they are nevertheless her sisters in the eyes of the patriarchy: "This woman has brought shame upon us all, and ought to die" (p. 51). Further, they acknowledge that as a representative female, Hester must be punished if society is to continue to control the women. If she is reprieved, "Then let the magistrates, who have made . . . [the law] of no effect, thank themselves if their own wives and daughters go astray!" (p. 52). Their fury is an index of their oppression. One of the clearest measures of the lack of true community in the Boston of *The Scarlet Letter* is the women's determination to deny Hester's sisterhood.[30]

As the narrative progresses, the issue of sisterhood takes several forms. After Hester's release from jail, isolated and reviled, the narrator writes that she intermittently "felt or fancied . . . [that] a mystic sisterhood would contumaciously assert itself." This sisterhood would apparently link her to other sinners, particularly to women who, although never accused, seemed to her to have engaged in forbidden sexual activity (pp. 86–87). But while noting that she felt herself a member of a sisterhood of sinners, the narrator comments that she fought against this sense of community, "struggling to believe that no fellow-mortal was guilty like herself" (p. 87).

He later discusses another kind of sisterhood. The people of Boston, he writes,

> perceived . . . that . . . Hester . . . was quick to acknowledge her sisterhood with the race of man, whenever benefits were to be conferred. . . . She came, not as a guest, but as a rightful inmate, into the household that was darkened by trouble . . . as if its gloomy twilight were a medium in which she was entitled to hold intercourse with her fellow-creatures. . . . She was a self-ordained Sister of Mercy. (Pp. 160–61)

Hester willingly shares a sense not of mutual sin, but of sickness; she shares the sorrow common to fallen humans in a fallen world.

Although Hester denies any knowledge of the community led by the Black Man, at least one Boston woman welcomes her membership in this grouping. This diabolical secret society is an assembly to which many thought Hester belonged. The reputed witch Mistress Hibbins, believing Hester's brand a sign of her membership and affirming their common sisterhood, interprets Hester's rejection as a clumsy effort to preserve organizational secrecy.

Despite these actual or imagined communities, however, near the end of *The Scarlet Letter*, when Hester stands at the foot of the scaffold as Arthur preaches his Election Sermon, she is again the center of a "magic circle of ignominy," and the women who had earlier condemned her are again among those surrounding her (p. 246). Their "cool, well-acquainted gaze at her familiar shame," along with that of the other townspeople, "tormented Hester Prynne, perhaps more than all the rest" (p. 246). Seven years—and twenty chapters—after her branding on the pillory, Hester remains rejected as a sister by the women of Boston.[31]

In addition to dramatizing the women's informal denial of Hester's sisterhood, the first scaffold scene also dramatizes the institutional denial of her identity. Hester's official transformation from woman to thing enacts the negation central to the institution of slavery—the denial of the humanity of one of God's reasoning creatures, the denial the abolitionists saw as sin. "Giving up her individuality," the narrator says, "she would become the general symbol at which the preacher and the moralist might point, and in which they might vivify and embody their images of woman's frailty and sinful passion" (p. 79).

The discourse of the antislavery feminists also functions as a subtext of *The Scarlet Letter* in connection with the question of Hester's womanhood. This is most apparent in the chapter called "Another View of Hester." At this point in the narrative, Hester, shocked by Arthur's distraught appearance in the second scaffold scene, has decided to try to rescue him from Roger's torture. Here the narrator pauses to explore Hester's identity seven years after her sentence and punishment. He places his examination within the context of a general discussion of the nature and condition of woman—a topic which by 1849 the antislavery feminists had been considering for more than a dozen years and which some of them had recently addressed in new, revolutionary ways at Seneca Falls.

Using a series of buried images and convoluted formulations, Hawthorne's narrator characterizes womanhood as conditional and woman as passive, fragile, and endangered. Imaging Hester first in terms of a group of static free-standing vertical objects—a blasted tree, a neoclassical sculpture —and generalizing on her nature, he comments that as a result of undergoing "an experience of peculiar severity" (figured as being crushed), a woman frequently loses "some attribute . . . the permanence of which has been essential to keep her a woman" (p. 163). He assures us that this lost womanhood can, however, be restored by another physical contact, "the magic touch to effect the transfiguration" (p. 164).

This description of Hester, which notes her "marble coldness" (seen as a result of her life having "turned . . . from passion and feeling, to thought") and observes that she is "standing alone," suggests a sculpture (p. 164). Activating this freestanding marble-like figure, the narrator evokes Hiram Powers's enchained *Greek Slave* as he describes Hester engaging in action: "She cast away the fragments of a broken chain. The world's law was not law for her mind."[32] This apparently revolutionary act, however, does not free her. Hester's chains, the narrator explains, were already broken.

> It was an age when the human intellect, newly emancipated, had taken a more active and a wider range than for many centuries before. Men of the sword had overthrown nobles and kings. Men bolder than these had overthrown and rearranged—not actually, but within the sphere of theory, which was their most real abode—the whole system of ancient prejudice, wherewith was linked much of ancient principle. (P. 164)

Hester is presented as the beneficiary of these male revolutionaries, not as a revolutionist herself. Likened to an intellectual whose radicalism stops short of "the flesh and blood of action," she might have been a revolutionist, it is suggested, but for the birth of her child (p. 164). The characterization of this event as "providential" implies that it may be a blessing that woman's reproductive role prevents her from becoming an activist. Had Pearl not been born, the narrator suggests, Hester might have become a religious leader or prophet, might have "come down to us in history, hand in hand with Anne Hutchinson, as the foundress of a religious sect. She might, in one of her phases, have become a prophetess. She might, and not improbably would, have suffered death from the stern tribunals of the period, for attempting to undermine the foundations of the Puritan establishment" (p. 165). But Hester does not become a link in this extraordinary chain of female revolutionists, the foremothers Abby Kelley Foster had eulogized, whom Hawthorne had condemned as fanatics in "The Gentle Boy." Instead, learning the lesson Ilbrahim's mother had failed to learn, Hester focuses her energies on motherhood.

Ironically, however, her efforts to fulfill this traditional female role inevitably raise precisely the line of revolutionary inquiry that the narrator suggests characterized the thought of women who assumed untraditional public roles. Concerning Pearl, "in bitterness of heart" Hester asks "whether it were for ill or good that the poor little creature had been born at all" (p. 165). It might seem peculiar that she had not become desperate much earlier. Hester had given birth to an illegitimate child before *The Scarlet*

*Letter* begins. However, unlike the drowned Martha Hunt (whom Hawthorne and the others had pulled out of the dark pond in 1845), and unlike the countless deceived maidens of American nineteenth-century fiction, she evidently had not attempted abortion, infanticide, or suicide. Only after seven years of dehumanization and ostracism does Hawthorne's female sexual rebel apparently consider adopting the destructive and self-destructive patterns assigned to "fallen women" in nineteenth-century American life and letters.

The questions she poses make clear that, despite her continued ostracism, she does not see her condition as fundamentally different from that of other women. "Indeed, the same dark question often rose into her mind, with reference to the whole race of womanhood. Was existence worth accepting, even to the happiest among them? As concerned her own individual existence, she had long ago decided in the negative, and dismissed the point as settled" (p. 165).

In the discussion that follows, the narrator initially intimates that the origins of the "woman question" may be social; this implies that public activity, like that of the antislavery feminists, could change woman's situation. But while suggesting that intense activity might result in reforms, this passage does not present woman as an active agent. Note the use of the passive voice:

> As a first step, the whole system of society is to be torn down, and built up anew. Then, the very nature of the opposite sex, or its long hereditary habit, which has become like nature, is to be essentially modified, before woman can be allowed to assume what seems a fair and suitable position. Finally, all other difficulties being obviated, woman cannot take advantage of these preliminary reforms, until she herself shall have undergone a still mightier change, in which, perhaps, the etherial essence, wherein she has her truest life, will be found to have evaporated. (P. 166)[33]

This analysis of woman's condition—that she is not permitted "a fair and suitable position"—appears similar to the analysis of the antislavery feminists. But here the cause of woman's oppression is identified differently, and the solution proposed is different from theirs.

Feminists such as Sarah Grimké, arguing that male domination is the source of woman's problems, had proposed that women actively oppose patriarchal restrictions and reassert their God-given role as corulers of the earth. Hawthorne's narrator suggests, however, that woman's condition is somehow a consequence of her female essence, of her essential nature.

Accordingly, she can rectify her oppressed social status neither by acting (like those "men of the sword" who had toppled aristocratic political structures), nor by thinking (like the "bold" men who had transformed ancient ideological structures). Instead, using an absolute negation and an equally absolute assertion, the narrator suggests that women remain passive and trust their physiology and their luck. Although women are ephemeral and in danger of "evaporation," he writes, their problems are equally ephemeral: "A woman never overcomes these problems by any exercise of thought. They are not to be solved, or only in one way. If her heart chance to come uppermost, they vanish" (p. 166).

Hester—"whose heart," we are told, "has lost its regular and healthy throb," now is seen not as a defeated queen or an enchained sculpture, but as a lost and fallen Eve (p. 166). The consequence of her single act toward self-liberation—throwing away her broken ideological chains—is not freedom, as it had been for Angelina Grimké. Although no longer bound by a repressive ideology, she is enslaved by her own nature. Tyrannized by her own ideas, tortured by thoughts of infanticide and suicide, she now wanders alone, a fallen Eve in a fallen world: "There was wild and ghastly scenery all around her, and a home and comfort nowhere" (p. 166). This entire passage, which recalls Angelina Grimké's early sense of bewilderment at finding herself on an "untrodden path," demonstrates the complex use, in *The Scarlet Letter*, of the antislavery feminists' structures of ideology and discourse. Unlike Grimké, who pursued her innovative course and redefined herself, Hester cannot successfully achieve womanhood and sisterhood unless Hawthorne's narrator changes his definition of woman or presents a narrative that contradicts these constructions.[34] Despite this, however, in the balance of the text we are intermittently presented with fragmentary views of Hester that figure her efforts to achieve these dual goals.

Hester's attempts to act out traditional female roles involve her with a number of issues Hawthorne's feminist contemporaries were raising. Her situation as Roger's wife, for example, dramatizes their demand for more adequate divorce laws, and her plight as a mother accused of unfitness addresses the feminist issue of a woman's right to her child.[35]

Hester's relationship to Arthur, it would appear, is by definition unconventional. Instead, however, it follows a standard pattern. Her functional role as Arthur's true wife becomes clear in the forest scene when she tells him that Roger is her legal husband. Here the question of a wife's duty, a question of deep interest to the feminists, is raised. Earlier, the narrator has revealed that Hester felt connected to Arthur in ways that the patriarchy

mandated that true women be connected to their husbands—as primarily
defined by this relationship, as primarily wives, and not (as the antislavery
women urged) as primarily God's creatures or as citizens. In this scene, the
narrator articulates Hester's lack of a sense of autonomy, her crucial dependence on her perception of Arthur's estimate of her: "All the world had
frowned on her. . . . Heaven, likewise, had frowned upon her. . . . But the
frown of this pale, weak, sinful, and sorrow-stricken man was what Hester
could not bear, and live!" (pp. 194–95). When Hester deliberately risks
Arthur's anger in an attempt to rescue him, she risks what—as every
traditional wife knows—amounts to annihilation. This explains the wild-
ness of her plea, following his fury: "Let God punish! Thou shalt forgive!"
(p. 194). Arthur's response, "I freely forgive you now. May God forgive us
both!" articulates his acceptance of the traditional husband's role as mediator between his erring wife and the Creator (p. 195).[36]

Their reconciliation, however, results in a reversal of the traditional
marital relationship. Fearing Arthur is endangered both physically and
spiritually as a result of his prolonged torture, Hester initially acts as a
traditional wife by urging him to save himself. But when Arthur claims he is
unable to choose, to act independently, when he urges her to assume a
dominant role—"Think for me . . . thou art strong. Resolve for me!" (p.
196); she does so—"Thou shalt not go alone!" (p. 198).

Following this exchange, the narrator pauses to present another detailed
view of Hester. She is no longer seen as a fallen, wandering Eve, but as the
quintessential enemy of Puritan civilization, an Indian at home in the vast
wild. "Her intellect and heart had their home, as it were, in desert places,
where she roamed as freely as the wild Indian in his woods" (p. 199).
Hester's new perspective recalls her shift in vision on the scaffold seven
years earlier. Then, she had reviewed her life in an effort to comprehend her
current situation and to validate her immediate perceptions. Now, however,
Hester looks outward. Her new vision of society is perhaps analogous to the
prospect viewed by Hawthorne's narrator after he was forced from the Custom House, or to the prospect from Henry David Thoreau's jail cell. "It
was," Thoreau had written, "like travelling into a far country. . . . It was to
see my native village in light of the middle ages. . . . It was a closer view of
my native town. . . . I had not seen its institutions before."[37]

From this new perspective, Hester identifies the institutional structures
of Boston, domestic as well as religious and political, with enemy eyes. She
now examines, we are told, "whatever priests or legislators had established;
criticizing all with hardly more reverence than the Indian would feel for the

clerical band, the judicial robe, the pillory, the gallows, the fireside, or the church" (p. 199). Hester is no longer like other women. The narrator explains: "The tendency of her fate and fortunes had been to set her free. The scarlet letter was her passport into regions where other women dared not tread" (p. 199).[38]

If, at this stage, Hester's development were to replicate the pattern described by the antislavery feminists, her new-found ability to identify the patriarchal society as her enemy would spark a new assertion of her identity, her womanhood. But Hester does not remain a wild Indian for long. Although after her agreement with Arthur she casts aside the dehumanizing scarlet letter and in the forest with him again becomes a woman, this renewal is presented as a consequence of her restored relationship with a man, as a result of his "magic touch." It is not shown as the result of her reawakened sense of her own identity—a consciousness that, in the case of the deeply religious antislavery feminists, grew from a sense of a renewed relationship with the Creator. Nevertheless, in the forest Hester appears an unfallen Eve in tune with Nature. When she again takes up the scarlet letter to suffer the "dreary change" into a thing, it is, she thinks, merely to "bear its torture . . . only a few days longer," until she can drown the dehumanizing brand in the deep sea (p. 211).

Her return is quickly followed by the third scaffold scene, which presents the carefully prefigured resolution of many of the problems the first scaffold scene had figured. Arthur confesses his crime in public; the spell binding Pearl is broken; the family is made complete; and Hester's relationship with Arthur is reordered to conform to a conventional marital pattern. When he calls, "Hester . . . come hither!" (p. 252), the woman who seven years earlier had defied the demands of husband, church, and state to name her partner in adultery—the woman who, we have just been told, sees all of Boston through the eyes of a "wild Indian"—obeys wordlessly "as if impelled by inevitable fate, and against her strongest will" (p. 252).

When Hester momentarily hesitates before reaching his side, Arthur reformulates and repeats his command: "Hester Prynne . . . in the name of Him, so terrible and so merciful, who gives me grace . . . come hither now, and twine thy strength about me!" (p. 253). Arthur's language gains added significance in the context of this display of female obedience and of Hester's unanswered question, "Shall we not spend our immortal life together?" (p. 256). His choice of words underscores the impression that this display of the completed nuclear family figures the standard wedding scene that climaxes much of our nineteenth-century fiction.

As Hawthorne wrote, use of the trope of the marriage of vine and elm became common in discussions of the woman question. The authors of the 1837 Pastoral Letter had used it to attack the Grimké sisters:

> If the vine, whose strength and beauty is to lean upon the trellis-work, and half conceal its clusters, thinks to assume the independence and the overshadowing nature of the elm, it will not only cease to bear fruit, but fall in shame and dishonor into the dust. We can not, therefore, but regret the mistaken conduct of those who encourage females to bear an obtrusive and ostentatious part in measures of reform, and countenance any of that sex who so far forget themselves as to itinerate in the character of public lecturers and teachers.[39]

In response, Sarah Grimké had presented a startling feminist variant. In her version, phallic objects that suggest both pastoral and military life apparently guard woman against some unnamed threat; but actually, they are woman's oppressors, not her defenders. Grimké's prose suggests that women who look to men for protection discover that males are at best weak and impotent, at worst dangerously rapacious. "Ah! How many of my sex feel in the dominion, thus unrighteously exercised over them, under the gentle appelation of *protection*, that what they have leaned upon has proved a broken reed at best, and oft a spear."[40]

The version of the trope presented in *The Scarlet Letter* is peculiar because in the third scaffold scene traditional gender roles are apparently reversed. The female vine is physically strong and the male elm, weak. Nonetheless, the physically stronger female submits against her will to the weaker male, who acts out the traditional husband's role of intermediary between his wife and the Creator. Thus Arthur: "Thy strength, Hester; but let it be guided by the will which God hath granted me. . . . Come, Hester, come! Support me up yonder scaffold!"[41] (p. 253).

Critics have pointed out that the final scaffold scene resolves many of the issues implicit in the first. But this scene fails to figure the resolution of the problems encoded in the earlier image of Hester exposed and enchained. Nor does it resolve the issues we have been examining: the official denial of Hester's womanhood and the informal denial of her sisterhood. As if acknowledging this, in the last chapter the narrator again turns to the twin issues of Hester's womanhood and sisterhood. Long after Pearl's humanization and Arthur's death on the scaffold, and long after Hester had taken Pearl away from Boston, he says, "Hester Prynne had returned, and taken up her long-forgotten shame. . . . [T]here was more real life for Hester Prynne, here, in New England, than in that unknown region where Pearl had found a home. Here had been her sin; here, her sorrow; and here was yet to be her penitence" (pp. 262–63). Hawthorne's feminist readers might find this promising. Despite the narrator's earlier statements about women, perhaps here, in contrast to most nineteenth-century fiction, a woman's life will not be seen as defined by a single event; perhaps here a female character will finally be treated as autonomous. While Hester's womanhood has been seen as contingent on her relationship with a man, and while her sisterhood is still denied, despite stirrings in the community, surely now that the narrator has returned to these issues, he will resolve them—although the comment that she must still become penitent perhaps presents a problem.

But the book ends on the next page. Her "real life" (p. 262)—inevitably involving her womanhood and sisterhood, inevitably involving her "sin . . . sorrow and . . . penitence" (p. 263), inevitably involving the sequence of views of Hester that we have been charting—is disposed of in eleven sentences in the next to last paragraph of *The Scarlet Letter*.

This passage begins with an announcement that the signification of her brand has been transformed. The "scarlet letter ceased to be a stigma which attracted the world's scorn and bitterness, and became a type of something to be sorrowed over, and looked upon with awe, yet with reverence too" (p. 263). Its changed signification, however, alters neither the form nor the force of Hester's dehumanizing brand. Although she is no longer identified as a threat but as a source of support, as "one who had herself gone through a mighty trouble," Hester evidently has not again regained the womanhood stripped from her on the scaffold and so briefly restored during her forest meeting with Arthur (p. 263). Apparently in the world of *The Scarlet Letter*, only a man's potent touch can restore lost womanhood; here a woman is defined neither as God's moral creature nor as a female member of society, but as the object of a man's love.

This passage reveals a triple vision. At its center, in a scene that finally does function as a pendant to the opening scene of Hester exhibited in the Market Place, the narrator shows her inside her hut, surrounded by the women of Boston. This glimpse of Hester among the women appears to resolve many of the tensions figured by the denial of her sisterhood in that first scaffold scene, and it perhaps even suggests the kind of women's discussion group that Margaret Fuller had created, which Sophia Peabody Hawthorne had attended. Actually, however, it is very different. What troubles the "wretched" "demanding" females surrounding Hester are not the complexities of the woman question that we are told had once tortured her, complexities that, by 1849, feminist intellectuals and activists had been

addressing for years: the nature of woman as God's creature and the character of woman's oppression by the patriarchy. Instead, the women around
Hester focus on private problems resulting from their sexual experiences
with men: on the consequences of breaking the patriarchal rules restraining
female "passion," or on the sense of worthlessness they feel because they
are "unvalued and unsought" by men (p. 263). Like the women surrounding
her, Hester now focuses on these private and domestic aspects of women's
lives. And like them, she does so in private.

Leaving implicit an assertion with which the feminists certainly agreed
— that "the whole relation between man and woman" requires basic change
— Hester makes explicit a series of ideas about how this change is to come
about, ideas with which they certainly disagreed (p. 263). What she says
counters feminist assertions that women are competent to analyze their
situation and to conceptualize the changes needed, that the time for these
changes is now, and that women acting together can successfully achieve the
necessary reforms. Instead, Hawthorne's narrator writes that Hester assures
the women around her that the inevitable change must be based on a new
revelation, that it will not occur now, and that it will not result from any
actions of hers or of their own: "at some brighter period, when the world
should have grown ripe for it, in Heaven's own time, a new truth will be
revealed" (p. 263). Hawthorne would repeat both the meter and the matter
of these phrases. Four years later, rejecting antislavery activism in his
campaign biography of Franklin Pierce, he would echo his rejection of
feminist activism in *The Scarlet Letter*. A wise man, he would assert, "looks
upon slavery as one of those evils which divine Providence does not leave to
be remedied by human contrivances, but which, in its own good time, by
some means impossible to be anticipated, but of the simplest and easiest
operation, when all its uses shall have been fulfilled, it causes to vanish like
a dream."[42]

At the end of *The Scarlet Letter*, we are told that Hester sketches, for the
women around her, alternative versions of the female figure who, she asserts,
will herald the "new truth." She dismisses the first: It is a vision of Hester
herself as a "destined prophetess" (p. 263) publicly proclaiming a revolution
in "the whole relation between man and woman." She rejects this figure
although it would appear to climax and to culminate the fragmentary series
of views of Hester that we have been tracing — as queen, as woman, and as
sculpture, all in chains; as fallen, lost Eve; as wild Indian; and as
prelapsarian Eve. And she rejects it although the narrator's comment that
she herself had once "vainly imagined" (p. 263) she might fulfill this role

underscores the intellectual and aesthetic inevitability of Hester's transformation into the "destined prophetess."

In refusing this vision of herself, Hester evidently repudiates the feminist subtext—the language and iconography of the antislavery women, the images of women in chains, of female figures erect in space—that has fueled *The Scarlet Letter*. Clearly, she now repudiates tactics like those of the antislavery feminists who were defying social taboos in an effort to move other women to action, polemicizing, lecturing, and preaching in public, and prophesying a change in "this whole relation between man and woman."

Just as clearly, she repudiates their ideology. Although finally surrounded by women and acknowledging her connections with these everyday sinners (and thus by extension with women like those who, in Hawthorne's time, were held in slavery and with those who, although legally free, identified so deeply with their sisters in chains that they figured themselves as slaves), she now denies the central assertion of the antislavery feminists: "that any mission of divine and mysterious truth should be confided to a woman stained with sin, bowed down with shame, or even burdened with a life-long sorrow" (p. 263). With these words, Hester denies that any of them (she herself, the women around her, or by extension nineteenth-century women literally and figuratively in chains) can act to end patriarchal oppression, can break her own chains and the chains of her sisters.

Instead, we are told that Hester has endorsed a different ideology. She now asserts that a woman unlike herself and her audience will function as "the angel and apostle of the coming revelation" (p. 263). In accordance with this new idea, she projects a new iconography. The figure she envisions, the antithesis of the woman in chains, is a divine female rescuer "lofty, pure, and beautiful; and wise . . . through . . . the ethereal medium of joy" (p. 263). Instead of proselytizing in public like the "destined prophetess"—and like the antislavery feminists who figured themselves as self-liberated liberators—this rescuer will deliver her message in private. Instead of engaging in debate and agitation like the antislavery feminists, the rescuer will present her message by example, simply showing "how sacred love can make us happy, by the truest test of a life successful to such an end!" (p. 263). Five years after publication of *The Scarlet Letter*, Coventry Patmore's poem would provide this female culture figure with a name. The image Hester here envisions and endorses, a superhuman, privatized, and domesticated version of the Liberator of the double antislavery emblem, is the patriarchy's paradigm of true womanhood, the Angel in the House.[43]

Ironically, Hester's new vision does not resolve the division between women that the first scaffold scene had dramatized; it simply reverses it. Now on one side is a happy lone figure; on the other, among women "stained . . . bowed down . . . and burdened," crouches Hester. She counsels those around her to comfort each other in private, to be patient, and to have faith. Formulated in the terms of the antislavery emblem, she advises them to function as sisters, as members of their human community, but not as women, God's autonomous moral creatures.

The final lines of *The Scarlet Letter* powerfully reinforce its opening scene. The free-standing vertical "slab of slate"—placed not over Hester's grave but between it and Arthur's, marked not with her name or his or even the word naming their relationship, but with the brand that signaled, for her, the denial of both womanhood and sisterhood—this gravestone recalls our first view of Hester Prynne (p. 264). Then, on the scaffold of the pillory, a young woman dressed in gray and branded with red was forced to expose herself as a punishment for breaking patriarchal laws restricting sexuality and as a device for controlling the behavior of other women in the colony. As then in the Market Place, so now in the cemetery, both her womanhood and her sisterhood are denied. Marked with a symbol whose meanings "perplex" (p. 264) their nineteenth-century viewers (and become available to us only through the intervention of Surveyor Pue and his decapitated successor, male officials of governments succeeding the Puritan theocracy), this "slab of slate" represents the ultimate denial of Hester's humanity and her membership in the community.[44] What we remember is the reassertion of the iconography of the antislavery feminists, now used to counter their definitions of true womanhood; we remember Hester's final exclusion from sisterhood with the dead, her final reduction from woman to nameless thing.

With the *Greek Slave* and *The Scarlet Letter*, the emblem of a woman exposed and enchained, of a woman pleading, again signifies a female victim, as it had before Angelina Grimké's excited realization that to appeal is to assert power. The antislavery feminists had recoded the suppliant image to express woman's struggle against oppression and to announce their own self-liberation. But the emblem of the female in chains was reappropriated and again recoded. Over time, as patriarchal discourse became utterly dominant, the speeches and writings of the antislavery feminists were marginalized. Then they disappeared from the page.

# CODA
# Women Silenced

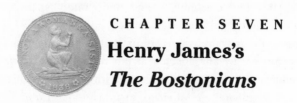

CHAPTER SEVEN

# Henry James's
# *The Bostonians*

*Although we do not wish to be unduly sensitive, we must submit that had Mr. James entitled his novel "The Cranks"* . . . *we should have found no fault.*

—The Woman's Journal[1]

The structures that the antislavery feminists had appropriated and encoded were, in turn, coopted by their opponents: Powers's *Greek Slave* was used to endorse woman's passivity, and Hawthorne's Puritan female rebel shrank into a weathered tombstone without a name. The fate of the antislavery feminists as the subject of literary discourse was perhaps even worse. The female activists who struggled to define themselves as women and sisters had been made the subject of both adulatory writings and vituperative attacks during the years of their public agitation against slavery and for women's rights. Then, a generation later, in his satirical novel *The Bostonians* Henry James etched them indelibly in the character of Miss Birdseye, "an old, weary, battered and simple-minded woman."[2]

By the 1880s, James had begun developing his own critique of American womanhood, and his decision to model Miss Birdseye on Elizabeth Peabody shaped the fate of the antislavery feminists in American literature. Had he chosen to pattern his character on Maria Weston Chapman, for example, or on Caroline Sturgis Tappan, doubtless the treatment of the antislavery feminists as a literary subject would have been very different. But James chose Peabody, who was, by the time he wrote, a notorious eccentric. Peabody,

although a reformer, had not been an antislavery activist in the 1830s and
1840s; she had never been a committed feminist. Yet, recast as the foolish
Miss Birdseye, a woman whose essential nature conformed to patriarchal
definitions of true womanhood but who, in her youth, had perversely blun-
dered into the public sphere, Peabody has come to characterize the antislavery feminists in the American literary canon.[3]

When James wrote *The Bostonians*, the antislavery feminists were dying
out. They had consciously and deliberately spent their lives protesting
against traditional true womanhood but at death were often eulogized in
terms of the patriarchy's Angel in the House. Angelina Grimké was praised,
for example, by one speaker at her funeral for applying her extraordinary
talents to the domestic sphere: "With a mind high and deep and broad
enough to grasp the relations of justice and mercy, and a heart warm enough
to sympathize with and cherish all that live, what a home she made!"[4]
Similarly, biographers of these women tended to reinterpret their lives to
conform to patriarchal patterns, and those historians who recalled them at
all characteristically judged them important because they had influenced
prominent men.[5]

As the antislavery feminists' political writings were allowed to go out of
print, Child was remembered only for moving Channing with her *Appeal* and
for her children's poems: her verse beginning "Over the river and through
the woods / To Grandmother's house we go" was republished so often that it
became accepted as folk culture. The continued popularity of Child's ballad
is certainly easy to understand.[6] A juvenile recital of a vulgar version of the
American Dream, it describes a stimulating but unthreatening journey
through a known landscape. Climaxing with the repossession of a familiar
domestic scene, it chronicles a success achieved without effort and actually
assured from the beginning: even "the horse knows the way." This juvenile
verse contrasts dramatically with Child's political writings in denying any
need for, or any possibility of, social change. It concludes with neither a
refreshment of spirit nor a renewal of material necessities, but with a
celebration of affluence in a domestic American setting: "Hurrah for the
pumpkin pie!"

Not puddings and pies, however, but public issues, including a redefinition of womanhood, were the recurrent motifs in the discourse of the feminists of Child's generation, as Henry James well knew. Although *The
Bostonians* centers on the turn-of-the-century reformers, it presents the
definitive treatment, in American letters, of that earlier generation. James's
Miss Birdseye, a relic of that time, embodies the historic connections

between abolitionism and feminism. Remarking that in her youth she had carried Bibles to the slaves, she announces that today she wants to carry to women "the Statute-book; that must be our Bible now" (p. 122).

These historic connections are articulated when Olive Chancellor, James's new-model feminist, links southern antebellum mastery of slaves with the mastery of women. Remarking that her antifeminist sister, Mrs. Luna, might appropriately marry the southerner Basil Ransom, Chancellor describes him as "a man who, no doubt, desired to treat women with the lash and manacles, as he and his people had formerly treated the wretched coloured race" (p. 172). Chancellor later evokes the image of the female supplicant when, haunted by visions of abused wives, mothers, and maidens, she comments that the "interminable dim procession seemed to stretch out a myriad hands to her" and describes women as oppressed by "the intolerable load of fate. It was they who sat cramped and chained to receive it" (p. 191). In addition, Chancellor uses antislavery feminist discourse to confront Ransom: "You hold us in chains, and then, when we writhe in our agony, you say we don't behave prettily!" (p. 255). And the southerner, too, acknowledges his familiarity with this rhetoric. Seeing Chancellor's delight at the triumphant platform appearance of her protégée, Verena Tarrant, he imagines her demanding, "*now* do you think that women are meant to be slaves?" (p. 266).

Although James's post-Civil War white feminists freely use the language of their antislavery feminist predecessors to signify their own oppression, they appear to lack interest in the black men and women whose earlier enslavement had structured this discourse. There are no blacks among the feminists in *The Bostonians*. When a single African-American appears in the novel—he is "a negro in a white jacket" who announces lunch in Olive's New York boardinghouse—the women seem totally uninterested despite the widespread northern racism suggested, at the end of the book, by a Boston policeman's casual use of the term *nigger* (pp. 284, 419). Is James here commenting on the white racism which, by the time he wrote at the end of the century, openly plagued the women's movement?[7]

Whatever the answer, women like Mrs. Farrinder, whom Olive Chancellor encounters as she involves herself in organized feminism, represent a new generation of reformers. They are not the contemporaries of the Grimkés, of Child, or of Sojourner Truth and Harriet Jacobs. Like Chancellor, they know of these foremothers only through Miss Birdseye, presented as the sole survivor of the antebellum band of women and sisters. And like James's turn-of-the-century feminists, today's readers of the American literary canon

know the early antislavery feminists only in the person of James's Miss
Birdseye.[8]

James was in Boston in 1883 when he wrote his first notes about *The
Bostonians*, curiously couching them in the past tense as if the book were
finished. "I wished to write a very *American* tale, a tale very characteristic
of our social conditions, and I asked myself what was the most salient and
peculiar point in our social life. The answer was: the situation of women, the
decline of the sentiment of sex, the agitation on their behalf."[9] James's
biographer Leon Edel has pointed out that earlier, the novelist had scrawled
the single word "Reformers" across the flyleaf of the *Correspondence of
Thomas Carlyle and Ralph Waldo Emerson*. The passage he noted
—Emerson's 1840 comment, "We are all a little wild here with numberless
projects of social reform"—indicates an interest in the antebellum movements for social change. Sketching out his new book for his publisher,
James connected the current women's movement with the earlier reformers,
whom he grouped together indiscriminately.

> The scene of the story is laid in Boston and its neighborhood; it relates an
> episode connected with the so-called "woman's movement." The characters
> who figure in it are for the most part persons of the radical reforming type, who
> are especially interested in the emancipation of women, giving them the
> suffrage, releasing them from bondage, co-educating them with men, etc.
> They regard this as the great question of the day—the most urgent and sacred
> reform. The heroine is a very clever and "gifted" young woman, associated by
> birth and circumstances with a circle immersed in these views and in every
> sort of new agitation, daughter of old abolitionists, spiritualists, transcenden-
> talists, etc. She herself takes an interest in the cause; but she is an object of
> still greater interest to her family and friends, who have discovered in her a
> remarkable natural talent for public speaking by which they believe her capa-
> ble of moving large audiences and rendering great aid in the liberation of her
> sex.[10]

He realized that to bring off his feminist orator, he would need to include "as
many little pictures as I can introduce of the women's rights agitation."[11]

James had been intimate with the reformers since childhood, a familiarity
grounded in the Swedenborgianism of his father. Regarding the antislavery
effort, he later recalled the rich reminiscences of Henry James, Sr., about
the "almost epic" Billy Taylor, a black servant, and remembered his own
boyhood encounters with an African-American couple who sold hot sticky

waffles to him and his schoolmates at Forest's.[12] More important, James recorded his recollections of the slaves Aunt Sylvia and her son Davy, brought to New York City by Kentuckians who had taken a house near his family. "Davy," he wrote, "mingled in our sports and talk, he enriched, he adorned them with a personal, a pictorial lustre that none of us could emulate." And he reports his reactions upon learning one day that both mother and son had fled. "They had never been for us so beautifully slaves as in this achievement of their freedom; for they did brilliantly achieve it—they escaped, on northern soil, beyond recall or recovery. I think we had already then, on the spot, the sense of some degree of presence at the making of history."[13]

James's familial experiences with white antislavery activities were almost as dramatic. His younger brothers, Bob and Wilky, were sent to Frank Sanborn's experimental school at Concord, where they joined, as school-boarders, a daughter of John Brown. Executed as a traitor only months before, Brown was mourned as a patriot by Sanborn and other abolitionists. Later, during the Civil War, Wilky enlisted as an officer in the Fifty-fourth Massachusetts, the first regiment of black soldiers organized in the North. He was wounded in the bloody attack on Fort Wagner, where Robert Shaw, son of Child's abolitionist friends, died with his men. Wilky was, James's father wrote, committed to "the negro-soldier cause; believes (I think) that the world has existed for it; and is sure that enormous results to civilisation are coming out of it." Henry James later recorded his own conflicted responses at seeing the black troops and their white officers:

> though our sympathies, our own as a family's, were, in the current phrase, all
> enlisted on behalf of the race that had sat in bondage, it was impossible for the
> mustered presence of more specimens of it, and of stranger, than I had ever
> seen together, not to make the young men who were about to lead them appear
> sacrificed to the general tragic need in a degree beyond that of their more
> orthodox appearances.[14]

Nonetheless, he reports that his father had confidence in the righteousness of the cause and believed, "Once we get rid of Slavery the new heavens and new earth will swim into reality."[15]

But if Henry James's familiarity with the slavery issue was immediate and personal, his experience with antebellum feminism was certainly thin. Indeed, after publication of *The Bostonians*, he commented, "I had the sense of knowing terribly little about the kind of life I had attempted to describe." The only instances I have found in which James even mentions

hearing women speak from the public platform are in a letter he wrote from
New York in 1863. He reported the preaching of the sensational Mrs. Cora
V. L. Hatch:

> She holds forth in a kind of underground lecture room in Astor Place. The
> assemblage, its subterraneous nature, the dim lights, the hard-working, thought-
> ful physiognomies of everyone present quite realised my idea of the meetings
> of the early Christians in the Catacombs. . . . Three individuals from the
> audience formed themselves into a committee to select a subject for Cora to
> discuss — and they were marshalled out of the room by a kind of fat showman,
> who, as I wittily suggested, was probably Mr. Chorus V. L. Hatch. They chose:
> "the Evidence of the continued existence of the Spirit after death." For some
> moments Cora remained motionless; probably, as Bob Temple said, "silently
> invoking her maker." Then she began to speak. Well, the long and short of it
> is, that the whole thing was a string of such arrant platitudes, that after about
> an hour of it, when there seemed to be no signs of a let-up we turned and fled.
> So much for Cora.[16]

And he described a second experience:

> I went with the ever faithful Bob Temple to a service held by the so-called
> "congregation of the new dispensation" just up Broadway. I haven't time to
> decribe it at length, tho' it was all extraordinary. — In fact my letter is so long
> already that I won't bother you with describing it at all. I enclose a little
> scribble of the platform. We had a grand oration (tremendous) from the female
> on the right and singing from her on the left.[17]

James's "scribble" does not display the iconography of antislavery feminism; he did not sketch either of the women standing exposed before an audience. Instead he shows them seated, with their male colleagues, in a high
space in which the absence of enclosure, the obtrusive lighting, and the po-
sitioning of the furniture suggest a public platform (fig. 27).[18] James's image
of the women seated in this space and turning their faces away from us certainly is less easily read than either the icon of the female orator as self-
liberated liberator or the icon of the sexually deviant woman on public display.

Many years later, James was again made aware of female lecturers. In the
spring of 1881, the National Woman's Suffrage Association met in Boston.
The feminists announced that their object was "to secure to women their
right to the ballot, by working for national, State, municipal, school, or any
other form of suffrage"; and their timing was right. In 1879, in response to

Fig. 27. Illustration in Henry James letter to Thomas S. Perry [1 November 1863].

meetings and petitions, the Massachusetts legislature had passed an act granting women the right to vote for members of school committees, and subsequently more than eight hundred Boston women had registered to vote in school board elections. At their 1881 Boston convention, the feminists were addressed by prominent speakers including Elizabeth Cady Stanton, Rev. Olympia Brown, Matilda Joslyn Gage, and Susan B. Anthony. Instead of being mobbed and reviled, as in earlier times, they were invited to meet the governor and the mayor and to dine with local dignitaries and reformers at the Parker House.[19]

That year, when Henry James and his sister Alice returned from Europe to Boston, woman's suffrage was the leading political question. Alice James's biographer reports that Katherine Loring, her companion, had supported the feminists at least to the extent of inviting friends to meet May Wright Sewall, who had spoken at the 1881 convention; she writes that both Jameses and Loring "watched the flurry of feminist activity with interest."[20]

Alice James's letters and journal document her acquaintance with feminists both at home and abroad.[21] While neither she nor Loring became involved with organized feminism, her writings repeatedly express the ideas and concerns that structured the women's movement. She voices woman's fundamental right to self-determination, for example, with a brief rhetorical question: "When will women begin to have the first glimmer that above all other loyalties is the loyalty to Truth, i.e., to yourself, that husband, children, friends and country are as nothing to that."[22] Although born a generation after the antislavery feminists, Alice James testifies to her familiarity with the motto encircling their emblem when, commenting on a detail in a memoir, she exclaims, "this touch of vanity maketh of an abbess of the 17th cent[ury] a woman and a sister!"[23]

Just as Alice James's complex ideas and actions, including what her biographer terms her "Boston marriage" to Katharine Loring, suggest one context for a reading of Henry James's fictional post-Civil War feminist Olive Chancellor, so the ideas and actions of transcendentalist Elizabeth Palmer Peabody provide a context for a reading of his pre-Civil War feminist, Miss Birdseye.[24]

Discussing the antislavery struggle late in life, Peabody commented on her distance from the abolitionist women when she wrote that during the early years she had been "so thoroughly buried in my school, that I had neither time nor opportunity to go to Antislavery meetings—though my heart and judgment were always on the Antislavery side from my earliest infancy when my mother induced us children all to refuse to eat sugar because it was the fruit of slave labor."[25] Her complaint in 1835 that the Garrisonian women were not sufficiently grateful for Harriet Martineau's support, and her suggestion that Martineau dissociate herself from them following their mobbing, testify to her differences with the Boston antislavery women.[26] By 1840, however, Peabody seems to have been within the abolitionists' circle of influence: after publishing Channing's *Slavery*, she apparently offered the pamphlet at cost to the American Antislavery Society. In 1849, Peabody echoed Garrison's disapproval of the Mexican War, and later, with her father, she moved to Eagleswood, the hotbed of feminism and abolition that the Grimké sisters and Theodore Weld had established in New Jersey.[27] In 1855—twenty years after Martineau's "martyrs"—Peabody was expressing antislavery convictions to her sister Sophia in England in a "manuscript pamphlet on the Abolition question." Although she did not publish this, she continued to write to her sister and to her niece on slavery.[28]

Then in 1859, John Brown's raid catapulted Peabody into abolitionist activism. She helped collect money, clothing, and hospital supplies to be taken south by Brown's wife and daughters, who were staying with the Alcotts. In March 1860, she traveled to Virginia in an effort to save the life of Aaron Dwight Stevens, one of Brown's followers.[29] After this, Peabody was consistently identified with the antislavery reformers. She endorsed Child's 1860 emancipationist pamphlet, *The Right Way, the Safe Way*; four years later, she actively aided the establishment of the Orphan's Home for Colored Children in Georgetown, D.C., and solicited autographs from her famous friends to be sold at a fair to raise money for the black regiments.[30]

Peabody's involvement in the struggle for woman's rights is much less clear. In 1859, criticizing feminist Caroline Healey Dall, she reviewed her historic estrangement from organized feminism: "I do not like conventions of women for Women's Rights—as you know—I did not when I first heard of them & would not sign the first call that was made—I like them still less in practice."[31] Peabody was particularly critical of those feminists who followed Stewart, Grimké, Rose, Kelley, and the others who stood to speak in public:

> Women do not seem to be able to divest themselves of a certain consciousness of their own personality—bodily or mental—and so make fools of themselves in public by thrusting *their own personality* before the audience. Of course there are exceptions—I suppose that when the subject matter that they have to speak of so absorbs them that they forget the Ego—*they will not do this* —But where they go into public to make an impression of the talents & power they always betray it in this way—& become the object of the pity of the audience—.[32]

Not for another ten years would Peabody advocate public agitation on women's issues. Then, addressing the "terrible evils and sorrows, produced by the industrial and moral circumstances of the working-women of our American, no less than of European, large cities," she wrote: "But public speeches, and even strong writing, are not enough to meet the evil. There must be effective activity to change the conditions from which, by the unchangeable logic of cause and effect, it flows. If ever there was necessity for large associations for reform and guidance, it is in this case."[33] Although through the decades her name was associated with humanitarian causes, from 1859 onward Elizabeth Palmer Peabody devoted her life neither to abolitionism nor to women's rights but to the kindergarten movement. Nevertheless, she was memorialized after her death by both Douglass and Stanton, and the abolitionists and feminists alike claimed her as one of their own.[34]

Writing of Peabody in his 1879 essay on Hawthorne, Henry James noted that she had "acquired . . . a very honourable American fame as a woman of benevolence, of learning, and of literary accomplishments."[35] Yet Edward Emerson recalled James's father offering a stuttered description of Peabody as "one of the most d-d-dissolute old creatures that walks the earth!" and reported that in response, the James family

> shouted with joy, though knowing well the saintly, if too optimistic character of the lady, at the Jamesian felicity of the adjective. For they saw, in memory, the gray hair falling down under the bonnet askew, the spectacles slipping down with resulting radiant upturned face, the nondescript garments and general dissolving effect, symbolizing the loose reasoning and the charity falling all abroad—yes, in a sense a dissolute personality.[36]

When his brother accused him of "having painted a 'portrait from life' of Miss Peabody" in *The Bostonians*, the novelist responded that he was "appalled." He asserted that his "Miss Birdseye was evolved entirely from my moral consciousness, like every person I have ever drawn."[37] James did, however, confess that "after I had got going [I] reminded myself that my creation would perhaps be identified with Miss Peabody—*that* I freely admit." Further, he acknowledged, "The one definite thing about which I had a scruple was some touch about Miss Birdseye's spectacles—I remembered that Miss P.'s were always in the wrong place."[38] Despite this "scruple," however, James makes Miss Birdseye's faulty eyesight a telling metaphor: "the whole moral history of Boston was reflected in her displaced spectacles" (pp. 61–62). It is almost as if he had read Hawthorne's angry response in 1857 to his sister-in-law Elizabeth Peabody's antislavery pamphlet: "like every other Abolitionist, you look at matters with an awful squint, which distorts everything within your line of vision; and it is queer, though natural, that you think everybody squints except yourselves. Perhaps they do; but certainly *you* do."[39]

James's Miss Birdseye, we are told, had before Emancipation gone far beyond the proposals that Angelina Grimké had made to the "Christian Women of the South" and the "Women of the Nominally Free States" by traveling south to break the laws and teach slaves to read. The history of activism that he assigns to Miss Birdseye in an amalgam of the experiences of a number of antislavery feminists. Like Lucretia Mott, whose male cospeaker was mobbed, Miss Birdseye's companions "had been tarred and feathered." Like Margaret Douglass, imprisoned in Virginia for teaching free blacks, Miss Birdseye had "spent a month in a Georgia jail."[40]

Early in the novel, James's narrator describes Miss Birdseye as

a confused, entangled, inconsequent, discursive old woman, whose charity
began at home and ended nowhere, whose credulity kept pace with it, and who
knew less about her fellow-creatures, if possible, after fifty years of humanitarian zeal, than on the day she had gone into the field to testify against the
iniquity of most arrangements. (P. 55)

While to James's brother this sentence apparently easily suggested Peabody,
it contrasts sharply with the novelist's sketch of another female reformer of
the older generation, his father's Transcendentalist friend Caroline Sturgis,
who had married into the abolitionist Tappan family:

With an admirable intelligence, of the incurably ironic or mocking order, she
was such a light, free, somewhat intellectually perverse but socially impulsive
presence (always for instance insatiably hospitable) as our mustered circle
could ill have spared. If play of mind, which she carried to any point of
quietly-smiling audacity that might be, had not already become a noted, in
fact I think the very most noted, value among us, it would have seated itself
there in her person with a nervous animation, a refinement of what might have
been called soundable sincerity, that left mere plump assurance in such
directions far in the lurch. And she was interesting, she became fairly historic, with the drawing-out of the years, as almost the only survivor of that
young band of the ardent and uplifted who had rallied in the other time to the
"transcendental" standard. [41]

A fictional female reformer resembling Tappan apparently could not, however, "embody in a sympathetic, pathetic, picturesque, and at the same
time grotesque way, the humanity and *ci-devant* transcendental tendencies
which," he wrote in 1885, "I thought it highly probable I should be accused
of treating in a contemptuous manner in so far as they were otherwise
represented in the tale."[42] For his story, James judged that he needed not a
Carolyn Sturgis Tappan, but an Elizabeth Palmer Peabody, a Miss Birdseye.

Although Basil Ransom, James's hero, impudently notes old Miss
Birdseye's absence of feminine curves, his final judgment is that he will
remember the aged activist "as an example of what women are capable of"
(p. 388). And in every way but physically, Miss Birdseye indeed fits the
profile that Ransom's patriarchal theories define as feminine: warm-hearted
and soft-headed, she is essentially selfless. In contrast to James's modern
feminist, Olive Chancellor, Miss Birdseye is a traditional true woman who
all her life has sacrificed her own well-being for the welfare of others. She

has not, however, restricted herself to the domestic sphere; those others have been not a husband and children, but oppressed Native Americans, Hungarians, Poles, and blacks. Miss Birdseye is thus presented as a true woman perverted, as someone who has misspent her life, who never (even in her youth) entertained a personal sentiment. "She was in love, even in those days, only with causes, and she languished only for emancipations" (p. 56). James's narrator sharply questions this humanitarianism. Noting that "Since the Civil War much of her occupation was gone," he comments in one of his more hostile asides: "It would have been a nice question whether, in her heart of hearts, for the sake of this excitement, she did not sometimes wish the black back in bondage" (p. 56).

Other than Miss Birdseye, the only character in any way identified with the antislavery movement is the mother of Verena Tarrant, James's young heroine. Mrs. Tarrant is no liberated woman. She conforms to traditional true womanhood in defining herself as a daughter (of a prominent abolitionist), as a wife (of a shoddy spiritualist), and as the mother of the gifted Verena. Aware that her marriage has lowered her status, Mrs. Tarrant's social consciousness appears limited to her hope that her daughter can regain respectability.

Although the ostensible subject of *The Bostonians* is organized feminism, the feminists' view of woman's autonomy is never seriously at issue; this signals the connections between James's book and Hawthorne's *Blithedale Romance*—and the distance of both from *The Scarlet Letter*.[43] Because James's young heroine Verena is essentially selfless, there is never any possibility that she will achieve autonomy. *The Bostonians* dramatizes another question: will Verena take Miss Birdseye's path and follow the Bostonian Olive Chancellor in waging a public crusade for woman's rights, or will she marry the southerner Basil Ransom and lead the private life of a traditional woman?

Olive and Basil are equally determined to win Verena. In Basil's view, the risk is that, like Miss Birdseye, the girl will give herself to the public rather than to a husband and home. He expounds patriarchal theories, including the doctrine of separate spheres and the efficacy of male domination, and he acts to enforce his will upon the woman he loves. Olive's practice, however, radically contradicts her theory: she asserts that men are women's oppressors, but what we see is her domination of Verena. And even Olive's theories fail. She grounds her ideas on her belief that women prefer independence and autonomy, while Basil assumes that they prefer dependence—but as far as Verena is concerned, he is right. If, in the world of *The Bostonians*, the validity of feminism stands or falls with Verena Tarrant, it must inevitably fall. Instead of believing, in Alice James's words, "that above all other loyalties is the loyalty to Truth, i.e., to yourself," Verena desires to please others. Indeed, this appears to be her dominant characteristic; James's narrator repeatedly describes her "sweetness," her pliability, and her "extraordinary mixture of eagerness and docility" (p. 125). Verena, we are told, was "the most good-natured girl in the world. . . . [s]he had always done every thing that people asked" (p. 317). "It was in her nature to be easily submissive, to like being overbourne" (p. 322). "A part of her essence was the extraordinary generosity with which she would expose herself, give herself away, turn herself inside out, for the satisfaction of a person who made demands on her" (p. 370).

A conformist born and raised within a circle of nonconformists, Verena amiably endorses the reformers' views; she has never even heard any other ideas until she meets Basil. Although to the public the red-haired Verena appears an independent "new woman," she is never even remotely autonomous. Essentially passive, she appears first as her father's creation; watching her being molded by Olive Chancellor, we understand that even when mouthing woman's cause, she is not her own person. In *The Bostonians*, Verena's autonomy is never an issue; the only question is whose dependent she will become.[44]

It was not, however, James's treatment of Verena—or even of Olive— that distressed his early readers. James' correspondence records an "assault" by his brother William, his aunt Kate, and James R. Lowell concerning his characterization of Elizabeth Palmer Peabody as Miss Birdseye.[45] Noting that at the end of the book this cruel portrait is softened, some commentators have speculated whether James may have been responding to these critics. Certainly Miss Birdseye's death, late in the story, moves us; to me, it resonates with James's appreciation of his father's

> constitutional optimism . . . fed so little by any sense of things as they were or are, but rich in its vision of the facility with which they might become almost at any moment or from one day to the other totally and splendidly different. . . . The case was so really of his . . . feeling so vast a rightness close at hand or lurking immediately behind actual [social] arrangements that a single turn of the inward wheel, one real response to pressure of the spiritual spring, would bridge the chasms, straighten the distortions, rectify the relations and, in a word, redeem and vivify the whole mass.[46]

Yet even at the end, Miss Birdseye is perhaps most positively characterized as exhibiting "benignant perversity" (p. 386). In a sense, her entire
death scene is a farce. The old woman, who has been instrumental in
creating Basil's conspiracy against Olive, is consistently characterized as
self-deceived; her penultimate self-deception is the notion that Verena has
converted Basil to feminism. We watch her read the developing situation
and, as she has done all of her long life, misinterpret what she sees. On her
deathbed, clinging to her "last theory," she believes that Verena has made a
convert of Basil when in fact he has by now almost succeeded in converting
her.

Seeing, as always, with a squint, Miss Birdseye is wrong not only about
Verena and Ransom, but also about Verena and Olive. The dying old woman
reviews her life, thinking that she "can measure the progress," believing
that Verena and Olive "will do more" than she has done, that in relation to
woman's cause, they will "see justice done" (p. 387). The last words we hear
her say, addressed to Olive, are couched in a visual metaphor: "I should
like to see what you will see" (p. 388). But James's few remaining chapters
recount the failure of Olive's effort to control Verena—and his twentieth-
century readers know that neither Olive nor Verena could have lived long
enough to see "justice done." Miss Birdseye's female physician, Dr. Prance,
characterizes her late patient as "one of the old school." And it is as "one of
the old school," as a quintessential antislavery feminist, that *The Bostonians*'s
Miss Birdseye has been codified in American literature (p. 389).

Reviewing Miss Birdseye's death, the narrator comments: "She had been
almost celebrated, she had been active, earnest, ubiquitous beyond any one
else, she had given herself utterly to charities and creeds and causes; and
yet the only persons, apparently to whom her death made a real difference
were three young women in a small 'frame-house' on Cape Cod" (p. 389).
That is, although she had worn herself out in the public sphere, she was not
valued by the public; instead, like more traditional women who stayed
within domestic boundaries, she was mourned by only a few intimates.[47]

And what was the effect of her death on this handful? Verena's exclama-
tions at first make it appear that the sad event has wedded her to the cause:
"You are our heroine, you are our saint. . . . We will think of you always,
and your name will be sacred to us, and that will teach us singleness and
devotion" (pp. 387–88). Yet she chooses not feminism but marriage. Fore-
seeing this, Olive prophesies truly: "I shall see nothing but shame and
ruin!"[48]

The image of a woman lecturing on a public platform stands at the center of *The Bostonians*. In Verena Tarrant, James presents a direct descendant of the young Angelina Grimké. Now, however, the focus is neither on her ideas nor on her words, but on the spectacle she produces. Verena's first appearance at Miss Birdseye's moves Olive deeply. But instead of paraphrasing or transcribing her speech, for a page and a half James's narrator presents Basil's responses to it. To him, we are told,

> The effect was not in what she said, though she said some such pretty things, but in the picture and figure of the half-bedizened damsel (playing, now again, with her red fan), the visible freshness and purity of the little effort. . . . the argument, the doctrine, had absolutely nothing to do with it. It was simply an intensely personal exhibition, and the person making it happened to be fascinating. (P. 84)

We are, however, given Verena's closing words. In them, she parodies Grimké speaking against the Pennsylvania Hall mob; Verena contrasts the violent world men have organized with "what the great sisterhood of women might do if they should all join hands, and lift up their voices above the brutal uproar of the world. . . . [T]he sound of our lips would become the voice of universal peace!" (p. 86).

Foolish Mrs. Luna provides our only report of Verena's speech at the Female Convention; although Verena recounts to Ransom her impressions of the occasion, we are not allowed to read any of her text. The narrator does, however, devote more than seven pages to her address at the Burrage home in New York. Two of these give us Verena's words; the other five concern Basil's responses, mainly to the sound of her "golden voice" and to the spectacle. He "became aware," we are told, "that he was watching her in very much the same excited way as if she had been performing high above his head, on the trapeze" (pp. 263, 265).

This is the sum of Verena's public speeches that James renders. Later, however, on Cape Cod, Basil stops to listen to the sound of her voice as she practices her Music Hall address. Entitled "A Woman's Reason," this is the speech that Verena never delivers, the speech that neither her audience —nor James's—will ever hear. But evidently it is not worth listening to. When Dr. Prance comments to Basil that he is too far away to decipher the words, he responds, groaning, "Oh, I know the words!" (pp. 381, 349).

Much as we might wish to listen to them, "the words" that Henry James apparently judged not worth hearing had been similarly dismissed, earlier, by the feminist Louisa May Alcott. In her semiautobiographical novel, *Work* (1873), Alcott had chosen to climax the growth of her female protagonist

Christie with a public address on behalf of women.[49] Unlike James, Alcott, who was easily familiar with the feminist movement, presents a detailed description of the meeting where Christie speaks. She parodies a series of feminists—ladies who lecture their working-class audience with "unconscious condescension"; an "accomplished creature" who "delivered a charming little essay on the strong-minded women of antiquity"; an "eloquent sister" who "made them eager to rush to the State-house *en masse*"; and another who "closed with a cheerful budget of statistics, giving the exact number of needle-women who had starved, gone mad, or committed suicide during the past year." Yet, foreshadowing James, Alcott omits Christie's speech. She does, however, carefully make the point that her protagonist addresses her audience from the lowest step to the platform—that instead of separating herself from the women around her, she rises among them. And Alcott uses the language of antislavery feminism to characterize the response of Christie's audience: "They saw and felt that a genuine woman stood down there among them like a sister . . . , an example to comfort, touch, and inspire them." Moved by this experience, Christie, too, responds within the discursive codes of the antislavery feminists. A latter-day abolitionist, she recognizes that "others have finished the emancipation work." Then, speculating that "this new task seems to offer me the chance of being among the pioneers . . . of a new emancipation," and announcing herself "'strong-minded,' a radical, and a reformer," she declares, "I accept the task, and will do my share faithfully with words or work, as shall seem best." Alcott's female speaker appears as "an example to comfort, touch, and inspire"; James's apparently is a phenomenon. Neither novelist is interested in her "words."

Alcott's new generation of feminists, of course, responded to James's satire. L. Maria Child had dismissed his early stories by commenting that "the writer who sketches shoddy fashionables wastes his talents." Doubtless, had she lived to read *The Bostonians*, she would have approved of his subject and condemned his treatment of it.[50] The *Woman's Journal* reviewer commented:

> The book is evidently intended as a tremendous satire on the whole "woman question," though we believe no direct allusion whatever is made to women's suffrage. . . . Mr. James is by no means true to nature, and merely conveys the idea which he assumes the leaders of the "woman movement" to hold. It seems hardly worth while to take the trouble to issue a protest against this caricature.[51]

Nevertheless, Henry James prophesied correctly when, discussing the portrayal of Peabody as the Miss Birdseye of his book, he wrote, "I believe the story will remain longer than poor Miss P's name or fame."[52]

If today the antislavery feminists are recalled as the subject of literature, they are likely to be remembered in terms of James's caricature, as true women gone wrong—as perhaps heroic but certainly ridiculous, like Miss Birdseye:

> She had a sad, soft, pale face, which (and it was the effect of her whole head) looked as if it had been soaked, blurred, and made vague by exposure to some slow solvent. The long practice of philanthropy had not given accent to her features; it had rubbed out their transitions, their meanings. The waves of sympathy, of enthusiasm, had wrought upon them in the same way in which the waves of time finally modify the surface of old marble busts, gradually washing away their sharpness, their details. (P. 55)

Contrast this with John Jay Chapman's characterization, in *Memories and Milestones*, of his grandmother Maria Weston Chapman and her comrades:

> She looked and bore herself like bronze and marble, and made upon all observers the impression of heroic womanhood. . . . I cannot help thinking of the antislavery people as being earth-born, titanic creatures, whom Nature spawned to stay a plague—and then withdrew them, and broke the mold. Heroic they remain. . . . A Cause like this solves all questions whether they be matters of metaphysical doubt or of practical life. One's business is ruined, of course. A child dies; alas, it is severe, but let the Cause consume our grief. All social ties were snapped long ago; it is a trifle. The old standard-bearers are dropping out from time to time through death; peace be unto them, we have others.
>
> The discipline of such a life—so unusual, so singular—wore down men and women into athletes; the stress made them strong. Thus the antislavery fighters grew hardy through a sort of Roman endurance, which shows in their physiognamy. It is a force behind the stroke of fate that we see in people's faces, —the power behind the die that mints themselves. . . . [E]veryone who speaks of my grandmother always dwells upon the way she looked. It is her looks they cannot forget.[53]

Seeing a daguerrotype of Maria Weston Chapman, it is easy to share this vision (fig. 28). Apparently it was shared by the artist Edmonia Lewis, who made a small portrait bust of her. Yet while male antislavery activists like

Fig. 28. *Maria Weston Chapman* (ca. 1846).

Garrison and Phillips were memorialized full-length in three-dimensional "bronze and marble," the antislavery women did not become the subject of major sculpture. And after *The Bostonians*, they functionally vanish as a literary subject.[54]

But fragments of the discursive codes of the antislavery feminists survived into the twentieth century in feminist political imagery, in American elite culture, and in the African-American vernacular. As the language and the icons of the antislavery feminists became incorporated into other structures, however, their complex dialectic was fractured.

Writing and rewriting the female supplicant slave in chains, the antislavery feminists had developed multiple interpretations of their emblem. Recurrently, they saw it as signifying both the situation of women in a patriarchal society and the situation of blacks in a slave society. This reading enabled even privileged white women to identify with black women oppressed by slavery; but it also permitted them to collapse the racist, sexist, and class oppression of black women into a common oppression of gender. Similarly, privileged white antislavery feminists recurrently saw the double emblem as signifying not their struggle for their own autonomy, but their rescue of other women who were passive and victimized. This reading, too, erased the figure of a black woman struggling for freedom.

The absence of black women in early twentieth-century feminist discourse was certainly a response to the political, social, and sexual climate of the time. But it was a response in accord with the discourse shaped by the abolitionist emblems that persisted in American feminism as a subtext. Its force is evident in Elizabeth Cady Stanton's opening sentence in the *History of Woman Suffrage*: "The prolonged slavery of woman is the darkest page in human history."[55]

By the turn of the century, feminists abandoned the image of a supplicating woman in chains; they, in fact, abandoned most visual images. Two of their designs, however, recall antislavery iconography. A pin commemorating the release of activists from prison refers directly to the image of the enchained female supplicant, but it shows a subject who is white (fig. 29). "Votes for Women" depicts a vibrant young woman with cropped hair and loose robes whose bare feet tread on broken chains. She is pictured emerging from an entrance; its lintel traces an arc above her head, and its barred doors have been thrown open. Like the flying birds behind her, and like her outstretched arms, they signal her newfound liberty. At her feet, broken chains signify her recent bondage. These chains forge the connecting link between this white feminist and the black supplicant of antislavery iconography.[56]

Better known is the figure of the Bugler Girl, which also recalls antislavery feminism (fig. 30). Although early twentieth-century American women borrowed this design from England, it had strong native antecedents. Nineteenth-century American activists had made many references to Joan of

Fig. 29. *Votes for Women* (ca. 1910–1915).

Arc and had repeatedly used medieval images of heraldry and of bugling: Abby Kelley Foster helped establish the *Anti-Slavery Bugle*; another abolitionist newspaper was called *The Herald of Freedom*; and Lucy Stone, praising Angelina Grimké's public lecturing, characterized her example as "a Bugle-call to all other women."[57] The Bugler Girl was described in the British feminist press as "a woman trumpeter, standing on ramparts, flag in hand, and blowing an inspiriting call to the women of Great Britain to come out and stand by their sisters in this fight." Neither a powerless supplicant nor a supplicant who, empowered, would break her own chains, her figure instead suggests the chain-breaking rescuer of the double antislavery emblem. But now no second figure is present. The adoption by the American feminists of the Bugler Girl merits analysis in relation to turn-of-the-century imperialism and the white racism rampant within the feminist movement. A herald of twentieth-century American feminism, she apparently also heralds the obliteration—or at least, the marginalization—of black women in feminist discourse.[58]

Remnants of antislavery feminist iconography also survived in American sculpture. The most interesting is *Forever Free* by the black artist Edmonia Lewis, where the female figure replicates the posture, gesture, and expression of the slave emblem (fig. 31). Now fully clothed and with her chains

Fig. 30. Illustration, sheet music cover. *Marching on to Victory* (ca. 1913).

broken, she appears a newly freed woman giving thanks for her freedom. Her kneeling figure contrasts dramatically with that of the erect male who, with one hand protectively on her shoulder, raises his other to display the broken chains in a triumphant gesture signaling Emancipation. But the contrast between Lewis's figures involves not only gender, posture, and gesture: while the curling hair of the male identifies him as African, the

Fig. 31. Edmonia Lewis, *Forever Free* (1867).

female has flowing hair not usually associated with women of African descent. Does this detail suggest connections between Lewis's supplicant and women who are not Africans? Is the contrast in posture and gesture between these male and female figures a comment on the continued repression of all women in patriarchal societies? Lewis's kneeling woman, although now no longer seminude and no longer enchained, certainly is not presented as one of the self-liberated liberating women Sarah Grimké had envisioned who would "arise in all the majesty of moral power, in all the dignity of immortal beings, and plant themselves side by side on the platform of human rights, with man."[59]

Sculptures showing the influence of Powers's *Greek Slave*—and thus, at one remove, of abolitionist iconography—do not even allude to black women, nor do they refer to American slavery. The best known, Erastus Dow Palmer's *White Captive*, identifies its pathetic subject as a young white girl captured by Native Americans (fig. 32). Like Palmer's victim, Abastenia St. Leger Eberle's *White Slave*, a protest against prostitution, is specifically identified as white (fig. 33).[60]

Remnants of the discourse of antislavery feminism also survived in American literature. Throughout nineteenth-century fiction, paired light and dark women who are somehow connected, are somehow "sisters," recur obsessively; they recapitulate the structures of power, race, and gender encoded in the emblems, speeches, and writings of the antislavery feminists. Similarly, the figure of the Tragic Mulatto, which embodies one set of antislavery feminist structures of race and gender, is obsessively replicated. Following its invention by L. Maria Child, this character appears in American fiction over generations, in works by white women (E. D. E. N. Southworth, Rebecca Harding Davis, Mary Haydon [Green] Pike, Harriet Beecher Stowe, and Kate Chopin); by white men (Epes Sargent, William Dean Howells, George Washington Cable, Mark Twain, and William Faulkner); and in African-American writings by black women (Frances Ellen Watkins Harper, Pauline Hopkins), and by black men (William Wells Brown, Frank Webb, Charles W. Chesnutt, and James Weldon Johnson).[61]

But while the discourse of the antislavery feminists, whitened and fragmented, lived on in American elite culture and in feminist political culture, it also lived on in African-American popular culture. The motto of the antislavery feminists became part of the black vernacular. Sixty years after Emancipation, the African-American journalist Alice Dunbar-Nelson, lightheartedly anticipating criticism from her black readers, quoted the abolitionists when she wrote that she expected "a howl . . . from the Man and

Fig. 32. Erastus Dow Palmer, *White Captive* (1859).

Fig. 33. Cover illustration for *The Survey* (3 May 1913). Abastenia St. Leger Eberle. *White Slave*.

Brother and the Woman and Sister." More recently, by choosing to entitle her anthology *Black Sister*, critic Erlene Stetson testified that the language of the antislavery feminists continues to resonate in the writings of African-American women poets.[62]

Although the antislavery feminists vanished as a literary subject, and although their version of true womanhood became so utterly absorbed by the Angel in the House that even the next generation of feminists often imaged a figure who was less a Woman and a Sister than an Angel in the Hall, fragments of the structures of oppression and self-liberation that they encoded have survived. In the nineteenth century, the image of a pleading female in chains moved women beyond domestic boundaries to claim a place in the public sphere and to speak out. Today, the slave emblem urges us to reclaim their lost voices and to explore further the uncharted territory of oppositional discourse in America.

# Notes

## Preface

1 The lyrics reproduced here include the first verse and chorus only.
2 See Thomas Wentworth Higginson, "The Invisible Lady," *Women and the Alphabet: A Series of Essays* (1881; rpt., New York: Arno Press, 1972), pp. 65–70.
3 For a twentieth-century view of nineteenth-century "true womanhood," see Barbara Welter, "The Cult of True Womanhood," *Dimity Convictions: The American Woman in the Nineteenth Century*, ed. Barbara Welter (Columbus: Ohio University Press, 1975). Coventry Patmore's poem *The Angel in the House*, 2 vols. (London: Macmillan, 1863), provided a name for one version of this cultural model. Patmore's poem originally appeared in four segments: *The Angel in the House: The Betrothal* (London: Parker, 1854), *Book 2, The Espousals* (London: Parker, 1856); *Faithful For Ever* (London: Parker, 1860); *The Victims of Love* (London: MacMillan, 1863). For more, see chapter 1.
4 For a plea for the transformation of literary criticism into "culture criticism," see Gerald Graff and Reginald Gibbons, "Introduction," *Criticism in the University*, ed. Gerald Graff and Reginald Gibbons, *Triquarterly* Series on Criticism and Culture, no. 1 (Evanston, Ill.: Northwestern University Press, 1985), pp. 7–12.
5 In M. M. Bakhtin, *The Dialogic Imagination*, ed. Michael Hilquist, trans. Caryl Emerson and Michael Hilquist (Austin: University of Texas Press, 1981), p. 427, *dialogism* is defined as "the characteristic epistemological mode of a world dominated by *heteroglosia*. Every thing means . . . there is a constant interaction between meanings, all of which have the potential of conditioning others." Fredric Jameson, *The Political Unconscious* (Ithaca: Cornell University Press, 1981), p. 85.
6 For the history of the relationships between the ideology of abolitionism and nineteenth-century feminism, see for example Aileen Kraditor's *The Ideas of the Woman Suffrage Movement, 1890–1910* (New York: Columbia University Press, 1965) and *Means and Ends in American Abolitionism* (New York: Pantheon Books, 1969); and chapter 2, below.

7   Jameson, *Political Unconscious*, p. 86.
8   Erwin Panofsky long ago discussed the dependence of artists on a vocabulary of forms; see *Meaning in the Visual Arts* (Garden City, N.Y.: Anchor Books, 1955). And Rudolf Arnheim argued not only the validity but the primacy of "visual thinking" in *Visual Thinking* (Berkeley: University of California Press, 1969).
9   *Sensational Designs* (New York: Oxford University Press, 1985), p. xv. For discussions of cultural texts—whose interpretation Alan Trachtenberg has characterized as necessarily "dialogic and contextual"—see two articles by Jules Prown: "Mind in Matter: An Introduction to Material Culture Theory and Method," *Winterthur Portfolio* 17 (Spring 1982): [1]–19; and "Style as Evidence," *Winterthur Portfolio* 15 (Autumn 1980). The quotation is from Trachtenberg's unpublished commentary presented at the American Studies Association, November 1987. For more, see chapter 1.
10  Roland Barthes, *Mythologies*, trans. Annette Lavers (New York: Hill and Wang, 1972), p. 112.
11  Umberto Eco, *Theory of Semiotics* (Bloomington: Indiana University Press, 1976), p. 271.
12  Raymond Williams, *Marxism and Literature* (New York: Oxford University Press, 1977), p. 114.

## Chapter One

1   Angelina E. Grimké, *Appeal to the Christian Women of the South* (New York: American Anti-Slavery Society, 1836), pp. 32–33.
2   Lyon G. Tyler, *Letters and Times of the Tylers*, 3 vols. (Richmond, Va.: Whittet and Shepperson, 1884–94), 1:573–81. I am grateful to Marilyn T. Williams for calling my attention to this passage.
3   For President Jackson's message to Congress, 7 December 1835, denouncing abolitionist prints, see Wendell P. and Francis J. Garrison, *William Lloyd Garrison: The Story of His Life Told by His Children*, 4 vols. (1885; reprint, New York: Negro Universities Press, 1969), 2:73. For the abolitionists' response, see Massachusetts Anti-Slavery Society, *Fourth Annual Report* (Boston: Isaac Knapp, 1836), pp. 17, 20. For Frederick Douglass's review of Gerrit Smith's 1836 condemnation of attempts to suppress abolitionist graphics, see Rochester, N.Y., *Douglass' Monthly*, January 1861, p. 389. Also see W. Sherman Savage, *The Controversy Over the Distribution of Abolition Literature, 1830–1860* (Washington, D.C.: n.p., 1938), pp. 9–42; and Frank Luther Mott, *American Journalism* (New York, 1950), p. 307.
4   *Proceedings* (New York: W. S. Dorr, 1837), p. 14.
5   Jules Prown, "Style as Evidence," *Winterthur Portfolio* 15 (Autumn 1980), p. 210; also see Umberto Eco, *A Theory of Semiotics* (Bloomington: Indiana University Press, 1976), p. 193: "In the iconic experience certain perceptual mechanisms function which are of the same type as the one involved in the perception of an actual object"; and Rudolf Arnheim, *Visual Thinking* (Berkeley: University of California Press, 1969).
6   See Peter Marzio, "Illustrated News in Early American Prints," in *American Print Making Before 1876* (Washington, D.C.: Library of Congress, 1975), p. 60. A standard listing of abolitionist publications remains Dwight Lowell Dumond, *A Bibliography of Antislavery in America* (Ann Arbor: University of Michigan Press, 1967). For a sampling of

antislavery images, see Dumond's *Antislavery: The Crusade for Freedom in America* (Ann Arbor: University of Michigan Press, 1961). For the Renaissance emblem tradition, see Mario Praz, *Studies in Seventeenth Century Imagery*, 2d ed. (Rome: Edizioni di storia e letteratura, 1964); Rosemary Freeman, *English Emblem Books* (1948; republished New York: Octagon, 1966); Peter M. Daly, *Literature in the Light of Emblem* (Toronto: University of Toronto Press, 1979); and Ronald Paulson, *Emblem and Expression: Meaning in English Art of the Eighteenth Century* (Cambridge: Harvard University Press, 1975). Use of the emblematic tradition in American art is discussed in various writings by Roger B. Stein, including "Thomas Smith's Self-Portrait: Image/Text as Artifact," *Art Journal* 44 (Winter 1984): 316–27; "Charles Willson Peale's Expressive Design," *Prospects* 6 (1981): 139–85; and *Seascape and the American Imagination* (New York: Clarkson N. Potter, 1975).

7 Thomas Clarkson, *History of the Rise, Progress, and Accomplishment of the Abolition of the African Slave Trade by the British Parliament*, 2 vols. (London: R. Taylor, 1808), 1:450–51. For earlier depictions of slavery, see "Esclavage," in Hubert F. L. Gravelot, *Iconologie par figures* (Paris, 1791; reprint, Geneva: Minkoff, 1972), 3:34; these plates were previously issued in *L'Almanach iconologique lattre* (1761–81) according to Henry Cohen and Seymour DeRicci, *Guide de l'amateur de livres a gravures du 18c* (Paris: Librarie a. Rouquette, 1912), col. 456. Hugh Honour speculates that the motto may derive from John Wesley's 1773 antislavery argument, which quoted from Genesis: "'The blood of thy brother,' (for whether thou wilt believe it or not, such is he in the sight of Him that made him) 'crieth against thee from the earth'" (Wesley, *Thoughts upon Slavery*, in *Works*, vol. 16, pp. 456, 464, in Honour, *Slaves and Liberators*, part 1 of *From the American Revolution to World War 1*, vol. 4 of *The Image of the Black in Western Art*, 4 vols. [Cambridge, Mass.: Harvard University Press, 1989], p. 63).

8 Clarkson, *History*, 2:191. For a discussion of the new technology, see Robin Reilly, *Wedgwood Portrait Medallions: An Introduction* (London: Barrie and Jenkins, [1973]).

9 Franklin is quoted in Alison Kelly, *The Story of Wedgwood* (New York: Viking, 1963), p. 42. For Wedgwood's antislavery correspondence, see *The Selected Letters of Josiah Wedgwood*, ed. Ann Finer and George Savage (London: Cory, Adams and Mackey, 1965), pp. 309–12.

10 Angelina E. Grimké, *Appeal*, p. 23. No systematic effort has been made to list antislavery artifacts in America. For antislavery coins and tokens, see Herbert Aptheker, "Antislavery Medallions in the Martin Jacobowitz Collection," *Negro History Bulletin* 33 (May 1970): 115–21; Melvin Fuld and George Fuld, "Antislavery Tokens," *Numismaticist* 70 (April 1957): 395–409; and *Journal of the Token and Medal Society* 2 (January-February, March-April, September-October 1962); Robert J. Lindesmith, "Edward Hulseman, Hard Times Engraver," *TAMS Journal* (June-July 1967): 71–82; Thomas Sheppard, *Medals, Tokens, etc. Issued in Connection with William Wilberforce and the Abolition of Slavery*. Hull Museum Publications no. 109 (Hull: n.p., 1916); "The Anti-Slavery Movement and its Coins and Medals," *The Coin Collectors Journal* (November 1884): 161–65. Examples of the motif on ceramics can be found in America, for example, in the collections of the Friends Historical Library, Swarthmore College, and the Society for the Preservation of New England Antiquities; and in England, at the Victoria and Albert, Brighton, and Liverpool museums; also see W. D. John and Warren Baker, *Old English Lustre Pottery* (Newport: R. H. Johns, 1951), p. 124. Examples of the motif in needlework and beadwork are in the collections of the Wedgwood Museum,

Barlaston, Staffordshire; of the Friends Historical Library, Swarthmore College; and of
Emma and Sidney Kaplan.

11    Lundy published sixteen volumes of *The Genius* (1821–39) at various locations. Lundy's
      publication continued as *Genius of Liberty* (1840–42); as *Western Citizen* (1842–53);
      and as *Free West* (1853–55). For Garrison's 1829 connection with *The Genius*, see
      Lundy's *Life, Travels and Opinions*, comp. Thomas Earle (Philadelphia: William D.
      Parrish, 1847), pp. 28–29. Whittier's 1834 poem—published as an antislavery
      broadside—was omitted from his *Complete Poetical Works* (Boston and New York:
      Houghton Mifflin, 1894).

12    Anti-Slavery Convention of American Women, *Proceedings* (New York: W. S. Dorr,
      1837), p. 7. The origins of this design remain unclear; it may well be an invention
      making use of archetypal elements such as praying hands, kneeling, and chains,
      according to a private communication from Huston Diehl to Jean Fagan Yellin, 19 May
      1987. But see the suggestive scholarship presented in Jean Vercoutter et al., *From the
      Pharaohs to the Fall of the Roman Empire*, vol. 1 of *The Image of the Black in Western
      Art* (New York: William Morrow, 1976); and Jean Devisse et al., *From the Early
      Christian Era to the "Age of Discovery,"* 2 pts., vol. 2 of *The Image of the Black in
      Western Art* (New York: William Morrow, 1979). Andre Grabar, *Christian Iconography: A
      Study of Its Origins* (Princeton: Princeton University Press, 1968), p. 126 discusses
      the kneeling or prostrate personifications of conquered cities or provinces on Roman
      coins. Also see the discussion of the origins of Ghilberti's *Sacrifice of Isaac* in Richard
      Krautheimer, *Lorenzo Ghilberti* (Princeton: Princeton University Press, 1956); and Ber-
      nard de Montfaucon, *Antiquity Explained and Represented in Sculpture*, trans. David
      Humphries, 2 vols. (London: J. Tonson and J. Watts, 1721), 1:65–66, pl. 27, which
      shows depictions of Marsyas that include the figure of a kneeling supplicant, variously
      identified as the Scythian or Olympus. I am grateful to Ann Coffin Hanson and to
      Sidney Kaplan for this source. For a somewhat different interpretation of this emblem,
      see Hugh Honour, *Slaves and Liberators*, part 1 of *From the American Revolution to
      World War 1*, vol. 4 of *The Image of the Black in Western Art*, 4 vols. (Cambridge, Mass.:
      Harvard University Press, 1989), pp. 63–64. For Sarah Grimké's comment, see Anti-
      Slavery Convention of American Women, *Proceedings*, p. 7.

13    The Afro-American Bicentennial Corporation, *A Study of Historic Sites in the District of
      Columbia of Special Significance to Afro-Americans* (typescript, Martin Luther King
      Public Library, Washington, D.C., 1972), pp. 76–77. Thomas Ball's sculpture *Eman-
      cipation Group* (1865) is in Washington, D.C.; a duplicate is in Boston.

14    See the figure of Poverty in "Fortune," from Cesare Ripa, (1758), in *Baroque and Rococo
      Pictorial Imagery: The 1758-60 Hertel edition of Ripa's Iconología*; trans. Edwin A.
      Maser (New York: Dover, 1971), p. 152; also see the illustration of "Pauvrete" from
      Boulard, *Iconologie* (Parma, 1759) in Mario Praz, *Studies in Seventeenth Century Imag-
      ery*, 2d ed (Rome, Edizioni di storia e letteratura, 1964), 202.

15    Artistic conventions associating nudity with purity conflicted with racial conventions
      associating nudity with savagery; see Kenneth Clark, *The Nude: A Study in Ideal Form*
      (Princeton: Princeton University Press, 1956); William Gerdts, *The Great American
      Nude* (New York: Praeger, 1975); and *The Image of the Black in Western Art*.

16    For changing gender patterns among abolitionists, see Lawrence J. Friedman, *Gregari-
      ous Saints* (New York: Cambridge University Press, 1982), chap. 5.

17    Soyez Libres et Citoyens, signed P. Rouvier, inv. et del; C. Baily, sculp, frontispiece, M.

Frossard, *La cause des esclaves Negres*, 2 vols. (Lyon: Amie de la Roche, 1789), 1. This scene is described in the concluding paragraph, which reads: "Behold! I see this beneficent Genius, charged by the King of the Universe for the well-being of France . . . content with his work, cross the seas and soar above the Antilles. He descends into those regions inhabited by despotism, terror and death. Sweet pity is in his gaze; goodness enlivens all his features. An enslaved people gathers about him. Accustomed to fear, those unfortunates experience before him a feeling which was unknown to them until that moment. A sacred confidence seizes their soul. They surround this defending Angel, they fall at his feet, they struggle to raise up to him their arms loaded with chains; and, their eyes fixed on his august face, they await in respectful silence, the decree which he will pronounce. —Soon, with that voice which reassures the heart and prepares it for generous reward . . . France blesses her Monarch: 'she begins to enjoy this fortunate and constant order which she owes to him.' Share her joy: Be Free men and Citizens." I am grateful to Hugh Honour for bringing this illustration to my attention, and to my colleague Philip Fulvi for this translation.

18  Female Society for Birmingham, etc., for the Relief of British Negro Slaves (later Ladies Negro's Friend Society of Birmingham), *First Report* (Birmingham: Richard Pearl, 1826), *Second and Third Reports* (1826–27, 1827–28) in [Female Society for Birmingham] *Album* [c. 1828], pp. 20–21. For the passage the Birmingham women referred to in their *Second Report*, see l'Abbe Guidicelly, *Observations sur la traite des noirs* (Paris: Chez les Marchands de Nouveautés, 1820), pp. 22–23. The origins of the female figure, like those of the male supplicant, remain obscure.

19  Ladies Negro's Friend Society, *Retrospect of the Work of Half-a-Century* (London: E. Newman, 1875), p. 6.

20  McLean's broadside is dated 23 February 1830. The antislavery papers appeared in *The Westminster Review* 11, no. 22 (October 1829): 275–90. For additional publications of British abolitionist women, see for example *The Negro's Friend, or, the Sheffield Anti-Slavery Album* (Sheffield, 1826); and *The Anti-Slavery Album* (London: Howlett and Bremmer, 1828). While these do not include the kneeling supplicant, this design does appear in the frontispiece of *Scripture Evidence of the Sinfulness of Injustice and Oppression* (London, 1828). The supplicant was one of the many stereotypes of blacks. For eighteenth-century depictions of bestial blacks seen as comical in fancy-dress, see the discussion of Hogarth's works in Hugh Honour, *Black Models and White Myths*, part 2 of *From the American Revolution to World War 1*, vol. 4 of *The Image of the Black in Western Art*, 4 vols. (Cambridge, Mass.: Harvard University Press, 1989).

21  *The Genius*, 3d ser., vol. 1 (May 1830), pp. 24–25; n.s., vol. 1 (8 September 1827): pp. 74–75; n.s. 4 (2 September 1829): p. 5. Elizabeth Margaret Chandler (1807–34) was an important figure in the history of female antislavery in America; we need a modern biography. Her collected *Works* are cited below.

22  "Mental Metempsychosis," *The Genius*, 3d series, 1 (February 1831): 171.

23  3d Series, 1 (May 1830): 41, 44.

24  2 (17 March 1832): 42.

25  Douglass to Chandler, Philadelphia, 1 March 1833, Chandler Papers, Michigan Historical Collections, Bentley Historical Library, University of Michigan; Elizabeth Smith Album, Francis J. Grimké Papers, Spingarn-Moorland Collection, Howard University. For other examples of the stationery, see Angelina Grimké to Stephen S. Foster, 17 July [1837]; and Sarah M. Douglass to Abby Kelley, Philadelphia, 18 May 1838, American

Antiquarian Society. For a British example of the female emblem on stationery, see
Henry W. Williams to Stephen S. Foster, 27 February 1846, American Antiquarian
Society. For the motif inked on cloth, see "poor little slave" artifact in the collection of
the Clements Library, University of Michigan.

26  *Appeal* (New York: Allen and Ticknor, 1833; republ. New York: Arno, 1968); "The
Slave's Address to the British Ladies. For the Chelmsford Female Anti-Slavery Association" (Covent Garden: I. Sturz, n.d.); *Oasis* (Boston: Allen and Ticknor, 1834), p. xvi.

27  *The Slave's Friend* 1, no. 8 (1836), title page.

28  Aaron M. Powell, *Personal Reminiscences of the Anti-Slavery and Other Reforms and
Reformers* (New York, 1899), pp. 1–2; Judith C. Breault, *The World of Emily Howland*
(California: Les Femmes, 1976), p. 10.

29  Weld to Angelina and Sarah Grimké, 15 December 1837, in Gilbert H. Barnes and
Dwight L. Dumond, eds., *Letters of Theodore Dwight Weld, Angelina Grimké Weld, and
Sarah Grimké, 1822–1844*, 2 vols. (1934; reprint, New York: De Capo, 1970), 1:490.
*The Fountain* (New York: John S. Taylor, 1836). A listing of materials concerning
Reason is included in Lynn Moody Igoe, *250 Years of Afro-American Art: An Annotated
Bibliography* (New York: R. R. Bowker, 1981), pp. 1046–48. Although the role of
abolitionists as patrons of Reason—or of other Afro-American artists—has not been
systematically examined, my spot check of antislavery publications yields a number of
announcements featuring Reason's work.

30  Amy Post to Abby Kelley Foster, 4 December 1843, Abby Kelley Foster Papers, American Antiquarian Society. I am grateful to Nancy Hewitt for bringing this letter to my
attention.

31  *Poetical Works of Elizabeth Margaret Chandler with a Memoir by Benjamin Lundy*
(Philadelphia: L. Howell, 1836); *Essays Philanthropic and Moral* (Philadelphia: L.
Howell, 1836). In 1839, *The Liberator* announced a new elaborate version, complete
with decorative chains, to ornament "a beautiful contribution box" designed for the
faithful to use as a depository for their weekly pledges to the cause. See issue of 20
December 1839, 202ff. Widely reproduced in antislavery publications, this image
became the cover graphic of *The Monthly Offering*, a publication connected with the
prominent abolitionist Maria Weston Chapman. See *The Emancipator*, 1 October 1840;
and *The Monthly Offering*, 1 (1841) and 2 (1842). I am grateful to the late Marilyn Baily
for help in tracing this version.

32  See André Grabar, *Christian Iconography*, p. 126. For views of bound vanquished
Africans in Egyptian, Greek, and Roman art, see *The Image of the Black in Western Art*,
vol. 1, figs. 42, 64, 65, 276, 277; for portrayals of victors and vanquished, see fig. 126.

33  For the development of an American Liberty and for Britannia Libertas as an abolitionist emblem, see Frank H. Sommer, "The Metamorphoses of Britannia," in Charles
F. Montgomery and Patricia E. Kane, eds., *American Art: 1750–1800: Towards Independence* (Boston: New York Graphic Society, 1976), pp. 40–49; also see Joshua C. Taylor, *America as Art* (Washington, D.C.: Smithsonian Institution Press, 1976); Hugh
Honour, *The European Vision of America* (Cleveland: Cleveland Museum of Art, 1975);
Robert C. Smith, "Liberty Displaying the Arts and Sciences: A Philadelphia Allegory
by Samuel Jennings," *Winterthur Portfolio* 2 (1965): 84–102; and two articles by
McClung Fleming, "The American Image as Indian Princess, 1763–1783," *Winterthur
Portfolio* 2 (1965): 65–81; and "From Indian Princess to Greek Goddess: The Ameri-
can Image, 1783–1815," *Winterthur Portfolio* 3 (1967): 37–66. For representations of

revolutionary America, see M. Dorothy George, "America in English Satirical Prints," *William and Mary Quarterly*, n.s. (1933): 511–37; Clarence S. Brigham, *Paul Revere's Engravings* (Worcester, Mass.: American Antiquarian Society, 1954), pp. 21–25, 91–92; and Michael Kammen, "From Liberty to Prosperity: Reflections upon the Role of Revolutionary Iconography in National Tradition," in American Antiquarian Society, *Proceedings* 76, pt. 2 (1976): 237–72. The iconography of Revolutionary France is discussed in *L'art de l'estampe et la revolution Francaise* (Exhibition catalog) (Paris: Musée Carnavalet, 1977); Maurice Agulhon, *Marianne au combat: L'imagerie et la symbolique republicaines de 1789 à 1880* (Paris: Flammarion, 1979); and James Cuno, *French Caricature and the French Revolution, 1789–1799* (catalog) (Chicago: University of Chicago Press, 1988).

34 The leather purse printed with this image that Chandler owned is in the collection of the Museum of the Daughters of the American Revolution, with another purse imprinted with antislavery designs. Similar antislavery "work-bags" are in the collection of The Friends Historical Library of Swarthmore College. Other examples in the Textile Collection, Victoria and Albert Museum, are stuffed with pamphlets; I am indebted to Winifred Lubell for telling me about them. For Cowper's work for abolition, see *The Life and Works of William Cowper* by Robert Southey, 15 vols. (London: Baldwin and Cradock, 1836), 2:314–16; also see Norma Russell, *A Bibliography of William Cowper to 1837* (Oxford: Clarendon Press, 1963), pp. 149–52.

35 L. Maria Child in *The Liberator*, 2 January 1837; in Walter M. Merrill and Louis Ruchames, eds., *The Letters of William Lloyd Garrison*, 6 vols. (Cambridge: Harvard University Press, 1971), 2:195; I am grateful to Sidney Kaplan for this reference.

36 *Authentic Anecdotes of American Slavery*, 2d ed. (Newburyport: Charles Whipple, 1838). For the English medal showing her as Justice, see n. 10, above.

37 In the King James Version, Ps. 2:3 reads: "Let us break their bands asunder, and cast away their cords from us."

38 See André Grabar, *Christian Iconography*. Although *The Liberator* masthead initially included no graphics, each of the three illustrated versions was increasingly elaborate. The earliest of these (1831) showed a slave auction. The next (1850) contrasted the scene of a slave sale on the left with a depiction of emancipation on the right. Figure 8 shows the third and final illustrated masthead, published in 1850 and signed by Hartwell; for contemporary responses to these mastheads, see Wendell P. and Francis J. Garrison, *William Lloyd Garrison*, 1:231–33.

39 For stationery with this double image, see for example Mary N. B. Smith to Abby Kelley, 16 August 1841, American Antiquarian Society. Maria Weston Chapman, editor of the Boston Female Anti-Slavery Society's annual giftbook, *The Liberty Bell*, included two versions in the 1839 edition. The chain-breaker appears as Truth in Patrick Reason's engraved frontispiece "Truth Shall Make You Free;" she is Freedom of the Press in an unsigned engraving, "Lovejoy, the First Martyr to American Liberty, Murdered for Asserting the Freedom of the Press" p. 69.

40 According to Eric P. Newman, "The Promotion and Suppression of Hard Times Tokens," in a *Festschrift* for Vladimir and Elvira Clain-Stefanelli, ed. R. G. Doty and T. Hackens (Wetteren, Belgium: Cultura, 1989), the New York City *Emancipator* of 23 November 1837 announced that "some Anti-Slavery COPPER MEDALS" showing "a female slave, in chains, in an imploring attitude, with the motto, 'Am I not a woman and a sister?'" had been manufactured by "an artist in New Jersey." For the stereotype cut, see Boston Type

Foundry *Specimen Book*, (1845), American Type Foundry Specimen Book Collection, Special Collections, Columbia University Libraries.

41  See Henry Louis Gates, Jr., "Writing 'Race' and the Difference It Makes," *"Race," Writing and Difference*, ed. Henry Louis Gates, Jr. (Chicago: University of Chicago Press, 1986), pp. 1–20; and see chapters 2 and 3, below.

42  For a helpful discussion of "the phallocentricity of the symbolic order," see Kaja Silverman, *The Subject of Semiotics* (New York: Oxford University Press, 1983), p. 131. A number of twentieth-century studies discuss the social restrictions placed on nineteenth-century women. See, for example, Barbara Welter, "The Cult of True Womanhood," *Dimity Convictions: The American Woman in the Nineteenth Century* (Athens, Ohio: Ohio State University Press, 1976); here purity, piety, chastity, and obedience are characterized as a "cult of domesticity" projected as an ideal for American women; and see Nancy F. Cott, *The Bonds of Womanhood: "Woman's Sphere" in New England, 1780–1835* (New Haven: Yale University Press, 1977). Some of the ways in which this ideology was acted out during the revolutionary period are explored in Linda Kerber, *Women of the Republic* (Chapel Hill: University of North Carolina, 1980). The issue of the complex relationships between gender identification and feminism is raised in Cott and in the work of Ellen DuBois, Nancy Hewitt, Lee Chambers-Schiller, Mary Ryan, and other historians. The shift that transformed the supplicant slave from male to female also permitted it to be read as an evocation of the biblical type of Judea Capta; this allowed the use of the image in connection with Ps. 68:31, "Ethiopia shall soon stretch out her hands unto God"; see chapter 2.

## Chapter Two

1  L. Maria Child to E. Carpenter, 20 March 1838, in *Lydia Maria Child: Selected Letters, 1817–1880*, ed. Milton Meltzer and Patricia G. Holland (Amherst: University of Massachusetts Press, 1982), pp. 71–72.

2  The connections and disjunctions between gender consciousness and feminist consciousness, between organized benevolence and organized feminism, are explored in Eleanor Flexner, *Century of Struggle: The Women's Rights Movement in the United States* (Cambridge: Harvard University Press, 1959); Nancy F. Cott, *The Bonds of Womanhood: "Woman's Sphere" in New England, 1780–1835* (New Haven: Yale University Press, 1977); Caroll Smith-Rosenberg, "The Female World of Love and Ritual: Relations between Women in Nineteenth-Century America," *SIGNS* (Autumn 1975): 1–29; Blanche Glassman Hersh, *The Slavery of Sex: Feminist-Abolitionists in America* (Chicago: University of Illinois Press, 1978); Ellen DuBois, *Feminism and Suffrage: The Emergence of an Independent Women's Movement in America, 1848–1869* (Ithaca: Cornell University Press, 1978); and Nancy A. Hewitt, "Feminist Friends: Agrarian Quakers and the Emergence of Women's Rights in America," *Feminist Studies* 12 (Spring 1986): 27–50.

3  Angelina Grimké, Diary, April 1829, Weld-Grimké Collection, William L. Clements Library, University of Michigan; also see entries for 19 December 1828; 9 February 1829; 29 August 1829; 31 August 1829; and 11 September 1829. For a description of the Charlestown jail, see Karl Bernard, Duke of Saxe-Weimar Eisenach, *Travels Through North America During the Years 1825 and 1826*, 2 vols. (Philadelphia, 1828), 2:8–10; excerpted in Willie Lee Rose, ed., *A Documentary History of Slavery in North America*

(New York: Oxford University Press, 1976), p. 243.

My discussion of Grimké is based on unpublished papers in the Weld-Grimké Collection and on published works by Angelina Grimké, Sarah Grimké, and Theodore Weld, on correspondence appearing in Gilbert H. Barnes and Dwight L. Dumond, eds., *Letters of Theodore Dwight Weld, Angelina Grimké Weld, and Sarah Grimké, 1822–1844*, 2 vols. (1934; reprint, New York: Da Capo Press, 1970), and on three biographies: Catherine Birney, *The Grimké Sisters: Sarah and Angelina Grimké, the First Woman Advocates of Abolition and Woman's Rights* (Boston: Lee and Shepard, 1885); Gerda Lerner, *The Grimké Sisters from South Carolina: Pioneers for Woman's Rights and Abolition* (New York: Schocken Books, 1967); and Katharine Du Pre Lumpkin, *The Emancipation of Angelina Grimké* (Chapel Hill: University of North Carolina Press, 1974). Sections of this chapter were presented at the Modern Language Association in New York in 1978.

4   For a discussion of the construction of a self in and through diary keeping, and of the formal literary issues involved, see "Introduction," *A Day at a Time*, ed. Margo Culley (New York: Feminist Press, 1985), pp. 3–26. For Poe's racist imagery, see Sidney Kaplan's classic introduction to *The Narrative of Arthur Gordon Pym* (New York: Hill and Wang, 1960).

5   Grimké's response was not, however, characteristic of the radical Quaker women; see the brief discussion of Lucretia Mott, below.

6   A. E. Grimké to Jane Smith, New York, 19 November 1836.

7   Grimké's letter appeared in *The Liberator*, 19 September 1835, and was widely republished. Writing to George W. Benson on 12 September 1835, Garrison commented on Grimké's "soul-thrilling epistle . . . with a spirit worthy of the best days of martyrdom" (*The Letters of William Lloyd Garrison*, ed. Walter M. Merrill and Louis Ruchames, 6 vols. [Cambridge: Harvard University Press, 1971–1981], 1:527). Also see Wendell P. and Francis J. Garrison, *William Lloyd Garrison, 1805–1879: The Story of His Life Told by His Children*, 4 vols. (New York: Century Company, 1885–89), 1:518. It is possible that a letter from a highly respectable southern lady "exposing conditions in the Charleston Work-House" published in *The Liberator*, 16 May 1835, was written by Grimké; I am grateful to Dorothy Sterling for this citation.

8   *Appeal to the Christian Women of the South* (New York: American Anti-Slavery Society, 1836). Rev. and republ. *The Anti-Slavery Examiner*, 1:2 (September, 1835). Page references are to this edition. For Grimké's epigraph, see Esther 4:16.

9   *Appeal to the Christian Women*, p. 21.

10  *An Appeal to the Women of the Nominally Free States* (New York: W. S. Dorr, 1837).

11  *Proceedings of the Anti-Slavery Convention of American Women, Held in the City of New-York, May 9th, 10th, 11th, and 12th, 1837* (New York: W. S. Dorr, 1837), p. 8. Conventions were also held in 1838 and 1839. The history of the female antislavery societies has not been written, although the New York society is the subject of one unpublished master's thesis: Amy Swerdlow, *An Examination of the New York City Female Anti-Slavery Society, 1834–1840* (Sarah Lawrence College, 1974). A very brief retrospective summary appears in Mary Grew, "Annals of Women's Anti-Slavery Societies," *Proceedings of the American Anti-Slavery Society at Its Third Decade, Held in the City of Philadelphia, December 3d and 4th, 1863* (Philadelphia, 1864; republished, New York: Negro Universities Press, 1969). The quoted passage is from the 1837 *Proceedings*, p. 8.

12  Sarah Grimké wrote the tract the convention addressed to African-Americans. For

Angelina and Sarah Grimké on the problem of white racism within women's antislavery organizations, see their letters: to Jane Smith, New York, 22 March 1837; to Sarah Douglass, New York, 3 April 1837; to Jane Smith, New York, 17 April 1837; and to Jane Smith, 20 May 1837.

Concerning the interracial composition of this convention, which passed 53 resolutions, issued 6 publications, and planned another convention for the following year, one participant reported that "about one-tenth of our number were colored. They did not take part in the general business, but when the subject of Colonization was taken up they spoke with earnestness. They responded also upon prejudice against color" (Sarah Pugh, *Memorial of Sarah Pugh: a Tribute of Respect from Her Cousins* [Philadelphia: J. B. Lippincott, 1888], p. 18). In its final form the product of an interracial committee, the moralistic pamphlet Sarah Grimké worked on appeared as *An Address to Free Colored Americans* (New York, 1837).

13  *An Appeal to the Women*, p. 21.

14  Edward Savage, *Liberty as Goddess of Youth* (1796), stipple engraving, Library of Congress, Washington, D.C. Also see Samuel Lovett Waldo's oil painting (c. 1805), Lyman Allyn Museum, New London, Conn.

15  *An Appeal to the Women*, p. 67.

16  Angelina Grimké left a running account of this lecture tour in letters to her friend Jane Smith. For the Salem meetings, see her letter of 16 July 1837; for Concord, where Lydian Emerson was one of her "delighted hostesses," according to Ralph L. Rusk, *The Life of Ralph Waldo Emerson* (New York, 1949), p. 260, see her letter of 15 September 1837. For Lydian Emerson's "zealous" membership in the antislavery society beginning in 1840, and for her participation in organized feminism, see Ellen Tucker Emerson, *The Life of Lydian Jackson Emerson* (Boston, 1980). For the mobbings, see Russel B. Nye, *Fettered Freedom: Civil Liberties and the Slavery Controversy, 1830–1860* (Michigan: Michigan State University Press, 1963), p. 203.

17  See Wendell P. and Francis J. Garrison, *William Lloyd Garrison, 1805–1879*, 2:133–36. Angelina E. Grimké, *Letters to Catharine E. Beecher, in Reply to an Essay on Slavery and Abolition, Addressed to A. E. Grimké* (Boston: Isaac Knapp, 1838). These thirteen letters first appeared in *The Liberator* in response to Beecher, *An Essay on Slavery and Abolitionism with Reference to the Way of American Females, Addressed to Miss A. E. Grimké* (Philadelphia: Henry Perkins; Boston: Perkins & Marvin, 1837). The standard work on Beecher is Kathryn Kish Sklar, *Catharine Beecher: A Study in American Domesticity* (New Haven: Yale University Press, 1973). The historian Richard Hildreth, an abolitionist, immediately saw the contradiction in Beecher's position. In *Brief Remarks on Miss Catharine E. Beecher's Essay on Slavery and Abolitionism, by the Author of Archy Moore* (Boston: Isaac Knapp, 1837), he pointed out that in writing and titling her pamphlet, Beecher had made herself visible in the public sphere—which was precisely what she argued women must not do. Beecher, however, may have felt called upon to address Grimké because Grimké's second *Appeal* had used as an epigraph lines Beecher had written: "The trembling earth, the low murmuring thunder, already admonish us of our danger; and if females can exert any saving influence in this emergency, *it is time for them to awake.*"

18  *Letters to Catharine E. Beecher*, p. 114.

19  *Letters to Catharine E. Beecher*, pp. 112–13.

20  Gerda Lerner, "The Political Activities of Antislavery Women," *The Majority Finds Its Past* (New York: Oxford University Press, 1979), pp. 112–28.

21  *Letters to Catharine E. Beecher*, pp. 116–19.

22  Nancy F. Cott, *Bonds of Womanhood*, p. 1.

23  Angelina Grimké to Jane Smith, 29 May-5 June-7 June 1837; 26 June 1837; and 26 October 1837.

24  Angelina Grimké to Jane Smith, 9 May-5 June-7 June 1837.

25  Lerner, "Political Activities of Antislavery Women," p. 124.

26  Grimké's speech before the Legislative Committee of the Massachusetts Legislature, 11 February 1838, was published in *The Liberator*, 2 March 1838.

27  Angelina Grimké to Sarah M. Douglass, 25 February 1838; the text is published in Barnes and Dumond, eds., *Letters of Theodore Dwight Weld, Angelina Grimké Weld, and Sarah Grimké*, 2:574. A rebel song of the Revolution was "The World Turned Upside-Down."

28  *Letters on the Equality of the Sexes and the Condition of Woman: Addressed to Mary Parker, President of the Boston Female Anti-Slavery Society* (Boston: Isaac Knapp, 1838). These were first published as a series in the *New England Spectator* in 1838.

29  *On the Equality*, p. 10.

30  References are to Angelina Grimké's diary entries of 29 March, 31 March, and 30 May 1829, as quoted in Birney, pp. 85, 89. For the shifting referends of the "root of bitterness," see Angelina Grimké's Diary entry of 26 December 1828; her letter to Thomas Grimké, quoted in Birney, p. 110; and *On the Equality*, p. 126.

31  *Letters on the Equality*, p. 45.

32  Eliza J. Davis to the 1838 Anti-Slavery Convention of American Women, *Proceedings* (Philadelphia: Merrihew & Gunn, 1838), p. 15.

33  Sarah M. Grimké, quoted in Birney, *Grimké Sisters*, p. 239.

34  Lydia Maria Child to E. Carpenter, 10 March 1838, quoted in *Letters of Lydia Maria Child with a Biographical Introduction by John G. Whittier and an Appendix by Wendell Phillips* (Boston and New York: Houghton, Mifflin, 1882), p. 26.

    Commenting on Angelina Grimké's speech before the Massachusetts Legislature, a reporter wrote, "It was a noble day, when for the first time in civilized America, a Woman stood up in a Legislative Hall, vindicating the rights of women"; see *Boston Mercantile Journal* as quoted in *The Liberator*, 29 April 1839; cited in Lerner, *The Grimké Sisters*, p. 11. After first hearing Angelina Grimké at Charlestown, Massachusetts, Garrison exulted, "No wonder that . . . the proslavery heads and tails of society know not what to do, when WOMAN stands forth to plead the cause of her degraded, chain-bound sex"; see *The Liberator*, 1 September 1837 as quoted in Lumpkin, *Emancipation of Angelina Grimké*, p. 125. Years later, recalling the impact of one of her public speeches during that summer of 1837, Samuel J. May concluded, "if there was a person there who went away unaffected, he would not have been moved though an angel instead of Angelina had spoken to him"; see *Some Recollections of Our Anti-Slavery Conflict* (Boston: Fields, Osgood, 1869), pp. 235–36.

35  Rebecca M. C. Capron to Amy Post, 1 April 1850, Post Family Papers, University of Rochester. I am grateful to Nancy Hewitt for showing me this letter. A study of this support network would immeasurably enhance the individual biographies of these unconventional women that are now being published.

36  Quotations about the Grimké sisters are taken from the Boston *Gazette*, 9 March 1838; the Pittsburgh *Manufacturer* as republished in *The Liberator*, 11 May 1838; and the Boston *Morning Post*, 25 August 1837; and published in Lerner, *The Grimké Sisters*,

pp. 11, 205. The letter, from Mary N. B. Smith to Abby Kelley, 16 August 1841, is in the Abby Kelley Foster Papers, American Antiquarian Society.

37  For Frances Wright, see Celia Morris Eckhardt, *Fanny Wright: Rebel in America* (Cambridge: Harvard University Press, 1984); and Barbara Taylor, *Eve and the New Jerusalem: Socialism and Feminism in the Nineteenth Century* (New York: Pantheon, 1983). For Rose, see Yuri Suhl, *Ernestine Rose and the Battle for Human Rights* (New York: Reynal, 1959). Because the abolitionists articulated egalitarian ideas about race and slavery, and especially because they shared egalitarian ideas about women, they were identified with Frances Wright. Garrison was accused "of Fanny Wrightism—of advocating the equal division of property, the prostration of all law, the abrogation of marriage, and the promiscuous intercourse of the sexes"; see Wendell P. and Francis J. Garrison, *William Lloyd Garrison*, 2:249. Angelina Grimké, internalizing such comments, in 1836 reported to a female friend her fears of giving a lecture by writing that she was warned "that it would be called a Fanny Wright meeting"; see Angelina Grimké to Jane Smith, 17 December 1838.

38  Passages by Stewart are quoted from *Productions of Mrs. Maria Stewart, Presented to the First African Baptist Church and Society, in the City of Boston* (Boston: Friends of Freedom and Virtue, 1835), pp. 6, 51–52, 54–55. See *Maria W. Stewart: America's First Black Woman Political Writer. Essays and Speeches*, ed. Marilyn Richardson (Bloomington: Indiana University Press, 1987); Dorothy Sterling, ed. *We Are Your Sisters: Black Women in Nineteenth Century America* (New York: W. W. Norton, 1984), pp. 153–59; and Edward T. James et al., eds., *Notable American Women*, 3 vols. (Cambridge, Mass.: Harvard University Press, 1971). For connections between Stewart and other female African-American evangelists, see Sue E. Houchins, "Introduction," *Spiritual Narratives, The Schomburg Library of Nineteenth-Century Black Women Writers*, ed. Henry Louis Gates, Jr. (New York: Oxford University Press, 1988), pp. xxix–xliv; and "Introduction," *Sisters of the Spirit*, ed. William L. Andrews (Bloomington: Indiana University Press, 1986), pp. 1–22. No full-length biography of Stewart has been written. After leaving Boston, she moved to New York, where she trained herself by joining a female literary society, writing speeches and presenting declamations. She taught school in New York and later, in Washington, D.C., worked in the Freedmen's Hospitals and organized Sunday schools.

39  Stewart, *Productions*, p. 21.

40  Stewart, *Productions*, pp. 75, 76–77, 82. The biblical reference is Isa. 40:2. Although Garrison recalls Stewart's obvious "intelligence and excellence of character" and Alexander Crummell remarks on her "greed for literature and letters," neither records his response to her public appearances in the introduction to the second edition of Stewart's speeches, *Meditations from the Pen of Mrs. Maria W. Stewart, (Widow of the Late James W. Stewart,) Now Matron of the Freedman's Hospital, and Presented in 1832 to the First African Baptist Church and Society of Boston, Mass.* (Washington, D.C.: n.p., 1879).

41  Zip Coon [pseud.], "Abolition Hall," Library Company of Philadelphia. I am grateful to Phil Lapsansky for locating this print.

42  See *History of Pennsylvania Hall, Which Was Destroyed by a Mob, on the 17th of May, 1838* (Philadelphia, 1838; reprint, New York: Negro Universities Press, 1969). Grimké's speech appears on pp. 123–26.

43  Chapman's public appearance at Pennsylvania Hall is described in Wendell P. and Francis J. Garrison, *William Lloyd Garrison, 1805–1879*, 2:114; and in Harriet Marti-

neau, *The Martyr Age of the United States* (Newcastle upon Tyne: Finlay and Charlton, 1840), p. 41, republished from *The London and Westminster Review* (December 1838). There is in print no full-length biography of Chapman; Lee Chambers-Schiller is researching her life. For an unsympathetic discussion, see Jane H. and William H. Pease, *Bound with Them in Chains* (Westport, Conn.: Greenwood, 1972), chap. 3.

44  Dorothy Sterling is writing a full-length biography of Abby Kelley Foster. My discussion relies on materials in Margaret Hope Bacon, *I Speak for My Slave Sister: The Life of Abby Kelley Foster* (New York: Thomas Crowell, 1974); and Nancy H. Burkett, *Abby Kelley Foster and Stephen S. Foster* (Worcester, Mass.: Worcester Bicentennial Commission, 1976). In "Authority, Autonomy, and Radical Commitment: Stephen and Abby Kelley Foster," *Proceedings*, American Antiquarian Society, vol. 90 (Worcester, Mass., 1980), pp. 347–86, Joel Bernard comments perceptively on the application of the language of antislavery in their marriage. Kelley's speech at Pennsylvania Hall appears in *History of Pennsylvania Hall*, p. 126.

45  See the 1838 Album, Western Anti-Slavery Papers, Library of Congress, quoted in Blanche Glassman Hersh, *The Slavery of Sex: Feminists-Abolitionists in America* (Urbana: University of Illinois Press, 1978), p. 34; Abby Kelley to "Brother Rogers," 8 July 1841, New-York Historical Society. I am grateful to Dorothy Sterling for this passage. Hersh, p. 34; Burkett, *Abby Kelley Foster*, p. 18.

46  See Bacon, *Slave Sister*, p. 185.

47  From Kelley's letter to her daughter, Alla. Undated, possibly ca. 1883. Collection of the Worcester Historical Museum, Worcester, Mass. The biblical reference is Jer. 9:1.

48  For Kelley's impact on Lucy Stone, see Bacon, *Slave Sister*, pp. 127–28; and Elinor Rice Hays, *Morning Star: A Biography of Lucy Stone, 1818–1893* (New York: Harcourt, Brace and World, 1961). Nancy A. Hewitt, "Feminist Friends: Agrarian Quakers and the Emergence of Woman's Rights in America," *Feminist Studies* 12 (Spring 1986): 29.

49  For female ministers of the Society of Friends, see Margaret Hope Bacon, *Mothers of Feminism: The Story of Quaker Women in America* (San Francisco: Harper and Row, 1986). For Mott, see Bacon's biography, *Valiant Friend: The Life of Lucretia Mott* (New York: Walker, 1980); and Dana Greene, *Lucretia Mott: Her Complete Speeches and Sermons* (Lewiston, N.Y.: Edwin Mellen Press, 1980). In a letter to Jane Smith, New York, 17 December [1836], Angelina Grimké discussed her principled decision to disclaim any right to speak because of sectarian qualifications as a Quaker minister. For Sarah Grimké's early difficulties with the Friends concerning her qualifications as a preacher, see Lumpkin, *Emancipation of Angelina Grimké*. It is noteworthy that the Grimkés–like Kelley Foster and a number of the other women who spoke in public —did not write out their remarks but instead addressed their audiences extemporaneously, as did Mott and other Quaker ministers.

50  Abby Kelley Foster's remarks at the 1851 Worcester meeting are quoted in Burkett, *Abby Kelley Foster*, p. 31.

51  Lerner, "The Political Activities of Antislavery Women," pp. 123–24.


## Chapter Three

1  L. Maria Child, "To the Readers of the *Standard*," *National Anti-Slavery Standard* 1, no. 50 (20 May 1841).

2   Information on Child comes from Milton Meltzer and Patricia G. Holland, eds., *The Collected Correspondence of Lydia Maria Child, 1817–1880* (Millwood, N.Y.: Kraus Microform, 1980); Milton Meltzer and Patricia G. Holland, eds., *Lydia Maria Child, Selected Letters, 1817–1880* (Amherst: University of Massachusetts Press, 1982); Milton Meltzer, *Tongue of Flame* (New York: Thomas Crowell, 1965); William S. Osborne, *Lydia Maria Child* (New York: Twayne, 1980); John G. Whittier, ed., *Letters of Lydia Maria Child* (Boston: Houghton Mifflin, 1882); and Helene Baer, *The Heart Is Like Heaven* (Philadelphia: University of Pennsylvania Press, 1964). Also see Susan Conrad, *Perish the Thought* (New York: Oxford, 1976), pp. 104–16; and essays by Carolyn Karcher, including "Introduction" to Child's *Hobomok* (New Brunswick: Rutgers University Press, 1986); "Lydia Maria Child's *Romance*," *Slavery and the Literary Imagination*, ed. Arnold Rampersad and Deborah McDowell (Baltimore: Johns Hopkins University Press, 1989), pp. 81–103; and "Rape, Murder and Revenge," *Women's Studies International Forum* 9 (1986), 323–32. Karcher is writing a biography of Child.

3   *An Appeal in Favor of That Class of Americans Called Africans* (New York: John S. Taylor, 1836; reprint, New York: Arno and the New York Times, 1968), p. 148; *Selected Letters*, p. xi. The *Appeal* ruined Child's promising career as a popular writer. See Harriet Martineau, *The Martyr Age in the United States* (Newcastle upon Tyne: Finlay and Charlton, 1840) republished from the *London and Westminster Review* (December 1838): 8; Whittier's "Introduction" to Child's *Letters*, p. ix; Wendell Phillips "Appendix" to the *Letters*, pp. 264–65; and Samuel May, *Some Recollections of Our Anti-Slavery Conflict* (Boston: Fields, Osgood, 1869), pp. 98–99.

4   This frontispiece derives from an illustration of Mrs. Bowdich, "The Booroom Slave," in Frederic Shoberl, ed., *Forget Me Not: A Christmas and New Year's Present for MDCCCXXVIII* (London, [1828]), facing p. 37; the illustration is based on Henry Thompson's painting, *The Booroom Slave*, 1827, according to Hugh Honour, *Slaves and Liberators*, part 1 of *From the American Revolution to World War I*, vol. 4 of *The Image of the Black in Western Art*, 4 vols. (Cambridge; Mass.: Harvard University Press, 1989), p. 130. Thomas Wentworth Higginson connects Child's *An Appeal* with Walker's in James Parton et al., *Eminent Women of the Age* (Hartford: S.M. Betts, 1868) p. 47.

5   *An Appeal*, p. [111]; Thomas Wentworth Higginson, "Lydia Maria Child," in *Eminent Women of the Age*, p. 54.

6   *History of the Condition of Women, in Various Ages and Nations*, vols. 4 and 5, Ladies' Family Library (Boston: J. Allen, 1835.) Quoted passages refer to the 1849 edition, 2: 212, 214, 224. Other works by Child in this series include *Biographies of Lady Russell and Mme. Guion* (Boston: Carter, Hendee, 1832); *Biographies of Mme. de Stael and Mme. Roland* (Boston: Carter, Hendee, 1832); and *Good Wives* (Boston: Carter, Hendee, 1833).

7   *Condition of Women*, 1:vii.

8   *Condition of Women* cites the Greek and Roman classics, mythology, history, British letters, and women's biographies. It includes accounts of women famous for their accomplishments and of women known because of their connections with important men, as well as discussions of women in relation to historic events. In addition, Child discusses the varied observances of physiological and cultural events in anonymous women's lives: birth, menarche, betrothal, marriage, childbirth, menopause, widowhood, and death. For an innovative modern approach to women's history that utilizes similar materials, see

Gerda Lerner, *The Female Experience: An American Documentary* (Indianapolis: Bobbs-Merrill, 1977). Sarah Grimké, *Letters on the Equality of the Sexes and the Condition of Woman* (Boston: Isaac Knapp, 1838); see chapter 2. I am indebted to Belle Cheveney for pointing out that, while revising *Woman in the Nineteenth Century*, Margaret Fuller reviewed Child's *Condition of Women*; see the New York *Tribune*, 20 November 1845.

9   From 20 May 1841 to 4 May 1843, Child was managing editor of the *Standard*. Under her aegis, the paper published works by Emerson, Dana, Hawthorne, Longfellow, Lowell, and Whittier, by Nell and Douglass, and by Mrs. Trollope and Dickens.

10   "To the Readers of the *Standard*," *National Anti-Slavery Standard* 1, no. 50 (20 May 1841). Child's endorsement of the abolitionist feminists is clear in her companion piece published on the same page, "To the Abolitionists": "In America women heard that every human had rights to full and free development and some questioned their situation. When their husbands and brothers tried to prevent them from expressing themselves on the question of slavery because it is a political question, the nucleus of a new and agitating idea took to itself shape, as rapidly as the blossom bursts from its sheath."

11   Child to Ellis G. Loring, 24 November 1841, *Selected Letters*, p. 153.

12   *Selected Letters*, p. 108. The situation was complex. Although antislavery influence was increasingly felt throughout the North, the abolitionists had split organizationally —first in Massachusetts, ostensibly over the involvement of women, but actually over a range of issues, including the use of political activism. For backgrounds, see Aileen S. Kraditor, *Means and Ends in American Abolitionism: Garrison and His Critics on Strategy and Tactics, 1834–1850* (New York: Pantheon, 1968); and Lewis Perry, *Radical Abolitionism: Anarchy and the Government of God in Antislavery Thought* (Ithaca: Cornell University Press, 1973).

13   "Speaking in the Church," *National Anti-Slavery Standard* 2, no. 6 (15 July 1841). As Child makes clear, the relationship between the antislavery women and the clergy is antithetical to the relationship between mainstream women and the clergy described by Ann Douglas in *Feminization of American Culture* (New York: Knopf, 1977). Unusual in its good humor, Child's editorial is otherwise characteristic of the women's efforts, at the least, to stop the clergy from opposing women's rights and, at the most, to prevail on the clergy to support the cause of the antislavery women. *The Liberty Bell* includes a number of items on this subject.

14   "Coincidences," *National Anti-Slavery Standard* 2, no. 18 (6 October 1842): 70.

15   "The African Race," *National Anti-Slavery Standard* 3 (27 April 1843). For more on Child's views in the *Standard* concerning race, see "The Different Races of Men," "Letters from New-York," *National Anti-Slavery Standard* 3 (5 January 1843).

16   Sarah Forten, "We Are Thy Sisters," [Angelina Grimké] *Appeal to the Women of the Nominally Free States* (New York: William S. Dorr, 1837). We need a history of antebellum black women's organizations; for starters, of the Massachusetts Colored Female Anti-Slavery Societies, and of the Colored Ladies Literary Society of New York City and the Rising Daughters of Abyssinia, both of which contributed financially to the first Convention of American Women Against Slavery; see *Proceedings of the Anti-Slavery Convention of American Women* (New York: William S. Dorr, 1837) p. 15.

17   *The Liberty Bell* by Friends of Freedom (Boston: National Anti-Slavery Bazaar, 1839), pp. 56–58; see Ralph Thompson, "*The Liberty Bell* and Other Anti-Slavery Gift Books," *New England Quarterly* 7 (March 1934): 154–68.

18   *The Liberty Bell* (Boston: Massachusetts Anti-Slavery Fair, 1842), pp. 156–63.

19  *The Liberty Bell*, pp. 6–12.

20  "Letters from New York, Number 50: Women's Rights," *National Anti-Slavery Standard* 3, no. 141 (16 February 1843).

21  Lucretia Mott, "Diversities," *The Liberty Bell* (Boston, 1844), pp. 175–78; Abby Kelley, "What Is Real Anti-Slavery Work?" *The Liberty Bell* (Boston: Massachusetts Anti-Slavery Fair, 1845), pp. 202–8; Mott, "What Is Anti-Slavery Work," *The Liberty Bell* (Boston: Massachusetts Anti-Slavery Fair, 1846), pp. 253–57.

22  "Farewell," *National Anti-Slavery Standard* 3, no. 48 (4 May 1843).

23  Higginson, "Lydia Maria Child," *Eminent Women of the Age*, ed. James Parton, p. 53.

24  Part of the long passage on Child in Lowell's poem "Fable for Critics" reads:

> If her heart at high floods swamps her brain now and then,
> 'Tis but richer for that when the tide ebbs again

"Letters from New York," written for the Boston *Courier*, ran in the *National Anti-Slavery Standard* from 19 August 1841 to 4 May 1843. In the "Letters"—as always—Child's range is impressive. She writes about New York neighborhoods (the Battery) and environs (Brooklyn and Staten Island); about urban institutions reflecting the diverse population (a synagogue and a Catholic cathedral); about black New York; about establishment and antiestablishment social institutions (the women's prison on Blackwell's Island, the Washington Temperance Society, the Society of Friends' home for paupers); about urban high culture (the music of Guzikow and the engravings of Richter); about innovative ideas ("correspondences," speculation concerning relationships between matter and spirit, animal magnetism); about the history of antislavery (the Thompson mob); about reformers (the Millerites); about reform ideas (capital punishment, women's rights); and about nature in the city (a garden, a snowstorm).

Child edited and published *New York Letters* between covers in 1843; a second volume appeared in 1845. I am grateful to Patricia G. Holland for suggesting that I examine the "Letters" in the *Standard* where, in contrast to the more genteel revised versions, they display the rough-and-tumble of controversy.

25  "Letters from New York: Number 33," *National Anti-Slavery Standard* 2, no. 11 (18 August 1842). Perhaps because of its controversial subject, Child excluded this piece from her book, which she designed as a money-maker. For the incident Child here describes, see Child to Louisa Loring, 15 August [1835]; and to Ellis G. Loring, 22 August 1835, *Selected Letters*, pp. 31–33, 33–35; also see Wendell P. Garrison and Francis J. Garrison, *William Lloyd Garrison: The Story of His Life Told by His Children*, 4 vols. (New York: The Century, 1885–1889), 2:3.

26  Child to Ellis G. Loring, 22 August 1835, *Selected Letters*, p. 34; also see Garrison to Henry E. Benson, 4 August 1835, *Letters*, 1:486.

27  *Correspondence Between Lydia Maria Child and Governor Wise and Mrs. Mason, of Virginia* (Boston: American Anti-Slavery Society, 1860). Three hundred thousand copies of this pamphlet were sold. Calling it the "most notable of all my anti-slavery doings," Child later commented that "The Letter to Mrs. Mason, especially, was copied by hundreds of thousands; and it is a satisfaction to me to think of it as one of the innumerable agencies that were at work to prepare the mind of the North for the final great crisis." Because all of the writers involved were aware of their own importance and of the historic significance of the events they discussed, it is impossible to be certain which of the letters were meant as private communications and which were in fact

written for the audience of history. Child to Samuel J. May, 29 September 1867, in Meltzer and Holland, eds., *Lydia Maria Child, Selected Letters*, p. 474.

28    For Brown, see Stephen B. Oates, *To Purge This Land with Blood: A Biography of John Brown* (New York: Harper & Row, 1970). For Wise, see Barton Wise, *Life of Henry Alexander Wise* (New York: Macmillan, 1899). After 16 October 1859, when Brown and his black and white sixteen-man army struck at slavery by attacking the United States Arsenal at Harper's Ferry, Virginia, events moved rapidly. Within thirty-six hours, seventeen were dead and Robert E. Lee had captured the wounded insurrectionist, six of his men, and his papers—which implicated prominent abolitionists. Immediately, Brown was questioned by Governor Henry A. Wise and Senator James M. Mason of Virginia. Wise decided to prosecute him in state courts rather than turning him over to federal authorities, and in the next two weeks, Brown was indicted, tried, convicted, and sentenced. A month later he was hanged.

29    For the "John Brown Fund," see Daniel Rosenberg, *Mary Brown: From Harper's Ferry to California* (New York: AIMS, 1975), pp. 14ff. The response of African-American women is glimpsed in a letter from "the ladies of New York, Brooklyn, and Williamsburgh" to Mary Brown, offering sympathy for the widow of "our honored and dearly-loved brother" and announcing their intention to organize in black churches "a band of sisters to collect our weekly pence, and pour it lovingly into your lap" (The New York *Weekly Anglo-African*, 17 Dec. 1859, in Benjamin Quarles, ed., *Blacks on John Brown* [Urbana: University of Illinois Press, 1972], pp. 16–19).

    Child, the Welds, and others in the movement were also active in arranging for the education of Brown's daughters, who briefly attended Frank Sanborn's school at Concord, then studied nearer home at Fort Edward Institute. In 1865, when Annie Brown taught at a freedom school for African-American children housed in Governor Wise's former residence, she saw her father's portrait hung on the wall. See Wendell P. Garrison and Francis J. Garrison, *William Lloyd Garrison: The Story of His Life Told by His Children*, 4:133.

30    For Mason's comments, see *Correspondence Between Lydia Maria Child and Governor Wise*; references are to *Corresp.* as republ. in *Letters of Lydia Maria Child*, ed. John G. Whittier, pp. 120–23. For Angelina Grimké's *Appeal to the Christian Women of the South* (New York: American Anti-Slavery Society, 1836), see chapter 2.

31    *Correspondence Between Lydia Maria Child and Governor Wise* in *Letters of Lydia Maria Child*, ed. John G. Whittier, pp. 134–35.

32    Francis Graeter, "A Sewing Society," *History of the Condition of Women*, 2:271; for Higginson's negative view of Francis Graeter's illustration, see "Lydia Maria Child," in *Eminent Women of the Age*, ed. James Parton, p. 46.

33    "The Plot Exposed! Or, Abolitionism, Fanny Wright, and the Whig Party!" broadside [1838], Department of Popular Prints, Library of Congress.

34    "The Times that Try Men's Souls," *History of Woman Suffrage*, ed. Elizabeth Cady Stanton et al., 6 vols. (New York, 1881–1922; republ., New York: Arno, 1969), 1:82. "Lines Suggested on Reading an Appeal to the Christian Women of the South, by A. E. Grimké," *The Liberator* 6 (26 October 1836), reprinted in *Black Sister*, ed. Erlene Stetson (Bloomington: Indiana University Press, 1981), p. 17.

35    S. J., "The Female Abolitionists," *Genius of Universal Emancipation*, 5th series, vol. 1, p. 93.

36    "To a Female Abolitionist," *Genius of Universal Emancipation*, 5th series, vol. 1, p. 100.

37  "Lucretia Mott," *The Voice of Freedom* (2 March 1843): 156.

38  "C. C. C. to Maria Weston Chapman," *National Anti-Slavery Standard* 9 (27 April 1848).

39  Quoted by Margaret Hope Bacon, *I Speak for My Slave Sister* (New York: Thomas Crowell, 1974), p. 145.

40  "Lines . . . Written on Reading 'Right and Wrong in Boston, Containing an Account of the Meeting of the Boston Female Anti-Slavery Society, and the MOB Which Followed, on the 21st of the 10th Month, 1835,'" *Poems* (New York: John W. Lovell, n.d.), pp. 47–49. This was not included in Whittier's *Works*.

41  "The Pastoral Letter," reprinted in *History of Woman Suffrage*, ed. Stanton et al., 1:85–86.

42  William Wells Brown, *Clotel; or, The President's Daughter* (London: Partridge and Oakey, 1853; republ., New York: Arno, 1969), chaps. 6, 10, 18.

43  "The Kansas Emigrants," *New York Daily Tribune*, 23, 24, 25, 28 October and 4 November 1856.

44  Frances Ellen Watkins Harper, "The Two Offers," *The Anglo-African* (Sept.–Oct. 1859): 288–91, 311–13. It is important not to overread Harper, however; her story does not pose a choice between marriage for love and commitment to a cause and a career. Indeed, Harper implies that if these were the choices, Jeanette would opt for the marriage. For Harper, see Hazel V. Carby, "Introduction," *Iola Leroy* (Boston: Beacon Press, 1987); Maryemma Graham, "Introduction," *Complete Poems of Frances E. W. Harper*, The Schomburg Library of Nineteenth-Century Black Women Writers (New York: Oxford University Press, 1988); Frances Smith Foster, "Introduction," *Iola Leroy*, The Schomburg Library of Nineteenth Century Black Women Writers (New York: Oxford University Press, 1988); and *A Brighter Coming Day: A Frances Ellen Watkins Harper Reader*, ed. Frances Smith Foster (New York: The Feminist Press, 1989).

45  Anna Dickinson, *What Answer?* (Boston: Field, Osgood, 1869), p. 42. Dickinson's apparent endorsement of female orators is rendered ambiguous, however, later in the novel when Francesca's admirer—and Dickinson's audience—learn that she is a quadroon. This revelation raises the question, does a woman who mounts the platform become conventionally black, i.e., does she move beyond white patriarchal definitions of free white womanhood? Is it, then, impossible to be both a "white woman" and an antislavery lecturer?

46  Leslie A. Fiedler, *Love and Death in the American Novel* (1960; republ. Cleveland and New York: World Publishing, 1962); Lydia Maria Child, *Hobomok: A Tale of Early Times* (Boston: Cummings, Hilliard, 1824).

47  Discussing these ideas and texts, racist terminology appears to be inevitable. Here to be not "white" but "black" is to have at least one "nonwhite" forebear. Although in the language of this fiction, each degree of "whiteness" is carefully noted and distinctions are made between mulattoes, quadroons, and octoroons, I have included all of these groups in my analysis of the "mulatto." In the works discussed, however, most of the "tragic mulattoes" have only "one fatal drop" of "black blood." For plantation fiction and the slave narratives, see my *Intricate Knot: Black Figures in American Literature, 1776–1863* (New York: New York University Press, 1972). For more on the narratives, see, for example, Charles T. Davis and Henry Louis Gates, Jr., eds., *The Slave's Narrative* (New York: Oxford University Press, 1985); *The Art of Slave Narrative*, ed. John Sekora and Darwin T. Turner (Illinois: Western Illinois University, 1982); and

Frances S. Foster, *Witnessing Slavery* (Westport, Conn.: Greenwood Press, 1979); also see Henry Louis Gates, Jr., "Writing 'Race' and the Difference It Makes," in *"Race," Writing and Difference*, ed. Henry Louis Gates, Jr. (Chicago: University of Chicago Press, 1985). Angelina Grimké's diary is discussed in chapter 2.

48  Nina Baym, *Woman's Fiction: A Guide to Novels by and about Women in America, 1820–1870* (Ithaca: Cornell University Press, 1978), pp. 22, 51.

49  "The Quadroons," *The Liberty Bell* (Boston, 1842).

50  Child presents two classic versions of the Tragic Mulatto in "The Quadroons." Like Richard Hildreth, who in 1836 had published *The Slave, or Memoirs of Archy Moore*, the first American abolitionist novel, Child grounded her miscegenation plots on factual accounts by white travelers and African-American slave narrators, as well as on English and French fiction. As early as 1834, Child presented a long account of the pathetic slave woman Joanna, adapted from Captain John Stedman's *Narrative of a Five Years' Expedition Among the Revolted Negroes of Surinam*; see her antislavery collection *The Oasis* (Boston: Allen and Ticknor, 1834), pp. 65–105. Sources for later antislavery fiction include books like Frederick Douglass, *Narrative* (Boston: Anti-Slavery Office 1845); and Gustave de Beaumont, *Marie, ou l'esclavage aux Etats-Unis, tableau de moeurs Americaines* (Paris, 1835; reprint trans. Barbara Chapman. Stanford, Calif.: Stanford University Press, 1958).

For discussions of the Tragic Mulatto figure, see my *Intricate Knot*; George M. Frederickson, *The Black Image in the White Mind* (New York: Harper and Row, 1971); Penelope Bullock, "The Mulatto in American Fiction," *Phylon* 6 (1945): 78-82; Jules Zanger, "The 'Tragic Octoroon' in Pre-Civil War Fiction," *American Quarterly* 18 (Spring 1966): 63–70; Sterling Brown's "Negro Character as Seen by White Authors," *Journal of Negro Education* 2 (April 1933): 179–203, and his "A Century of Negro Portraiture in American Literature," *Massachusetts Review* 7 (1966): 63–70; and Blyden Jackson, "A Golden Mean for the Negro Novel," *College Language Association Journal* 2 (1959): 81–87.

51  *Fact and Fiction* (New York: C. S. Francis, 1846). "Annette Gray," an editorial Child signed with her initials in *The Standard*, sympathetically told the story of a young slave woman held in sexual bondage before her escape to Boston. Learning that she is in danger of being kidnapped back south, Child offers aid, then uses the discourse of the antislavery emblems to express her fury at the northern policy of accommodating slaveholders: "A thousand times has my pulse beat high with indignation, to find that I, too, a free born woman of Massachusetts, was a bond-slave of the South, obliged . . . to obey the dictates of my conscience by stealth" (*National Anti-Slavery Standard* 2, no. 7 [22 July 1841]).

52  A slave women who marries her French purchaser is described in Lewis and Milton Clarke's narrative. A number of writers of fiction—including Gustave de Beaumont, E. D. E. N. Southworth, Rebecca Harding Davis, and Epes Sargent—presented Tragic Mulattoes who discovered that they were slaves. Sargent and Mary Haydon (Green) Pike showed Tragic Mulattoes who discovered that they were black. Tragic Mulattoes who happily flee to France can be found in works by Stowe and William Dean Howells.

Chesnutt, like Cable and Twain, shows a Tragic Mulatto who denies her motherhood to free her child. Characteristically, however, when African-American writers dramatize a woman of mixed race, she is very different from the Tragic Mulatto; this woman embraces her black identity, lives in the black community, and chooses a black man.

See, for example, writings by Frank Webb, William Wells Brown, Frances Ellen Watkins Harper, and James Weldon Johnson.

53  James Fenimore Cooper, *The Last of the Mohicans* (1826); "Slavery's Pleasant Homes," *Liberty Bell* (Boston: Massachusetts Anti-Slavery Fair, 1843).

54  Mattie Griffiths, "Madge Vertner," serialized in thirty-eight chapters in the *National Anti-Slavery Standard* 20–21 (30 July 1859-5 May 1860). Failed female liberators also appear in Stowe's *Dred* and in Southworth's *Retribution.* In Brown's *Clotel*, the white liberator Georgiana frees her slaves on her deathbed, but this successful effort at emancipation is unusual.

55  *The Crisis* 37 (1930): 210.

56  *A Romance of the Republic* (Boston: Ticknor and Fields, 1867). Child had followed *Hobomok* with *The Rebels* (Boston: Cummings, Hilliard, 1825); and *Philothia* (Boston: Otis, Broaders, 1836).

57  Earlier, black and white babies had been switched in Joseph Holt Ingraham's *The Quadroone* (New York: Harper & Bros., 1841). This device would later be used in Mark Twain's *The Tragedy of Pudd'nhead Wilson* (Hartford: American Publishing, 1894).

58  For another positive treatment of miscegenation in fiction by another abolitionist feminist, see Dickinson, *What Answer*; also see James Kenney, *Amalgamation! Race, Sex and Rhetoric in the Nineteenth-Century American Novel* (Westport, Conn.: Greenwood, 1955). Child had earlier supported the petitions against miscegenation laws filed by the women of Lynn, Massachusetts; see *Selected Letters*, pp. 110–11.

59  Child, *A Romance of the Republic*, p. 440.

60  Child to Charles Sumner, 4 July 1870, *Selected Letters*, pp. 493–97.


## Chapter Four

1  This passage is from a letter from Harriet Jacobs to Amy Post, 18 June [1861], Isaac and Amy Post Family Papers, University of Rochester Library.

2  *Narrative of Sojourner Truth . . . with a History . . . Drawn from Her "Book of Life"* (Battle Creek, Mich.: For the Author, 1875; republ. New York: Arno, 1968), p. v. Information about Sojourner Truth is drawn from this source, as well as from Arthur H. Fauset, *Sojourner Truth* (Chapel Hill: University of North Carolina Press, 1938); and Hertha Pauli, *Her Name Was Sojourner Truth* (New York: Appleton Century-Crofts, 1962).

3  I treat Sojourner Truth's as-told-to narrative as a secondary source while presenting transcriptions of her speeches as primary texts. Her speech at the 1851 Akron Women's Rights Convention was rendered in dialect as prose by Frances D. Gage years later in *History of Woman Suffrage*, ed. Elizabeth Cady Stanton et al., 6 vols. (New York, 1881–1922), 1:115–17; in this century, it appears with standardized spelling and lined out as a poem in Erlene Stetson, ed., *Black Sister* (Bloomington: Indiana University Press, 1981), pp. 24–25.

4  [Harriet A. Jacobs], *Incidents in the Life of a Slave Girl, Written by Herself*, ed. L. Maria Child (Boston: For the Author, 1861; reprint, ed. Jean Fagan Yellin, Cambridge: Harvard University Press, 1987). Page numbers in my text refer to this new edition. A nineteenth-century English edition appeared under the title, *The Deeper Wrong: Or, Incidents in the Life of a Slave Girl. Written by Herself*, ed. L. Maria Child (London: W.

Tweedie, 1862). Information about Jacobs comes from her narrative, from letters in the Isaac and Amy Post Family Papers, and from other primary sources cited in the Harvard edition. Jacobs's authorship was established in Jean Fagan Yellin, *"Written by Herself*: Harriet Jacobs' Slave Narrative," *American Literature* 53 (November 1981): 479–86.

5 Major sources of primary materials include reports of the public speeches made by other women who had been held in slavery, such as Ellen Craft; the narratives of women such as Elizabeth Keckley, Mattie J. Jackson, Lucy A. Delaney, and Kate Drumgoold; the oral histories of former slaves; and the living African-American folk tradition.

6 For a discussion of the white racism in the antislavery movement, see Robert L. and Pamela P. Allen, *Reluctant Reformers* (Washington, D.C.: Howard University Press, 1974); Rosalyn Terborg-Penn, "Discrimination Against Afro-American Women in the Woman's Movement, 1830–1920," *The Afro-American Woman*, ed. Sharon Harley and Rosalyn Terborg-Penn (Port Washington, N.Y.: Kennikat Press, 1978), pp. 17–27. For one nineteenth-century white woman's private criticism of that racism, see S. A. Burtis to Abby Kelley, 17 January 1843, Abigail Kelley Foster Papers, American Antiquarian Society, Worcester, Massachusetts. I am grateful to Nancy Hewitt for this reference.

7 For the implications of this move in relation to black women in America, see, for example, *"Race," Writing and Difference*, ed. Henry Louis Gates, Jr. (Chicago: University of Chicago Press, 1986); and see Houston Baker, Jr., "Autobiographical Acts and the Voice of the Southern Slave," *The Journey Back* (Chicago: University of Chicago Press, 1980), pp. 27–52.

8 For the differences between the treatment of female slaves in narratives by men and women, see Frances Foster, "'In Respect to Females': Differences in the Portrayals of Women by Male and Female Slave Narrators," *Black American Literature Forum* 15 (Summer 1981): pp. 66–70.

9 Henry David Thoreau, *Walden* (1854), chap. 1.

10 See n. 3, above.

11 Here she quantifies intellect, as W. E. B. Du Bois later would quantify for his materialistic audience the demand for human rights by measuring them in terms of a "jot and tittle." See *The Souls of Black Folk* (Chicago: A. C. McClurg, 1903).

12 *Atlantic Monthly* (April 1863); this is quoted at length in *Narrative of Sojourner Truth*, pp. 151–73. Also worth noting are Stowe's comments showing Sojourner Truth good-naturedly trivializing the women's movement, ridiculing bloomers, and asserting: "Sisters, I a'n't clear what you'd be after. Ef women want any rights more'n dey's got, why don't dey jes' *take 'em*, and not be talkin' about it?" (p. 165).

13 *Narrative of Sojourner Truth*, p. 161.

14 *Narrative of Sojourner Truth*, pp. 167–68.

15 *Narrative of Sojourner Truth*, p. 169.

16 Story was completing his *Cleopatra* when Stowe visited his studio at Rome, and she commented on its unusual character. This *Cleopatra* is not aryan. For discussions of nineteenth-century interpretations of the racial heritage of the fabled queen, see William H. Gerdts, "Egyptian Motifs in Nineteenth-Century American Painting and Sculpture," *Antiques* (October 1966): 495–502; and Michael Grant, *Cleopatra* (New York: Simon and Schuster, [1973]), pp. 4–5. I am grateful to Sidney Kaplan for these sources.

17 Jan M. Seidler, *A Critical Reappraisal of the Career of William Wetmore Story, American Sculptor and Man of Letters* (Ph.D. diss., Boston University, 1985), p. 508.

18   Story to Charles Sumner, 22 June 1860; 6 December 1860; 13 May 1861; to Charles
     Eliot Norton, 15 August 1861; quoted in Seidler, pp. 503, 504, 511, 557; also see
     Henry James, *William Wetmore Story and His Friends*, 2 vols. (Boston: Houghton,
     Mifflin, 1903), 1:71.

19   *Harper's New Monthly Magazine* 27 (1863): 566–67; 133.

20   Annalina Calo Levi, *Barbarians on Roman Imperial Coins and Sculpture*, Numismatic
     Notes and Monographs no. 123 (New York: American Numismatic Society, 1952), figs.
     3.2; 4.1; Jocelyn M. C. Toynbee, *The Hadriatic School*, 2 vols. (New York: Cambridge
     University Press, 1935), vol. 2, figs. 11.26, 11.27, 12.19–23, 14.24, 25.1. *Judea
     Capta* is illustrated in 3.2.

21   Cotton Mather, *Humiliation Followed with Deliverances* (Boston: B. Green and J. Allen,
     1694), p. 31.

22   Erwin Panofsky, *The Life and Art of Albrecht Dürer* (Princeton: Princeton University
     Press, 1955), pp. 161, 162.

23   Joshua C. Taylor, *America as Art* (Washington, D.C.: Smithsonian Institution Press,
     1976), pp. 30, 34, 35.

24   Lydia Maria Child, *Selected Letters, 1817–1880* (Amherst: University of Massachusetts
     Press, 1982), p. 224; *The Liberty Bell*. By Friends of Freedom (Boston: Massachusetts
     Anti-Slavery Fair, 1842).

25   Panofsky, *Albrecht Dürer*, p. 163.

26   (Boston: For the author, 1861). For recent studies of the slave narrative, see Charles T.
     Davis and Henry Louis Gates, Jr., eds., *The Slave's Narrative* (New York: Oxford Uni-
     versity Press, 1985); John Sekora and Darwin T. Turner, eds., *The Art of Slave Narra-
     tive* (Illinois: Western Illinois University Press, 1982); and Frances Smith Foster, *Witnessing
     Slavery* (Westport, Conn.: Greenwood Press, 1979).

27   For black spiritual autobiography and its relationship to the slave narrative, see William
     L. Andrews, *To Tell a Free Story* (Urbana: University of Illinois Press, 1986).

28   Critics have identified changing attitudes toward the "fallen woman" in nineteenth-
     century American literature. The earliest fiction upheld feminine chastity as an abso-
     lute value. According to Margaret Wyman, "The Rise of the Fallen Woman," *American
     Quarterly* 3 (1951): 167–77, "Once a girl fell, she invariably faced dishonor and death,
     unless, indeed, she evaded public shame by prompt suicide" (p. 167). This female
     sinner disappeared from domestic antebellum fiction, where heroines maintained "purity
     against all temptation and patience under all affliction" (p. 168). Not until after the Civil
     War would novelists like Elizabeth Stuart Phelps and Louisa May Alcott dramatize the
     view that individual fallen women were "eminently redeemable" (p. 171). L. Maria
     Child's dramatizations, in the 1840s, of illegitimacy in "Elizabeth Wilson" and of
     infanticide in "Hilda Silfvering" were unusual (*Fact and Fiction: A Collection of Stories*
     [New York and Boston: C. S. Francis, 1847]). Also see my "From *Success* to *Experience*:
     Louisa May Alcott's *Work*," *Massachusetts Review* (1980): 527–39.

29   Once, however, she calls him "witness to my shame" (*Incidents*, p. 76).

30   The importance of *Incidents* is discussed in Andrews; in Hazel V. Carby, *Reconstructing
     Womanhood* (New York: Oxford University Press, 1987); and my "Text and Contexts of
     Harriet Jacobs's *Incidents in the Life of a Slave Girl*," in Davis and Gates, Jr., eds., *The
     Slave's Narrative*, pp. 262–82.

31   *Incidents* does, however, include one female slaveholder-turned-liberator (the dying wife
     of a sympathetic minister), and one failed female liberator (a mistress who had offered

her slaves their freedom but after marrying a tyrannical husband was powerless to help them.) See "Texts and Contexts of Harriet Jacobs's *Incidents in the Life of a Slave Girl: Written by Herself.*"

32   Linda perhaps implies her grandmother's sexual history when she comments bitterly that her mother's master had "died when she was a child; and she remained with her mistress till she married. She was never in the power of any master; and thus she escaped one class of the evils that generally fall upon slaves" (p. 78).

33   For "domestic feminism," see Kathryn Kish Sklar, *Catharine Beecher* (New Haven: Yale University Press, 1973).

34   *Incidents*, p. 55. I am grateful to Hazel Carby for helping me clarify this issue.

35   See Child, *Fact and Fiction*. In *Woman in the Nineteenth Century* (1845), Margaret Fuller judged Child's defense of prostitutes significant.

36   Harriet Jacobs to Amy Post, 14 February [1853], *Incidents*, p. 234.

37   See Paula Giddings, *When and Where I Enter: The Impact of Black Women on Sex and Race in America* (New York: William Morrow, 1984), p. 7.


## Chapter Five

1   S. F., W. Bloomfield, 25 September 1850, "The Greek Slave," *The North Star*, 3 October 1850.

2   New York *Tribune*, 15 September 1847, Hiram Powers Scrapbook, Hiram Powers Papers, Archives of American Art. For the *Greek Slave*, see Vivien M. Green, "Hiram Powers's *Greek Slave*: Emblem of Freedom," *American Art Journal* 14 (1982): 31–39; and Samuel A. Roberson and William H. Gerdts, "The Greek Slave," in the quarterly publication of the Newark Museum, *The Museum* n.s. 17 (1965): 1–32. For Powers, see Donald Martin Reynolds, *Hiram Powers and His Ideal Sculpture* (New York: Garland, 1977), and Reynolds, "The 'Unveiled Soul,': Hiram Powers' Embodiment of the Ideal," *The Art Bulletin* 59 (September 1977): 394–414. Also see Sylvia E. Crane, *White Silence: Greenough, Powers, and Crawford, American Sculptors in Nineteenth-Century Italy* (Coral Gables, Fla.: University of Miami Press, 1972); Margaret Farrand Thorp, *The Literary Sculptors* (Durham: Duke University Press, 1965); and Vivien Green Fryd, *Sculpture as History: Themes of Liberty, Unity and Manifest Destiny in American Sculpture, 1825–1865* (Ph.D. diss., University of Wisconsin, Madison, 1984). Unless otherwise identified, quoted passages are from the Powers Papers at the Archives of American Art.

3   L. Maria Child, "The Little Greek Girl," *Juvenile Miscellany* 3, no. 1 (September 1827): 13–14; L. Maria Child, *History of the Condition of Women* (Boston: J. Allen, 1835) 2:212, 269; Sarah Grimké, *Letters on the Equality of the Sexes and the Condition of Woman; Addressed to Mary Parker, President of the Boston Female Anti-Slavery Society* (Boston: Isaac Knapp, 1838), pp. 43–44, 51; Rose at the Seventh National Woman's Rights Convention, New York City, 1856, in *History of Woman Suffrage*, ed. Elizabeth Cady Stanton et al., 6 vols. (New York: 1881–1922; republ., New York: Arno, 1969) 1:666. Also see William Lloyd Garrison to the President of the Anti-Slavery Convention, 30 January 1836, in Walter M. Merrill and Louis Ruchames, eds., *The Letters of William Lloyd Garrison*, 6 vols. (Cambridge, Mass.: Harvard University Press, 1971–81), 2:30.

4   E. W. Southwick, "To the Ladies of Connecticut," *Freedom's Gift* (Hartford: S. S. Cowles, 1840), pp. 15–17.

5   Powers to J. S. Preston, 7 January 1841.

6   Powers to Preston, 28 September 1841; to Wheeler, 28 December 1842; Mrs. Powers to Mrs. Gibson, 20 February 1843. Notation of 11 September 1841, in Paul Revere Frothingham, *Edward Everett, Orator and Statesman* (Boston: Houghton Mifflin, 1925), 182. Kenneth Clark, *The Nude: A Study in Ideal Form* (Princeton: Princeton University Press, 1956), p. 79.

7   Kenneth Clark, *The Nude*; E. McSherry Fowble, "Without a Blush: The Movement Toward Acceptance of the Nude as an Art Form in America, 1800–1825," *Winterthur Portfolio* 9 (1974): 103–21; William H. Gerdts, "Marble and Nudity," *Art in America* 49 (1971): 60–67; and *The Great American Nude* (New York: Praeger, 1974). See my "Caps and Chains: Hiram Powers' Statue of 'Liberty,'" *American Quarterly* 38 (Winter 1986): 798–826. For European sculptures of enchained women, see Hugh Honour, *Black Models and White Myths*, part 2 of vol. 4, *From the American Revolution to World War 1*, *The Image of the Black in Western Art*, 4 vols. (Cambridge, Mass.: Harvard University Press, 1989), pp. 169–71.

8   Powers's wife and children remained in Cincinnati when he worked elsewhere. Henry W. Bellows, "Seven Sittings with Powers, the Sculptor," *Appleton's Journal* 1 (1869): 55.

9   Carter G. Woodson, "The Negroes of Cincinnati Prior to the Civil War," *Journal of Negro History* 1 (1916): 4. This discussion of Powers's Cincinnati is based on the following sources: Charles T. Hickock, *The Negro in Ohio, 1802–1870* (Cleveland, 1896); Richard C. Wade, "The Negro in Cincinnati, 1800–1830," *Journal of Negro History* 39:43–57; [Ohio Anti-Slavery Society], *Narrative of the Late Riotous Proceedings Against the Liberty of the Press in Cincinnati*, (Cincinnati: [n. p.], 1836); [Ohio Anti-Slavery Society], *Condition of the People of Color in the State of Ohio* (Boston: Isaac Knapp, 1839). I am grateful to the late Marilyn Baily for permission to examine two of her unpublished studies: "Conditions of Life for Black People in Cincinnati, Ohio, .1787–1829," and "From Cincinnati to Wilberforce."

10   Cincinnati *Journal*, 22 March 1833, quoted in Forrest Wilson, *Crusader in Crinoline: The Life of Harriet Beecher Stowe* (Philadelphia: J. B. Lippincott, 1941), 115–16.

11   *Specimen of Printing Type, from the Foundry of O. & H. Wells* (Cincinnati, 1827), pp. showing cuts 119–23; and 254–62. Also see *Specimen of Modern and Light Face Printing Types and Ornaments, Cast at the Cincinnati Type Foundry, 1834* (Cincinnati, 1834), p. showing cuts 870–71.

12   The Lane rebels were reprimanded by the seminary trustees and left for Oberlin. See Gilbert Barnes, *The Antislavery Impulse, 1830–1844* (1933; republ. Worcester, Mass.: Peter Smith, 1957); and "Introduction," *Letters of Theodore Dwight Weld, Angelina Grimké Weld, and Sarah Grimké: 1822–1844*, ed. Gilbert H. Barnes and Dwight L. Dumond, 2 vols. (1934; reprint, New York: Da Capo Press, 1970).

13   The "Cincinatti sisters" are discussed in *Letters of Theodore Dwight Weld, Angelina Grimké Weld and Sarah Grimké*, ed. Barnes and Dumond, 1:132–35, 178–80, 184–85, 189–94, 211–21, 250–54, 298–302, 312–15, 323–26; 2:995–96; and [Ohio Anti-Slavery Society], *Condition of the People of Color in the State of Ohio*, pp. 11–12, 24. Two Ohio women participated as delegates to the Convention held at New York in 1837; see Anti-Slavery Convention of American Women, *Proceedings* (New York: William S. Dorr, 1837), p. 4.

14  [Ohio Anti-Slavery Society], *Narrative of the Late Riotous Proceedings Against the Liberty of the Press in Cincinnati*; Leonard L. Richards, *"Gentlemen of Property and Standing"*: *Anti-Abolition Mobs in Jacksonian America* (New York: Oxford University Press, 1970), pp. 92–100.

15  Hickock, *The Negro in Ohio*, pp. 141–45; also see Albert B. Hart, *Salmon Portland Chase* (Boston: Houghton Mifflin, 1899), pp. 73–74.

16  Frances Trollope, *Domestic Manners of the Americans*, ed. Donald Smalley, New York: Knopf, 1949, p. 73.

17  Powers to Edward Greenway, 3 December 1850; Powers to Calvert, 22 June 1851.

18  Powers to Sidney Brooks, 31 December 1859.

19  Powers to Everett, 2 March 1861; Hickock, *The Negro in Ohio*, pp. 156, 157; also see Eric Foner, *Free Soil, Free Labor and Free Men* (New York: Oxford University Press, 1971).

20  Louis Leonard Tucker, "The Western Museum of Cincinnati, 1820–1867," *Curator* 8 (1965): 17–35.

21  [Miner Kellogg], *Powers' Statue of the Greek Slave* (New York: R. Craighead, 1847), p. 4.

22  [Kellogg], *Powers' Statue*, p. 30.

23  New York *Tribune*, 15 September 1847, in [Kellogg], *Powers' Statue*, p. 27.

24  Rev. A. Stevens, "Powers, the Sculptor," *Ladies Repository* 8 (1848): 323.

25  Stevens, "Powers," p. 326; also see W. H. F. in the Boston *Harbinger*, 24 June 1848, Powers Scrapbook. Quotation is from Rev. Orville Dewey, "Mr. Powers' Statues," *Union Magazine* (October 1847), reprinted in [Kellogg], *Powers' Statue*, p. 19.

26  [Kellogg], *Powers' Statue*, pp. 17, 18.

27  James Freeman Clarke, "The Greek Slave." For the notion of the morality of the *Slave*'s white marble, see Reynolds, "The 'Unveiled Soul': Hiram Powers's Embodiment of the Ideal," *The Art Bulletin* 49 (1977): 403–7.

28  Cincinnati *Daily Commercial*, 30 October 1848. Also see Kellogg to Powers, 6 November 1848; and N. Longworth to Powers, 18 November 1848.

29  Rev. A. Stevens, "Powers the Sculptor," *Ladies' Repository* 8 (1848): 326.

30  W. H. F., Boston *Harbinger*, 24 June 1848, Powers Scrapbook.

31  *Western Christian Advocate*, 29 November 1848. Powers Scrapbook.

32  New York *Saturday Emporium*, 8 September 1847, Powers Scrapbook.

33  *Citizen's Advertiser*, 1 November 1848, Powers Scrapbook.

34  *Christian Inquirer*, n.d., Powers Scrapbook. For pertinent allusions in Powers' correspondence, see Tuckerman to Powers, 16 December 1847; and Everett to Powers, 25 December 1848.

35  Washington, D.C., *National Era*, September 1847, Powers Scrapbook.

36  C. L. of L. H. P., New York *Herald*, September 1847, Powers Scrapbook. Lyon is identified in Linda Hyman, "The *Greek Slave* by Hiram Powers: High Art as Popular Culture," *Art Journal* 25 (1976): 222.

37  Kellogg to Powers, 14 April 1848.

38  S. F., "The Greek Slave," W. Bloomfield, 25 September 1850 *North Star*, 3 October 1850.

39  Powers to E. W. Stoughton, 29 November 1869; Powers to J. P. Richardson, 14 December 1853; also see Powers to Thomas Powers, 31 December 1849 and 8 January 1851; and Ellen Powers, "Recollections of My Father," *The Vermonter*, March 1907, 83. For a

nineteenth-century critique that interpreted the *Slave* as an Eve, see the *National Intelligencer*, 25 August 1847, Powers Scrapbook.

40 For the psychosexual implications of Powers' nude woman in bondage, see Hyman, "The *Greek Slave*," pp. 216–23.

41 New York *Courier and Enquirer*, 31 August 1847.

42 Anna G. Lewis, "Art and Artists in America," *Graham's Magazine* 10 (November 1855).

43 W. H. Coyle, quoted in Hyman, "The *Greek Slave*," p. 219.

44 Alice Stone Blackwell, *Lucy Stone: Pioneer of Women's Rights* (1930; reprint, Detroit: Grand River Books, 1971), pp. 89–90. I am grateful to Dorothy Sterling this citation.

45 15 September 1847; reprinted in [Kellogg], *Powers' Statue*, pp. 26–28.

46 Powers to John Grant, 18 February 1849; to Sampson Powers, 17 January 1849. For a fuller discussion of Powers' *America*, see my "Caps and Chains: The Iconography of Powers' *America*," pp. 798–826. For the development of an American Liberty, see Frank H. Sommer, "The Metamorphoses of Britannia," in Charles F. Montgomery and Patricia E. Kane, eds., *American Art: 1750-1800: Towards Independence* (Boston: New York Graphic Society, 1976), 40–49; Joshua C. Taylor, *America as Art* (Washington D.C.: Smithsonian Institution Press, 1976); and Hugh Honour, *The European Vision of America* (Cleveland: Cleveland Museum of Art, 1975). Important studies include Robert C. Smith, "Liberty Displaying the Arts and Sciences: A Philadelphia Allegory by Samuel Jennings," *Winterthur Portfolio* 2 (1965): 84–102; and three indispensable essays by E. McClung Fleming, "The American Image as Indian Princess, 1775–1783," *Winterthur Portfolio* 2 (1965): 65–81; "From Indian Princess to Greek Goddess: The American Image, 1783–1815," *Winterthur Portfolio* 3 (1967): 37–66; and "Symbols of the United States: From Indian Queen to Uncle Sam," *Frontiers of American Culture*, ed. Ray B. Browne et al., (Indiana: Purdue University Studies, 1968), pp. 1–24; for recent discussions, see Michael Kammen, "From Liberty to Prosperity: Reflections upon the Role of Revolutionary Iconography in National Tradition," American Antiquarian Society, *Proceedings* 76, pt. 2 (1976): 237–72; and Fryd, *Sculpture as History*, chap. 4.

47 Powers to Dr. Playfair, 9 December 1848.

48 There is no record of the history of the surviving plaster, which has been "pointed"; it apparently differs from the finished marble only in its depiction of defeated Despotism. Probably some time after 23 October 1850, by which date he had made various other iconographical changes, Powers had this plaster made up and displayed in his studio in hopes of attracting a British buyer. A second plaster, purchased from Charles W. Lemmi by the Pennsylvania Academy of Fine Arts in December 1916, has been lost. A photograph shows it crowned but undraped and without the fasces or the wreath; the identity of the object under its foot is unclear. An "enlarged copy" of *America*, intended for the exhibition of the Crystal Palace at Sydenham, was completed, but Powers thought it "botched" and had it destroyed. Several busts of *America* survive. Pennsylvania Academy of Fine Arts, reel P78, no. 0029, Archives of American Art; Powers to John L. Maquay, 13 February 1856 and 12 August 1856.

49 Powers to Dr. Playfair, 9 December 1848. Undated entry, Powers Journal; the previous fully dated item is 14 April 1841; the subsequent fully dated item is Thursday, 29 March 1842. For the uses of the female form in art, see Marina Warner, *Monuments and Maidens* (New York: Atheneum, 1985).

50 Fryd, "Sculpture as History," 127, 149 n.5.

51  Powers to J. P. Richardson, 14 December 1853. For Powers's trivializing views of feminism, see his letter to Richardson, 14 December 1853.

52  Powers to John Grant, 18 February 1849; Powers to Everett, 23 October 1850.

53  Thomas Branigan, "Description of the Frontispiece," *The Penitential Tyrant; or, Slave Trader Reformed*, 2d ed. (New York: Samuel Ward, 1807), p. 1.

54  "The Genius of America," *Freedom's Gift*, pp. 76–77.

55  *The Liberty Bell* (Boston: National Anti-Slavery Bazaar, 1852), pp. 250–51.

56  Powers to Longworth, 10 June 1853.

57  Powers to Sidney Brooks, 19 July 1854 and 20 July 1854.

58  Powers to Everett, 5 June 1855. *New York Times*, 16 September 1856.

59  Powers to Atlee, 10 February 1856.

60  Powers to Everett, 7 January 1857.

61  Powers to Brooks, 8 March 1865.

62  New York *Tribune*, 15 September 1847.

63  "America in Crystal," *Punch, or the London Charivari* (1851): 209. For other antislavery comment on *The Greek Slave* at the exhibition, see Henry C. Wright's furious denunciation of American hypocrisy, "The Great Exhibition," *The Liberator*, 16 September 1853; Wright asserts that by featuring *The Greek Slave* America implies that "slavery is abolished in the United States, as she is exhibited to the gaze of other nations!" Victor Schoelcher, "American Slavery, and the London Exhibition," *The Liberty Bell* (Boston: National Anti-Slavery Bazaar, 1852), pp. 157–69, asserts that the United States should have included exhibitions of "whips with knotted thongs, of iron collars, of heavy chains" along with the specimens of slave-produced goods, and he criticizes England for not prohibiting the exhibition of all goods produced with slave labor.

64  "The Virginian Slave," *Punch, or the London Charivari* (1851): 236.

65  William Farmer to Garrison, 26 June 1851, "Fugitive Slaves at the Great Exhibition," *The Liberator*, 18 July 1851; in William Still, *Still's Underground Railroad Records* (Philadelphia: The Author, 1886), pp. 374–77.

66  For Ellen Craft, see William Craft, *Running a Thousand Miles for Freedom* (London: William Tweedie, 1860); and Dorothy Sterling, *Black Foremothers: Three Lives* (Old Westbury, N.Y.: Feminist Press, 1979), pp. 25, 38, 41. Her portrait appeared in the *London Illustrated News*, 19 April 1851.

67  Grant to Powers, 27 November 1844? Powers to Stoughton, 26 November 1869.

68  The reference is to Harriet Beecher Stowe's *Uncle Tom's Cabin* (1852); for a discussion of the racism in Stowe's book, see my *Intricate Knot* (New York: New York University Press, 1972), chap. 7; for a discussion of the antifeminism in Stowe's book, see my "Doing It Herself: *Uncle Tom's Cabin* and Woman's Role in the Slavery Crisis," *New Essays on Uncle Tom's Cabin*, ed. Eric J. Sundquist (Cambridge: Cambridge University Press, 1986), pp. 85–106; "Letter from Grace Greenwood," *Philadelphia Saturday Evening Post*, 15 July 1848, Powers Scrapbook.

69  The text of Elizabeth Barrett Browning, "Hiram Powers' *Greek Slave*," in *The Poetical Works of Elizabeth Barrett Browning, Complete Edition* (New York: Thomas E. Crowell, n.d.), reads as follows:

> They say ideal beauty cannot enter
> The house of anguish. On the threshhold stands
> An alien Image with enshackled hands,

Called the Greek Slave! as if the artist meant her
(That passionless perfection which he lent her,
Shadowed, not darkened, where the sill espands)
To so confront man's crimes in different lands
With man's ideal sense. Pierce to the centre,
Art's firey finger! and break up ere long
The serfdom of this world! appeal, fair stone,
From God's pure heights of beauty against man's wrong!
Catch up in thy divine face, not alone
East grief, but west, and strike and shame the strong,
By thunders of white silence overthrown.

For Barrett Browning on Powers, see Frederick G. Kenyon, ed., *The Letters of Elizabeth Barrett Browning*, 4th ed., 2 vols. (London: Smith, Elder, 1898), 1:334, 347, 378;
2:97, 120, 131; and *Elizabeth Barrett Browning: Letters to Her Sister, 1846–1859*, ed.
Leonard Huxley (London: John Murray, 1929), pp. 24, 29, 38.

70    For Barrett Browning on slavery, see *The Letters*, 1:21, 23; 2:110–11. The poet permit-
ted Maria Weston Chapman and the Boston Female Anti-Slavery Society to publish her
"Runaway Slave at Pilgrim's Point" and "A Curse for a Nation"; see *The Liberty Bell*
(Boston: National Anti-Slavery Bazaar, 1848), p. 29; and (Boston: National Anti-
Slavery Bazaar, 1856), p. 1.


## Chapter Six

1    Elizabeth Cady Stanton, "Hester Vaughn," *The Revolution* (10 December 1868): 360–61.
2    Hawthorne scholarship has been transformed by the appearance of *The Centenary Edition of the Works of Nathaniel Hawthorne*, ed. by William Charvat, Roy Harvey Pearce,
and Claude M. Simpson, 20 vols. to date. (Columbus: Ohio State University Press,
1962–). References to *The Scarlet Letter* and other works by Hawthorne are to this
edition. References to the *American Notebooks* are to volume 8 of this edition. See also
*Hawthorne's Lost Notebook, 1835–1841*, transcribed by Barbara S. Mouffe (University
Park: Pennsylvania State University Press, 1978).

Hawthorne's letters are designated by dates and addresses in the text or in the notes;
quoted passages follow the texts established for *The Centenary Edition*. I am grateful to
L. Neal Smith, associate textual editor of *The Centenary Edition*, who made typescripts
and notes relating to this correspondence available to me before these texts appeared in
print.

Building on Robert Cantwell's *Nathaniel Hawthorne, the American Years* (New York:
Rinehart, 1948), relevant biographical studies include Arlin Turner's "Hawthorne and
Reform," *New England Quarterly* 15 (1942): 700–14; his "Needs in Hawthorne Biography," *Nathaniel Hawthorne Journal* 2 (1972): 43–45; and his *Nathaniel Hawthorne: A
Biography* (New York: Oxford University Press, 1980); as well as James R. Mellow,
*Nathaniel Hawthorne in His Times* (Boston: Houghton Mifflin, 1980). In addition to works
mentioned in the notes that follow, I have found the following critical studies particularly useful: Nina Baym's "Hawthorne's Women: The Tyranny of Social Myths," *Centennial Review* 15 (1971): 250–72; her "The Significance of Plot in Hawthorne's Romances,"

in G. R. Thompson et al., eds., *The Ruined Eden of the Present: Hawthorne, Melville, Poe* (Lafayette, Ind.: Purdue University Press, 1981), pp. 44–70; her "Passion and Authority in *The Scarlet Letter*," *New England Quarterly* 43 (1970): 209–30; and her full-length study, *The Shape of Hawthorne's Career* (Ithaca, N.Y.: Cornell University Press, 1976); Michael D. Bell's *Hawthorne and the Historical Romance of New England* (Princeton: Princeton University Press, 1971); Millicent Bell, "The Obliquity of Signs: *The Scarlet Letter*," *Massachusetts Review* 23 (1982): 9–26; Sacvan Berkovitch's *The American Jeremiad* (Wisconsin: University of Wisconsin Press, 1978); Richard Brodhead's *Hawthorne, Melville and the Novel* (Chicago: University of Chicago Press, 1976); Michael Colacurcio's "Footsteps of Anne Hutchinson: The Context of *The Scarlet Letter*," *ELH* 39 (1972): 459–94; and his *The Province of Piety* (Cambridge Mass.: Harvard University Press, 1984); Ronald J. Gervais, "A Papist Among the Puritans: Icon and Logos in *The Scarlet Letter*," *Journal of the American Renaissance* 25 (1979): 11–16; Lawrence S. Hall, *Hawthorne, Critic of Society* (New Haven: Yale University Press, 1944); Harry B. Henderson III, *Versions of the Past: The Historical Imagination in American Fiction* (New York: Oxford University Press, 1974); and Tony Tanner, *Adultery in the Novel: Contract and Transgression* (Baltimore: Johns Hopkins University Press, 1979).

3   See my "Hawthorne and the American National Sin," in *The Green Tradition in American Culture*, ed. H. Daniel Peck (Baton Rouge: Louisiana State University Press, 1989).

4   Horace Mann, speech of 23 February 1849, *Slavery: Writings and Speeches* (New York: Burt Franklin, 1969), pp. 153–54.

5   Although well documented in the holdings of the Essex Institute, the history of the Salem, Massachusetts, Female Anti-Slavery Society has not been written. See *The Liberator*, 7 January 1832 and 17 November 1832; *Proceedings, Third Anti-Slavery Convention of American Women 1839* (Philadelphia: Merrihew and Thompson, 1839), pp. 8–9; and Angelina Grimké to Jane Smith, 16 July 1837, Grimké-Weld papers, Clements Memorial Library, University of Michigan.

6   "Cuba Journal," p. 1; Sophia Peabody letters, 20 December [1833]-2 July [1834], Mary Peabody letters, 8 January-31 May [1834], Sophia Peabody to Mrs. Elizabeth Palmer Peabody, 21 March [1834], Henry W. and Albert A. Berg Collection, The New York Public Library, Astor, Lenox and Tilden Foundations. Used by permission.

7   Sophia Peabody Hawthorne to her mother, Mrs. Elizabeth Peabody, 15 November 1843. Unless otherwise stated, quoted passages from Sophia Peabody Hawthorne's correspondence are from The Henry W. and Albert A. Berg Collection, The New York Public Library, Astor, Lenox and Tilden Foundations, and are used by permission.

8   "The Great Lawsuit: Man versus Men; Woman versus Women," *The Dial* (July 1843); revised and republished as *Woman in the Nineteenth Century*, ed. Arthur B. Fuller (New York: Tribune Press, 1845). Sophia Peabody Hawthorne to her mother, Elizabeth P. Peabody, quoted in Julian Hawthorne, *Nathaniel Hawthorne and His Wife: A Biography* (Boston: Houghton Mifflin, 1884), 1:257.

9   Sophia Peabody Hawthorne to her mother, in Julian Hawthorne, *Nathaniel Hawthorne and His Wife*, 1:257.

10  Sophia Peabody Hawthorne to her sister Elizabeth P. Peabody, [Spring 1860], quoted in Louise Hall Tharp, *The Peabody Sisters of Salem* (Boston: Little, Brown, 1950), p. 288; and in Rose Hawthorne Lathrop, *Memories of Hawthorne* (Boston: Houghton Mifflin, 1923), p. 358.

11   Independently of Ferrin's efforts, the Know-Nothings, who dominated the legislature, passed a Married Woman's Property Act in 1853; a liberalized divorce law followed in 1855. See *History of Woman Suffrage*, ed. Elizabeth Cady Stanton et al., 6 vols. (New York, 1881–1922), 1:208–15. For Hawthorne and Upham, see Hawthorne to Horace Mann, Salem, 26 June 1849 and 8 August 1849; and to Burchmore, 17 September 1850, and 7 April 1851, in *Letters*, 16:284–86, 291–95; 364–66; 415–16. Also see Stephen Nissenbaum, "The Firing of Nathaniel Hawthorne," Essex Institute *Historical Collections* 114 (April 1978): 57–86.

12   For commentary that blamed the abolitionists for inciting the mob, see "Reported Riot in Boston" in the *American Monthly Magazine*, which Hawthorne would edit the following year, vol. 2 (1835): 164. Harriet Martineau, "The Martyr Age of the United States," *London and Westminster Review* (December 1838; republ. Newcastle upon Tyne: Finlay and Charlton, 1840): 43; *Autobiography of Harriet Martineau*, ed. Maria W. Chapman, 3 vols. (Boston: J. R. Osgood, 1877), 1:347–57. For Garrison's description of Chapman at Pennsylvania Hall, and of her subsequent illness, see his letter to his mother dated 19 May 1838; and to George Benson, 25 May 1838, in the *Letters of William Lloyd Garrison*, ed. Walter M. Merrill and Louis Ruchames, 6 vols. (Cambridge, Mass.: Harvard University Press, 1971–1981), 2:363, 366. Also see Lydia Maria Child to Caroline Weston, 28 July 1838, in *Selected Letters, 1817–1880*, ed. Milton Meltzer and Patricia G. Holland (Amherst: University of Massachusetts Press, 1982), pp. 79–82; Child to Louisa Loring, 3 June 1838; and to Lydia B. Child, 7 August 1838, in *The Collected Correspondence of Lydia Maria Child, 1817–1880*, ed. Patricia G. Holland and Milton Meltzer (Millwood, N. Y.: Kraus Microform, 1980).

13   For Whittier's poem, "The Branded Hand," see *The Complete Poetical Works of John Greenleaf Whittier*, Cambridge Edition (Boston and New York: Houghton Mifflin, Riverside Press, 1894), p. 296. Walker later lectured with Harriet Jacob's brother, John S. Jacobs. Daniel Drayton, too, later spoke for the abolitionists; he published an account of his ordeal in *Personal Memoirs* (Boston: Bella Marsh, 1855). For Mann's defense of Drayton, see Louisa Hall Tharp, *Until Victory: Horace Mann and Mary Peabody Mann* (Boston: Little, Brown, 1953), pp. 224–34. For the *Pearl* refugees, see Harriet Beecher Stowe, *Key to Uncle Tom's Cabin* (1853; reprint, New York: Arno, 1968), pp. 306–30. For Beecher's "slave sales," see William C. Beecher and Rev. Samuel Scoville, *A Biography of Henry Ward Beecher* (New York: C. L. Webster, 1888), pp. 292–300; and William G. McLaughlen, *The Meaning of Henry Ward Beecher* (New York: Knopf, 1970), pp. 200–1. Eastman Johnson, who had painted Hawthorne's portrait in 1846, made the Plymouth Church "slave sale" the subject of his oil painting *The Freedom Ring* after the magazinist Rose Terry Cooke, who was in the church, heard Beecher's plea and dropped her ring into the collection plate.

14   *The Autobiography of Harriet Martineau*, vol. 2, pp. 33–35. For the Manns, see Louise Tharp, *Until Victory*, especially pp. 224–34; and Jonathan Messerli, *Horace Mann* (New York: Knopf, 1972).

15   1835 entry, *American Notebooks*, 10.

16   Hawthorne lived at Brook Farm from April to November 1841. For his critical private views of reformers, see, for example, *American Notebooks*, 10, 136. For his critical public views, see, for example, "The Hall of Fantasy," *Pioneer* (February 1843), and a series of pieces in *The Democratic Review*, including "The New Adam and Eve" (Febru-

ary 1843); "The Procession of Life" (April 1843); "The Celestial Rail-road" (May 1843); "The Christmas Banquet" (January 1844); "The Intelligence Office" (March 1844); and "A Select Party" (July 1844). "Earth's Holocaust" appeared in *Graham's Magazine* in May 1844. All of these were collected in the 1846 edition of *Mosses from an Old Manse*.

17    *The Blithedale Romance* (1852); "Mrs. Hutchinson," Salem *Gazette*, 7 December 1830, republished in *Biographical Sketches*, Riverside Edition, vol. 17, pp. 217–26. Evidently Hawthorne did not think that female artists exposed themselves as female writers did. Yet while courting Sophia Peabody, long before *The Scarlet Letter*, he alternately fantasized about a life in which both of them would create art and expressed concern that efforts to do serious work as an artist would jeopardize her health. See Hawthorne to Sophia Peabody, 21 and 23 August 1839; 3 January 1840; 15 April 1840; 12 August 1841, in *The Letters*, vol. 15. pp. 339, 397, 440, 557. For Sophia Peabody Hawthorne as an artist, see Josephine Withers, "Artistic Women and Women Artists," *Art Journal*, 35 (1976): 330–36.

18    "The Gentle Boy" first appeared in *The Token* for 1832; it was collected in *Twice-Told Tales*. For an informed discussion, see Michael J. Colacurcio, *The Province of Piety*; pp. 63, 66–68 suggest connections between this text, "Mrs. Hutchinson," and *The Scarlet Letter*.

19    "The New Adam and Eve" first appeared in the *United States Magazine and Democratic Review* (12 February 1843); it was collected into *Mosses* in 1846 and 1854; see The Centenary Edition, vol. 10.

20    "The Hall of Fantasy," which first appeared in *The Pioneer* (1843), and "A Christmas Banquet," which first appeared in *Democratic Review* in 1844, were collected into *Mosses* in 1846 and 1854; for all, see the Centenary Edition, vol. 10. For Abby Folsom, see *The National Cyclopaedia of American Biography* (New York: James T. White, 1921), 2:394. Hawthorne's reference to Folsom—like his other references to contemporaries—was dropped when this piece was anthologized.

21    Sarah M. Grimké, *Letters on the Equality of the Sexes* (Boston: Isaac Knapp, 1838), letter 3, p. 14.

22    Margaret Hope Bacon, *I Speak for my Slave Sister: The Life of Abby Kelley Foster* (New York: Thomas Crowell, 1974), p. 131.

23    For echoes in *The Scarlet Letter* of the French Revolution, and of the European revolutions of 1848, see Larry J. Reynolds, *"The Scarlet Letter* and Revolutions Abroad," *American Literature* 57 (March 1985): 44–67. For the "decapitated surveyor" Hawthorne and Hester, see Stephen Nissenbaum, "The Firing of Nathaniel Hawthorne," *Essex Institute Historical Collections* 114 (April 1978): pp. 57–86.

24    "Hester Vaughn," *The Revolution* (10 December 1868), pp. 360–61.

25    For Harriet Hosmer's *Zenobia* (1858), see *Harriet Hosmer: Letters and Memories*, ed. Cornelia Carr (London: J. Lane, The Bodley Head, 1913), pp. 191–93, 199–204, 363–68; Lorado Taft, *History of American Sculpture* (New York: Macmillan, 1930); and Margaret F. Thorp, *The Literary Sculptors* (Durham: Duke University Press, 1965), pp. 87–88. A version of this work is at the Wadsworth Atheneum, Hartford. The subject of Zenobia, Queen of Palmyre, was of interest to the American feminists; Child discusses her in *History of the Condition of Woman*, 2 vols. (Boston: J. Allen, 1835). William Ware's 1837 novel is best known by its second title, *Zenobia: or, the Queen of Palmyra*. *The Blithedale Romance*, Hawthorne's comment on Brook Farm, was published in 1852.

26  Roberts's 1869 sculpture is in the collection of the Library Company of Philadelphia. See *Philadelphia: Three Centuries of American Art. Bicentennial Exhibition*, catalog (Philadelphia: Philadelphia Museum of Art, 1976), p. 34.

27  For the antislavery feminists and the figure of Queen Esther, see chapter 2, above.

28  For blacks in seventeenth-century Massachusetts, see, for example, Robert C. Twombly and Robert H. Moore, "Black Puritan: The Negro in Seventeenth-Century Massachusetts," *William and Mary Quarterly*, 3d series (April 1967): 224–42; and George H. Moore, *Notes on the History of Slavery in Massachusetts* (1866; reprint, New York: Negro Universities Press, 1968). For Hawthorne's early awareness of this historic black presence, see, for example, *American Notebooks* 21, p. 150; his continued interest in the history of African-Americans is expressed (p. 550). Also see "Old News," *The New-England Magazine* 1–3 (February-May 1835) in *The Snow Image* (1852); and *Grandfather's Chair* 2 (1841) in *True Stories: Writings for Children*, Centenary Edition, vol. 6; for more, see my essay "Hawthorne and the American National Sin," *The Green American Tradition*, ed. H. Daniel Peck.

29  The convergence of western structures signifying diabolism and spiritual enslavement, and western structures signifying Africans and the African slave trade, are discussed in *The Image of the Black in Western Art*, vol. 2, *From the Early Church to the "Age of Discovery,"* pt. 1, Jean Devisse, *From the Demonic Threat to the Incarnation of Sainthood* (New York: William Morrow, 1979); and in *The Image of the Black in Western Art*, vol. 2, *From the Early Christian Era to the "Age of Discovery,"* pt. 2, Jean Devisse and Michel Mollat, *Africans in the Christian Ordinance of the World*, Fourteenth to the Sixteenth Century (New York: William Morrow, 1979).

30  These women are so punitive that an anonymous man chides them. One, however—a young mother—sympathizes with Hester. Her comment about the badge—"Not a stitch in that embroidered letter, but she has felt it in her heart" (p. 54)—recalls a motto of the sewing circles organized by the female antislavery societies: "May the points of our needles prick the slaveholders' consciences."

31  If anything, Hester's isolation is now more complete. Although some have come to believe her *A* signifies "Able," we are not told that the women have stopped behaving like witches and distilling their poison for her ears; the tender-hearted young mother who initially sympathized with her has died in the seven-year interval.

32  For Powers's sculpture, see chapter 5, above. Miner Kellogg's promotional pamphlet *Powers' Statue of The Greek Slave* (New York: R. Craigshead, 1847) underscores Hester's connections with Powers's work; see especially p. 125.

33  The danger of women's evaporation was again voiced following the October 1851 Woman's Rights Convention at Worcester. When an article in the *Christian Inquirer* queried, "Place woman unbonneted and unshawled before the public gaze and what becomes of her modesty and her virtue?" feminist Ernestine Rose responded: "In [the writer's] benighted mind, the modesty and virtue of woman is of so fragile a nature, that when it is in contact with the atmosphere, it evaporates like chloroform. Such a sentiment," she continued, "carries its own deep condemnation" (*History of Woman Suffrage*, 1:245–46).

34  Angelina Grimké to Jane Smith, 9 May-5 June-7 June 1837; see chapter 2, above. For Nathaniel Hawthorne's ambivalence concerning the construction of gender, see Walter Herbert, Jr., "Nathaniel Hawthorne, Una Hawthorne, and *The Scarlet Letter*," *PMLA* 103 (May 1988): 285–97.

35  "Declaration of Sentiments," *History of Woman Suffrage*, 1:70–73.

36 For a contemporary feminist discussion of the duties of a wife and of the traditional role of a Christian husband as mediator between his wife and her Creator, see Sarah Grimké's *Letters on the Equality of the Sexes*, chapter 2, above. For a very different reading of Hester's relationship with Arthur and of the book's conclusion, see Nina Baym, "Thwarted Nature: Nathaniel Hawthorne as Feminist," *American Novelists Revisited: Essays in Feminist Criticism*, ed. Fritz Fleischmann (Boston: G. K. Hall, 1982), pp. 58–77.

   Hester's self-identification as Arthur's true wife is demonstrated by her refusal to name him in the first scaffold scene and in her prison interview with Roger; by the narrator's insinuation that her decision to remain in Boston after being released from prison is at least partially based on her feeling "connected in a union, that, unrecognized on earth, would bring them together before the bar of final judgement, and make that their marriage-altar" (p. 80); by her tenacious appeal to Arthur to intervene on her behalf with the Governor when her custody of Pearl is jeopardized; and by her sense of a responsibility and commitment to Arthur, her only "significant link" to anyone in the community. This commitment leads her to tell Roger that she has decided to break her promise and reveal his identity to Arthur.

   Hester's revelation of Roger's identity comments not only on her earlier promise to keep that identity secret and her refusal to name her lover to him, it also underscores her sense of herself as Arthur's wife by reversing the stock literary situation in which an adulterous wife finally identifies a secret lover to her husband.

37 In 1848, Thoreau had included these ideas in his talk on "Civil Disobedience" at the Concord Lyceum; Elizabeth Peabody had published his essay—along with Hawthorne's sketch "Main Street"—in *Aesthetic Papers* (May 1849); reprint, Gainesville, Fla.: Scholar's Facsimiles and Reprints, 1957.

38 The narrator does not entirely approve. He comments, "Shame, Despair, Solitude! These had been her teachers,—and they had made her strong, but taught her much amiss" (pp. 199–200).

39 The 1837 Pastoral Letter of "The General Association of Massachusetts (Orthodox) to the Churches under Their Care" is extracted in Stanton, *History of Woman Suffrage*, 1:81–82. The figure of the marriage of weak female vine and strong male elm appeared in classical writings by Virgil, in medieval emblem books, and in English masterworks by Spenser, Shakespeare, and Milton. I am indebted to A. Bartlett Giamatti for bringing to my attention Peter Demetz's "Elm and Vine: Notes Toward the History of a Marriage Topos," *PMLA* 73 (1958): 521–32.

40 Sarah Grimké, *Letters on the Equality of the Sexes* (Boston: Isaac Knapp, 1838), p. 21; see chapter 2, above.

41 The comments of Hawthorne's narrator about the events following Arthur's spectacular death reinforce the impression that Hester, like a true wife, has grounded her sense of self in her relationship with her man. Reporting that after the minister's death Roger "positively withered up" because revenge was "the very principle of his life" and with Arthur's death there was "no further material to support it" (p. 260), he comments on the similarities between love and hate and defines both as parasitic: "Each renders one individual dependent for the food of his affections and spiritual life upon another; each leaves the passionate lover, or the no less passionate hater, forlorn and desolate by the withdrawl of his object" (p. 260). References to connections between marriage and mosses and references to wives as "gentle parasites" recur throughout Hawthorne's work.

Here his account of Hester's disappearance after Arthur's death underscores the notion that she is a true wife, a gentle parasite deprived of her host.

42  *Life of Franklin Pierce*, Centenary Edition, 5:416–17.

43  Coventry Patmore, *The Angel in the House*, 2 vols. (London: Macmillan, 1863); Patmore's poem had been published in sections in 1854, 1856, 1860, and 1863. Hawthorne, who was familiar with Patmore's poetry, wrote that "The Angel in the House" was "a favorite" of his and of Sophia; he judged it "a poem for married people to read together." See Mellow, *Nathaniel Hawthorne in His Times*, pp. 40, 439; and *English Notebooks*, p. 620. I am deeply grateful to Milton R. Stern, whose comments, made so long ago, moved me to attempt an adequate reading of this passage, and who explores some of the complexities of Hawthorne's thought and production in "Nathaniel Hawthorne: Conservative After Heaven's Own Fashion," in Joseph Waldmeier, ed., *Essays in Honor of Russel B. Nye* (East Lansing, Mich.: Michigan State University Press, 1978), pp. 195–225.

44  For an awareness of the role of the government officials, I am indebted to Nina Baym's "George Sand in American Periodicals" (Paper delivered at the meetings of the Nathaniel Hawthorne Society, New York, 1983).

## Chapter Seven

1  L[ucia] T. A[mes], "The Bostonians," *The Woman's Journal* 17 (13 March 1886): 82–83.

2  *The Bostonians*, published by Macmillan in England and the United States in 1886, had appeared in installments in *The Century Magazine* from February 1885 to February 1886. The novel was not included in the twenty-six volume Scribner's New York edition (1907–1909) of James's collected works, although James judged it "tolerably full and good"; see Henry James to William Dean Howells, 17 August 1908, *Henry James. Letters of Henry James*, ed. Percy Lubbock, 2 vols. (New York: Scribner's, 1920), 2:100. Page numbers cited in my text refer to the edition edited by Charles B. Anderson (Middlesex, England: Penguin Books, 1984); this follows the text of *The Bostonians* in the complete edition of James's fiction published in thirty-five volumes by Macmillan (London, 1921–1923), a reprint of the first English edition (1886). This quotation is from Henry James to William James, 14 February 1885 *Letters*, ed. Leon Edel, 4 vols. (Cambridge: Harvard University Press, 1974–1984), 3:68–69.

3  My discussion of Peabody is based on the following sources: Ruth M. Baylor, *Elizabeth Palmer Peabody: Kindergarten Pioneer* (Philadelphia: University of Pennsylvania Press, 1965); Louisa Hall Tharp, *The Peabody Sisters of Salem* (Boston: Little, Brown, 1950); and *Letters of Elizabeth Palmer Peabody, American Renaissance Woman*, ed. Bruce A. Ronda (Middletown, Conn.: Wesleyan University Press, 1984). For the connections between Elizabeth Palmer Peabody and Henry James's Miss Birdseye, see below.

4  Catherine H. Birney, *Sarah and Angelina Grimké: The First American Women Advocates of Abolition and Woman's Rights* (1885; reprint, New York: Haskell House, 1970), pp. 215–16.

5  For example, the title of Helene G. Baer's biography of Child is *The Heart Is Like Heaven* (Philadelphia: University of Pennsylvania Press, 1964).

6  Lydia Maria Child, "Thanksgiving Day," in Mildred P. Harrington and Joseph H. Thomas, comps., *Our Holidays in Poetry* (New York: H. W. Wilson, 1929), p. 345.

7   See, for example, my "DuBois' *Crisis* and Woman's Suffrage," *Massachusetts Review* (1973): 365–75; Aileen Kraditor, *The Ideas of the Woman Suffrage Movement, 1890–1920* (New York: Anchor Books, 1971), chap. 7; Rosalyn Terborn-Penn, "Discrimination Against Afro-American Women in the Woman's Movement, 1830–1920," in *The Afro-American Woman*, ed. Sharon Harley and Rosalyn Terborg-Penn (Port Washington, N.Y.: National University Publications, 1978), pp. 17–28.

8   For controversy on the shaping of the American literary canon, see, for example, Jane Tompkins, *Sensational Designs: The Cultural Work of American Fiction, 1790–1860* (New York: Oxford University Press, 1985).

9   Item dated Boston, 8 April 1883, in *The Complete Notebooks of Henry James*, ed. Leon Edel and Lyall H. Powers (New York: Oxford University Press, 1987), pp. 18–20.

10  Leon Edel, *Henry James: The Middle Years: 1882–1895* (Philadelphia: J. B. Lippincott, 1962), p. 137; James's review, which first appeared in *The Century Magazine* (June 1883) is included in *The American Essays*, ed. Leon Edel (New York: Vintage, 1956), pp. 31–50. *The Complete Notebooks*, p. 18.

11  *The Complete Notebooks*, p. 19.

12  *A Small Boy and Others* (New York: Charles Scribner's Sons, 1914), pp. 269–70, 228.

13  *A Small Boy and Others*, p. 250.

14  *Notes of a Son and Brother* (New York: Charles Scribner's Sons, 1914), pp. 221, 374, 242.

15  *Notes of a Son and Brother*, p. 209.

16  For James's lack of familiarity with the woman's movement, see for example David Howard, *The Air of Reality: New Essays on Henry James*, ed. John Goode (London: Methuen, 1972), pp. 65, 66; Sara deSauesure Davis, "Feminist Sources in *The Bostonians*," *American Literature* 50 (1979): 570–87, makes the claim—which I find unconvincing—that a triangle involving Anna Dickinson, Susan B. Anthony, and Wendell Phillips (or, alternatively, a triangle involving Dickinson, Anthony, and Whitlaw Reid), may have been a source for *The Bostonians*. For more speculation regarding biographical sources, see Ruth Evelyn Quebe, "*The Bostonians*: Some Historical Sources and Their Implications," *Centennial Review* 125 (1980): 80–100. Henry James to William James, 13 June 1886, *Henry James: Letters*, 3:121. Henry James to Thomas Sergeant Perry, New York, [1 November 1863], *Henry James: Letters*, ed. Leon Edel, 1:44–47. For Hatch, see Howard Kerr, *Mediums, Spirit Rappers and Roaring Radicals* (Urbana: University of Illinois Press, 1972).

17  Henry James to Thomas Sergeant Perry, New York [1 November 1863], *Henry James: Letters*, ed. Leon Edel, 1: 44–47.

18  The sketch is in Henry James's letter to Thomas Sergeant Perry [1 November 1863], in the microfilm collection of the Manuscript Division, William P. Perkins Library, Duke University.

19  *History of Woman Suffrage*, ed. Elizabeth Cady Stanton et al., 6 vols. (New York, 1881–1922), 3:287, 273, 192–97.

20  For Alice James, see Jean Strouse, *Alice James: A Biography* (Boston: Houghton Mifflin, 1980); *The Death and Letters of Alice James*, ed. Ruth Bernard Yeazell (Berkeley: University of California Press, 1981); and *The Diary of Alice James*, ed. Leon Edel (New York: Penguin Books, 1981). For Sewall's speech, see *History of Woman Suffrage*, 3:193; Sewell is sketched in *Notable American Women*, ed. Edward T. James et al., 3 vols. (Cambridge, Mass.: Harvard University Press, 1971), 3:269ff. For the interest in

feminism of Henry James, Alice James, and Katherine Loring, see Strouse, *Alice James: A Biography*, p. 217.

21  See the references to Abby May Alcott in Alice James's letter to Sara Sedgwick, 1 February 1874; and the references to Rosalind Francis, her husband, George James Howard, and Sir Wilfred Lawson in Alice James's letter to Alice Howe Gibbens James and William James, [20 November 1887], in *Death*, pp. 136–37.

22  19 November 1889, entry, *The Diary of Alice James*, ed. Leon Edel. Published as *Alice James: Her Brothers—Her Journal* (1934); retitled and republished, New York: Penguin Books, 1982), p. 60.

23  17 December 1889, entry, *The Diary of Alice James*, p. 71. For other expressions of Alice James's feminist consciousness, see, for example, the entry of 21 February 1890, *The Diary of Alice James*, p. 95; Alice James to William James, 3–7 January [1886], *Death*, p. 107; Alice James to Francis Rollins Morse, 9 June [1889], *Death*, p. 172; Alice James to Anna Hazard Ward, 7 January 1883, *Death*, p. 87; Alice James to Alice Howe Gibbens James, 9 January 1890, *Death*, p. 179.

24  See Strouse, *Alice James*, pp. 191ff. For women's relationships in the nineteenth century, see Carroll Smith-Rosenberg, "The Female World of Love and Ritual: Relations Between Men and Women in Nineteenth-Century America," *Signs* 1 (Autumn 1975): 1–29.

25  Elizabeth Palmer Peabody to Theodore Weld, 11 November 1866, Robert Lincoln Straker Collection, Antioch College Library, quoted in Baylor, *Elizabeth Palmer Peabody*, p. 90.

26  The specific character of Peabody's antislavery commitment remains unclear; Margaret Neussendorfer's forthcoming biography of Peabody will no doubt resolve this question. Peabody to Mary Peabody Mann, [Summer? 1835?], Cuba Journals, pp. 223–24, no. 371363B, Henry W. and Alberta A. Berg Collection, The New York Public Library, Astor, Lenox and Tilden Foundations; *Harriet Martineau's Autobiography*, ed. Maria Weston Chapman, 3 vols. (Boston: J. R. Osgood, 1877), 2:33–35.

27  The 1841 edition of Channing's book appeared under the rubric of the American Antislavery Society; Tharp, *Peabody Sisters*, p. 139. "The Dorian Measure," *Aesthetic Papers* (May, 1849; reprint, Gainesville, Fla.: Scholars' Facsimiles and Reprints, 1957), pp. 109–10. Maude Greene, "Raritan Bay Union, Eagleswood, New Jersey," *Proceedings of the New Jersey Historical Society* 68 (January 1950): 9–10; *Letters of Elizabeth Palmer Peabody*, p. 276; Tharp, *Peabody Sisters*, pp. 230–31.

28  Hawthorne to Peabody, 13 August and 8 October 1857, *Letters of Nathaniel Hawthorne*, 18:89, 115. Sophia Hawthorn to Peabody [Spring, 1860]; see fn. 10, p. 207, above.

29  Although Peabody evidently met with Virginia Governor Letcher, her pleas were disregarded; Stevens, too, was hanged. The bodies of Stevens and of Albert Hazlett were buried at Eagleswood as a consequence of the efforts of Rebecca Spring, a member of the Eagleswood community who had also gone to Virginia; see Tharp, *Peabody Sisters*, pp. 283–85; Peabody's *Letters*, p. 315; and Oswald Garrison Villard, *John Brown, 1800–1859* (Boston: Houghton Mifflin, 1910), pp. 573–80.

30  Elizabeth Palmer Peabody to [William C.] Bryant, October 1864, Berg Collection, New York Public Library; to Longfellow, 15 October 1864, Elizabeth Palmer Peabody Correspondence, Houghton Library; quoted in Baylor, *Elizabeth Palmer Peabody*, p. 90. Also see Peabody's *Letters*, pp. 332–33. Meeting with Lincoln in 1865, Peabody presented the president with a copy of *The Liberator*; see Peabody's *Letters*, pp. 326–31.

31  Peabody to Dall, 21 February 1859, Peabody, *Letters*, pp. 297–98.

32  Ibid.

33  "Industrial Schools for Women," *Harper's Monthly Magazine* 40 (May 1870): 889; I am grateful to Margaret Neussendorfer for this citation.

34  The most prominent American proponent of Froebel's approach, Peabody established and edited the *Kindergarten Messenger* in 1873; in 1877, she organized the American Froebel Union and served as its first president. See Baylor, *Elizabeth Palmer Peabody*; International Kindergarten Union, *Pioneers of the Kindergarten in America* (New York: The Century, 1924), pp. 19–38; *History of Woman Suffrage*, 4:227.

35  Henry James, *Hawthorne* (1879; reprint, Ithaca, N.Y.: Cornell University Press, 1956), pp. 54–55.

36  Mark A. DeWolfe Howe, *The Later Years of the Saturday Club, 1870–1920* (Boston: Houghton Mifflin, 1927), pp. 156–57.

37  Henry James to William James, 14 February [1885], *Henry James: Letters*, ed. Leon Edel, 3:68.

38  Henry James to William James, 14 February [1885], *Henry James: Letters*, ed. Leon Edel, 3:69.

39  Nathaniel Hawthorne to Elizabeth Peabody, 13 August and 8 October 1857, *Nathaniel Hawthorne's Letters*, 13:89, 115.

40  *Bostonians*, p. 189. For Mott, see Otelia Cromwell, *Lucretia Mott* (Cambridge: Harvard University Press, 1958); *James and Lucretia Mott*, ed. Anna Davis Hallowell (Boston: Houghton Mifflin, 1896); and Margaret Hope Bacon, *Valiant Friend, The Life of Lucretia Mott* (New York: Walker, 1980). Margaret Douglass, *Educational Laws of Virginia: The Personal Narrative of Mrs. Margaret Douglass, a Southern Woman, who was imprisoned for one month in the common jail of Norfolk* (Boston: J. P. Jewett, 1854).

41  *Notes of a Son and Brother*, pp. 213–14.

42  Henry James to William James, 14 February [1885], *Henry James: Letters*, ed. Leon Edel, 3:68–69.

43  For connections between *The Bostonians* and Hawthorne's works, see Richard H. Brodhead, *The School of Hawthorne* (New York: Oxford University Press, 1986); Marius Bewley, *The Complex Fate* (London: Chatto and Windus, 1952); R. W. B. Lewis, "Hawthorne and James: The Matter of the Heart," *Trials of the Word* (New Haven: Yale University Press, 1965); and Robert Emmet Long, "The Society and the Masks: *The Blithedale Romance* and *The Bostonians*," *Nineteenth-Century Fiction* 19 (1964): 105–22.

44  For a provocative alternative reading of Verena, see Judith Wilt, "Desperately Seeking Verena: A Resistant Reading of *The Bostonians*," *Feminist Studies* 13 (1987), pp. 193–316. For Verena as a spiritualist medium, see Susan Wolstenholme, "Possession and Personality: Spiritualism in *The Bostonians*," *American Literature* 49 (1978): 580–91.

45  Henry James to William James, 14 February [1885], *Henry James: Letters*, ed. Leon Edel, 3:68.

46  On the shifting treatment of Miss Birdseye, see Bruce R. McElderry, Jr., *Henry James* (New York: Twayne, 1965), pp. 66–67; R. W. B. Lewis, *Trials of the Word*, p. 95; and David H. Heaton, "The Altered Characterization of Miss Birdseye in Henry James's *The Bostonians*," *American Literature* 50 (1979): 588–603. *Notes of a Son and Brother*, pp. 224–25. On possible connections between Henry James, Sr., and Miss Birdseye, see Henry Seidel Canby, *Turn West, Turn East: Mark Twain and Henry James* (Boston: Houghton Mifflin, 1951), p. 176.

47   Indeed, only a "dozen sympathizers" travel from Boston to attend her funeral; the others
     send Olive "pages of diffuse reminiscence" and expect her to provide them with "all
     particulars" (p. 396).
48   P. 389. It seems to me that she is correct—even if, as some critics have suggested, the
     speech she is forced to deliver after the book ends proves to be a success. She does not,
     after all, win Verena; and it was Verena, not "feminism," that she wanted.
49   Louisa M. Alcott, *Work: A Story of Experience* (1873; reprint, New York: Schocken,
     1977). Passages cited can be found on the following pages: 425–27, 429, 431, 437,
     442, and 449. See my article "From *Success* to *Experience*: Louisa May Alcott's *Work*,"
     *Massachusetts Review* (1980): 527–39.
50   Child to Sarah Shaw, 10 March 1879, *Lydia Maria Child: Selected Letters, 1817-1880*,
     ed. Milton Meltzer et al. (Amherst: University of Massachusetts Press, 1982), p. 557.
51   For *The Bostonians* as satire, see Charles R. Anderson's "Introduction" to the Penguin
     edition (Middlesex, England: 1984). L[ucia] T. A[mes], *The Woman's Journal* 17 (13
     March 1886): 82–83.
52   Henry James to William James, 15 February [1885], *Henry James: Letters*, ed. Leon
     Edel, 3:71.
53   John Jay Chapman, *Memories and Milestones* (New York: Moffat, Yard, 1915), pp. 209,
     216, 218, 221.
54   For the portrait bust of Chapman, see the entry concerning Edmonia Lewis in *Notable
     American Women*, 2:397ff. The work is pictured in James A. Porter, *Ten Afro-American
     Artists of the Nineteenth Century*, catalog (Washington, D.C.: Howard University, 1967),
     p. 19. Olin L. Warner's sculpture of Garrison was installed on Boston's Commonwealth
     Avenue in 1886; Wendell Phillips's statue stands on Boston Common. Antislavery
     feminists appear as sexually decadent New England schoolteachers in the Reconstruc-
     tion South in Faulkner's works.
55   *History of Woman Suffrage*, 1:1.
56   For this discussion of the use of images by turn-of-the-century feminists, I am indebted
     to Edith Mayo, whose paper, "Motherhood, Madonnas, and Social Ministry: The Mate-
     rial Culture of Woman's Suffrage," was read at a conference on Woman and the Progres-
     sive Era at the Smithsonian Institution in 1988. Mayo speculates that the pin was issued
     either by the Congressional Union or by the Woman's Party, probably between 1913 and
     1920. (Arrests of National Woman's Party pickets began in 1917).
57   For the antislavery feminists and Joan of Arc, see chap. 2, above; and see, for example,
     Lamartine, *Joan of Arc: A Biography*, translated from the French by Sarah Grimké
     (Boston: Adams, 1867); Lucy Stone is quoted in Catherine H. Birney, *Sarah and
     Angelina Grimké*, 215–16.
58   *Women's Franchise*, 25 May 1908, p. 564, quoted in Lisa Ticknor, *The Spectacle of
     Women: Imagery of the Suffrage Campaign, 1907–1914* (Chicago: University of Chi-
     cago Press, 1988), p. 80. Ticknor reports, p. 51, that the *Common Cause* glossed this
     image with "Now press the clarion on thy woman's lip," a line from Elizabeth Barret
     Browning's *Aurora Leigh*, Book 9. In Barret Browning's poem, this imperative is addressed
     to Aurora, who is urged to "blow all class-walls level as Jericho's / Past Jordan"—a
     demand resonating with the most egalitarian, and the most embattled, impulses of the
     feminist movement. For American versions of this image, I am indebted to Edith Mayo.
          The Bugler Girl, in her medieval armor, appears consonant with the chivalric model
     proposed by contemporary American idealogues of white supremacy. For white racism

within the American feminist movement, see, for example, *The Afro-American Woman: Struggles and Images*, ed. Sharon Harley and Rosalyn Terborg-Penn (Port Washington, N.Y.: Kennikat Press, 1978); Aileen Kraditor, *The Ideas of the Woman Suffrage Movement, 1890–1920* (New York: Columbia University Press, 1965); and Jean Fagan Yellin, "DuBois' *Crisis* and Woman's Suffrage," *Massachusetts Review* (Spring 1973): 365–75. Also see, for example, *The History of Woman Suffrage*, 6:81–82.

59    For Lewis, see Lynn M. Igoe, *250 Years of Afro-American Art: An Annotated Bibliography* (New York: R. R. Bowker, 1981), pp. 899–905; for *Forever Free*, see William H. Gerdts, Jr., *The White, Marmorean Flock: Nineteenth Century American Women Neoclassical Sculptors*, catalog (Poughkeepsie, N.Y.: The Vassar College Art Gallery, 1972), [12–13]. Sarah M. Grimké, *Letters on the Equality of the Sexes* (Boston: Isaac Knapp, 1838), p. 45.

60    For the *White Captive*, see Wayne Craven, *Sculpture in America* (New York: Thomas Crowell, 1968), pp. 162–64. For St. Leger Eberle's *White Slave*, see Louise R. Nouer, "Introduction," *Abastenia St. Leger Eberle, Sculptor*, catalog (Iowa: Des Moines Art Center, 1980), pp. 9–10. The tradition in painting, which presents slave women in Turkish slave markets, appears in works as diverse as those by American Lilly Martin Spencer and the French academician Jean-Leon Gerome; see Samuel A. Roberson and William H. Gerdts, "The Greek Slave," in the quarterly publication of the Newark Museum, *The Museum*, n. s. 17 (1965).

61    References are to Southworth, *The Brothers*; Davis, *Margaret Howth*; Pike, *Ida May*; Stowe, *Uncle Tom's Cabin* and *Dred*; Chopin, "Desiree's Baby"; Sargent, *Peculiar*; Howells, *An Imperative Duty*; Cable, "tite Paulette" and "Madam Delphine"; Twain, *Pudd'nhead Wilson*; Faulkner, *Absalom! Absalom!*; Harper, *Iola Leroy*; Hopkins, *Contending Forces*; Brown, *Clotel*, *Miralda*, and *Clotelle*; Webb, *The Gairies and Their Friends*; Chesnutt, "Her Virginia Mammy," and Johnson, *Autobiography of an Ex-Colored Man*.

62    "Une Femme Dit," *Pittsburgh Courier*, 20 February 1926, *The Works of Alice Dunbar-Nelson*, ed. Gloria T. Hull, 2:131, *The Schomburg Library of Black Women Writers*, ed. Henry Louis Gates, Jr., 30 vols. (New York: Oxford University Press, 1988). *Black Sister: Poetry by Black American Women*, ed. Erlene Stetson (Bloomington: Indiana University Press, 1981).

# Index

Abolitionist discourse: widespread distribution of, 4–5, 7, 12–17, 22–23, 44; slave emblems as motifs in, 7, 10, 15, 17, 19, 22; religious elements of, 33, 40–41, 58–59, 84. *See also* Abolitionist women; Abolitionists; Chandler, Elizabeth Margaret; Child, L. Maria; Christian evangelism; Christian resignation; Grimké, Angelina E.; Grimké, Sarah; Jacobs, Harriet; Liberator figures; Scriptural language; Slave emblems; Sojourner Truth; Stewart, Maria W.; Supplicant figures

Abolitionist iconography. *See* Abolitionist prints; Book illustrations; Liberator figures; Newspaper graphics; Slave emblems; Supplicant figures

Abolitionist prints, 3, 4–5, 15

Abolitionist women: and slave emblems, 3, 10, 15–17, 19, 22, 23; and nineteenth-century gender roles, 9–10; writings by, 12–14, 17, 29–52, 53–76, 77–96; free African-American, 15, 46–48, 58–59, 70, 77, 127; and pacifism, 21; and issues of race and gender, 23–26; Woman and Sister embodied by, 25–26, 52, 73, 77, 78–79, 123; true womanhood defined by, 26, 52, 61, 77, 78–79, 92, 96, 123, 178; clerical opposition to, 36, 38, 50–51, 59–60, 69, 133, 146; and "promiscuous" audiences, 44, 46; and sexual and racial taboos, 45–46, 48, 50–51, 62, 65; as literary subject, 59–60, 65–66, 68–71, 73, 132, 153–70 passim, 166–67, 168, 177; and writings and speeches of ex-slaves, 77–96 passim; racism among, 81, 155; iconography of, reinterpreted in elite culture, 99–100, 102, 110, 112, 118–19, 120–22, 123, 134, 171; and Powers's Cincinnati, 105, 106; and Hawthorne's Massachusetts, 128, 129, 140; survival of discourse of, in twentieth century, 170–78. *See also* Antislavery sewing societies; Antislavery societies, female; Boston Female Anti-Slavery Society; Cincinnati Anti-Slavery Society; Conventions of American Women Against Slavery; Feminism; Petitioning, right of; Public role of women

Abolitionists: and writings and graphics, 3, 4–5, 10, 12, 13, 15, 17, 18–19, 21, 22, 23, 44, 84, 115, 122; and women in public debate, 3, 26, 51–52, 55; and slave emblems, 5–7, 10, 19; and female supplicant figure, 10, 13, 15, 99; and